# Hard Times
# and New Deal
# in Kentucky
# 1929-1939

# Hard Times and New Deal in Kentucky 1929-1939

## GEORGE T. BLAKEY

THE UNIVERSITY PRESS OF KENTUCKY

Scholarly publisher for the Commonwealth,
serving Bellarmine College, Berea College, Centre
College of Kentucky, Eastern Kentucky University,
The Filson Club, Georgetown College, Kentucky
Historical Society, Kentucky State University,
Morehead State University, Murray State University,
Northern Kentucky University, Transylvania University,
University of Kentucky, University of Louisville,
and Western Kentucky University.

*Editorial and Sales Offices:* Lexington, Kentucky 40506-0024

**Library of Congress Cataloging-in-Publication Data**

Blakey, George T.
   Hard times and New Deal in Kentucky, 1929-1939.

   Bibliography: p.
   Includes index.
   1. Kentucky—History—1865-    . 2. New Deal,
1933-1939—Kentucky. 3. Kentucky—Economic conditions.
4. Kentucky—Politics and government—1865-1950.
5. United States—Economic policy—1933-1945. I. Title.
F456.B53 1986    976.9′042    86-1513
ISBN 0-8131-1588-4

# Contents

# Acknowledgments

I am indebted to the following for their assistance:

my parents, G.T. and Eulela Blakey, for their participation in and memories of the era;

Indiana University East for providing time and funds for this project;

librarians and archivists in Kentucky, Ohio, Indiana, New York, and Washington, D.C. for opening doors to the past;

my wife, Carolyn, for her patient listening and reading;

John E. Wilz and two anonymous readers for their acute criticism and suggestions.

The book is better for their contributions, but its interpretations and weaknesses are mine.

# Introduction

In all his sixty-four years, Ruby Laffoon probably never had to perform a sadder duty than the one he undertook early in the morning of March 1, 1933. As governor of Kentucky he closed the banks of the commonwealth. Late in the evening prior to this extraordinary act he had finished a long and tiring day by signing the official proclamation; now on Wednesday bankers across the state followed his request and either did not open their doors as usual or curtailed business to minimal levels.[1] Signed and declared as a last resort, the proclamation climaxed weeks of concern over the large number of banks that had collapsed in the previous months and the anticipated failure of many more in the near future. Perhaps by temporarily closing the remaining banks, the governor could calm the panic and halt the failures that threatened thousands of Kentuckians with bankruptcy.

Strangely, the governor's unpleasant action had to assume the guise of celebration; his grim proclamation used the festive words, "bank holiday." Kentucky law limited the governor's powers in such circumstances to declaring days of thanksgiving; so the financial wake Laffoon created ironically bore this cheerful title. Technically, these days of thanksgiving were voluntary, although most banks chose to observe them as though they were mandatory, hoping that his brief respite would enable them to find a solution to the crisis. A seemingly relentless series of bank closings had begun in 1930 when twenty Kentucky banks, twice the usual number, declared insolvency. The bankruptcies doubled again the following year, and in 1932 more than fifty banks that could not meet their obligations shut their doors.[2] Laffoon's holiday, therefore, provided reason for thanksgiving by halting the rash of closings, temporarily at least.

This scene in Frankfort could have been even sadder for Laffoon had it not been duplicated in thirty-three equally beleaguered states. More than half of America's governors had declared some form of holiday to protect their remaining banks and prevent revenues from flowing outside state borders.[3] Governor Laffoon of Kentucky merely played the same game. It was a testament to the widespread nature of the crisis that Franklin D. Roosevelt proclaimed a banking holiday for the entire nation on March 5, the day following his inauguration as president. When the president acted, the burden of saving the failing banks was shifted from the states to the federal government.

If the banking crisis of 1933 had been the only problem needing correction, solutions might have been easier to find. Other problems, unfortunately, demanded immediate attention at the same time. Idle factories and mines, millions of unemployed workers, depressed farm prices, and a rapidly eroding faith in the American future—all had to be addressed. Private enterprise, local and state governments, and the recently discredited Hoover administration had proven unable or unwilling to respond. Governor Laffoon joined other governors and millions of Americans in the hope that the new president's New Deal would offer solutions. The banking crisis can be seen as a microcosm of the situation in which millions of people and hundreds of institutions began looking to Washington, D.C., for answers. Governors, bankers, and individuals waited to see what course the new administration would chart, not so much admitting their own failures as hoping for better success.

The tacit admission by state governments and the private sector that the crisis was beyond their control created, in effect, a vacuum that Roosevelt's New Deal would move to fill. Civilian Conservation Corps camps, Work Projects Administration crews, Tennessee Valley Authority dams, the Blue Eagle, and Social Security payments all became familiar parts of the American scene, some temporary, some permanent. The New Deal accelerated the reform and regulation impulse of the earlier

Progressive era, expanded the "general welfare" clause of the Constitution, experimented with social and regional planning, flirted with ideological radicalism, and generated new political alignments. No one denies the influence of the New Deal; many disagree, however, about its merits and legacy. A vast library of publications chronicles and analyzes the phenomenon, testifying to the desire of scholars to understand the events and to the appetite of the public for recalling them after half a century. This book will discuss the New Deal and its impact on one state, Kentucky. Observation of the events of the late 1920s and early 1930s from this narrow perspective yields a better appreciation of the sense of urgency that heralded the New Deal in 1933. And by examining the programs from a local rather than a national level, we can better understand the unprecedented federal activities. An analysis of how the New Deal came to Kentucky and how it worked—socially, economically, and politically—will help to explain developments of the later twentieth century. Profound and enduring changes were wrought during the 1930s in Kentucky's relationship to the land and to the federal government. This breaking of old traditions and shaping of new ones—the transformations this national experiment brought to a rural, conservative, and comparatively poor state— can best be appreciated through a topical rather than chronological review. How Kentucky fared in and reacted to this decade of crisis and change can also be better understood through comparison with the commonwealth's neighbors in the South and Midwest. Was Kentucky typical or aberrant in its response to Roosevelt's efforts to cure a stricken nation? There are several answers to this question and they will become evident in subsequent chapters.

# 1. Hard Times in the Commonwealth

Prior to October 1929 and the stock market crash that ushered in the Great Depression, the phrase "progress and prosperity" seemed to permeate the American vocabulary. Rapid technological change following the Great War produced the obvious symbols of progress and prosperity and gave the impression—part real and part illusory—of social and economic improvement. Asphalt and concrete highways began to replace dirt and gravel roads, and Fords and Chevrolets drove horses and wagons into retirement. Once considered luxury items for the wealthy elite, these and other newly affordable automobiles now belonged to twenty-six million Americans in 1929.[1] They bridged the distance between rural and urban America and added new dimensions to the lives of their owners. Commercial radio stations began broadcasting for the first time in 1920 and soon were transmitting news and entertainment to the remotest villages. By 1929, 40 percent of the families in the United States owned at least one radio,[2] evidence of both spare cash and spare time. Ornate cinema palaces encouraged Americans to drive downtown and enjoy America's favorite recreational pastime, the movies. Hollywood film makers had rapidly advanced beyond their humble nickelodeon origins and now offered sophisticated fantasy and adventure to millions of patrons each week. These technological changes transcended state borders and aided in the breakdown of provincialism and the homogenization of culture. The infatuation with new cars, *Amos and*

*Andy* radio jokes, and Mary Pickford movies was an American phenomenon that had no difficulty crossing the Ohio River and Appalachian Mountains to make its impact on Kentuckians. Kentucky shared in this material display of progress and prosperity. Of the 2.6 million residents in the state, more than 300,000 owned automobiles by the end of the decade,[3] and car dealers advertised their inventory as the answer to everyone's vocational and recreational needs. Radio ownership in Kentucky in 1929 lagged behind the national average by one-half, but the gap was growing smaller.[4] Thanks to initial transmission from Louisville's station WHAS, devotees of thoroughbred racing in Europe could listen to the running of the Kentucky Derby that year, even though some Kentuckians only a few miles from Churchill Downs could not. Most Kentuckians, however, did live close enough to a movie theater to attend on occasion. Whether they lived in Lexington, Middlesboro, or Paducah, fans of the Marx Brothers could see them on the screen in the fall of 1929. More serious movie patrons could watch Greta Garbo in those same cities that year.

Accompanying such manifestations of progress and prosperity during the 1920s was an aggressive optimism that many observers referred to as "boosterism." Chambers of commerce and civic organizations extolled growth, expansion, and profit. Business was king during the decade and Republican officials were its courtiers. President Calvin Coolidge had helped to set the tone when he said, "The business of America is business."[5] Kentucky's Republican governor Flem Sampson acted in the spirit of Coolidge in 1928 when he appointed businessmen to the newly created Kentucky Progress Commission, whose mission was "to advertise Kentucky to the world."[6] Although a Democrat, Keen Johnson, editor and copublisher of the Richmond *Daily Register,* was obviously swept up in the same spirit when he told a gathering of public utilities officials early in 1929: "There is romance in the routine of industry, there is artistry in the architecture of the skyscraper; there is a melody pregnant with meaning in the symphony of sound which emanates from the plants of productivity. . . . There is poetry in progress be it expressed in asphalt or whirling dynamos."[7]

Sinclair Lewis's widely read novel *Babbitt* reflected this boosterish spirit of the 1920s, and many midwestern cities claimed to be the inspiration for its shining city, Zenith. Although Louisville was not one of those, it did possess a tall new skyline, dominated by the Brown Hotel, that had risen since the Great War. The older but still elegant Seelbach Hotel was only a short walk from the Brown down bustling Fourth Street and had, in fact, been the prototype for the fictional Muhlback Hotel in F. Scott Fitzgerald's *The Great Gatsby*, another popular novel of the day. Inside the Seelbach could be found many of the stereotypes of this boisterous age: flappers, jazz bands, and illicit liquor. Kentucky appeared eager not to be left behind in this booming decade.

Still, by almost every criterion Kentucky trailed the rest of the nation in the frenzied growth of the late 1920s. Progress and prosperity in the commonwealth were largely an urban phenomenon, and Kentucky was still mostly rural. Census reports for 1920 showed that for the first time a majority of Americans lived in towns and cities; in Kentucky barely more than a quarter of the people were urban. The national shift to the city continued throughout the decade, but by 1930 approximately 70 percent of Kentuckians still lived in the countryside.[8] By the end of the 1920s Louisville, with three hundred thousand people, was the ony genuinely urban area in the state. Its J.B. Speed Museum could boast of a small and impressive art collection, and its Bowman Field had just recently begun regularly scheduled airline flights, but most Kentuckians never saw such marvels. Covington, the second largest city with a population of sixty-five thousand, seemed content to bask in the shadow of Cincinnati just across the Ohio River rather than develop an identity of its own. With only forty-five thousand residents, Lexington ranked third in population and did not pretend to be urban, notwithstanding the measure of sophistication provided by the University of Kentucky and the community of thoroughbred breeders and racers.[9]

Another aspect of the 1920s boosterism, industrial development, also affected few Kentuckians. Less than 18 percent of the state's adult population was employed in industry, compared to almost 28 percent nationally, and much of that work—although technically industrial—was tied to agriculture. Many Kentuckians labored in lumber and flour mills and meat-packing plants.[10] In contrast to most American industries, which were booming at this time, two of Kentucky's major employers were in a serious decline. The "noble experiment" of Prohibition, begun in 1920, had all but dried up the distilleries and breweries of the state. Before the ratification of the Eighteenth Amendment, more than two hundred Kentucky distilleries and breweries had supplied bourbon and beer to international markets and had employed more than four thousand workers.[11] Only a handful of distilleries remained in operation in 1930, and their product was now marketed through narrowly constricted pharmaceutical channels.[12] Another leading Kentucky industry, soft coal mining, had also fallen on hard times by the late 1920s because of the high price of coal and the shift to alternative forms of energy such as electricity and oil. In 1927 more than 600 mines, employing sixty-four thousand miners, were operating in the state; by 1929 only 451 mines were still open, and only fifty-seven thousand miners worked there.[13]

One who wished that Kentucky could get in step with the nation's forward march was Governor Sampson. Kentuckians, he said, "desire to prosper and enjoy the fruits of profitable business enterprises. They can, if they will, display just as great a spirit of progress and enterprise as the people of other states." Meanwhile, his publicity organization boasted that the state already possessed the world's largest baseball bat manufacturer and the nation's largest casket factory.[14] Although these admonishments and advertisements tried to inspire confidence, sports and funerals were hardly destined to be high-growth in the near future.

The report of the Kentucky Progress Commission in 1930 revealed some of the reasons for slow industrial progress in the state. Several investors from outside the state had requested information about potential sites and resources for development in 1928. At that time the commission had no available statistics about water, utilities, and labor, so it sent questionnaires to gather the information from cities throughout the

state. No cities or towns could meet the necessary requirements, and "as a result several plants were apparently lost to
Kentucky." The commission consequently concluded that the
state could not hope to make commercial progress until more
towns and cities had the necessary facilities and the ability to
market them.[15] The commission might have added that other
factors holding back progress were the slow pace of electrification and highway construction. Kentucky lagged far behind its
neighbors Ohio, Indiana, and Tennessee in the production of
electricity and in the paving of its roads. Indeed, fewer than one-
third of its seventy-six thousand miles of highways were surfaced with asphalt or concrete.[16]

As a predominantly agricultural state, Kentucky did march in
step with the nation's unhappy agricultural situation. For the
most part, American farmers throughout the 1920s were producing too much and finding markets glutted and prices low.
Tobacco, Kentucky's leading agricultural crop and one of the
state's major sources of revenue, was an exception. Increasing
numbers of Americans were smoking, and the phosphorus-
calcium soil of central Kentucky could produce large quantities
of the popular burley leaf. Lexington had become the world's
largest loose-leaf market, and Kentucky tobacco farmers enjoyed an income of $71 million in 1929, considerably better than
the previous year. A majority of the state's farmers, unfortunately, did not share in this exceptional prosperity. The combined income for the remaining major market products—dairy
goods, corn, and livestock—amounted to only $95 million in
1929, down from the year before.[17] Kentucky's farmers also had
to work harder for these meager results than did farmers in
neighboring states. The percentage of farms in other states that
had electricity and its labor-saving conveniences was triple that
in Kentucky.[18] In 1929 the Kentucky Progress Commission had
little progress to report on the rural front. It spoke, on the
contrary, of the continuing problems affecting the typical farmer and the distressing number of abandoned farms. "Instead of
showing any improvement," the commission lamented, "the
situation is becoming worse each year."[19]

Thus, by most criteria Kentucky did not seem to share the

progress of the 1920s. Only a few exceptional economic areas were in harmony with national trends, and whatever small share Kentucky had of prosperity was lost when prosperity gave way to depression in 1929-1930. Kentucky was fully in step with rest of the country when the stock market crash ushered in the Great Depression.

The bull market that investors and speculators had enjoyed through most of the 1920s, which many people regarded as a gauge of the nation's economic health, turned into a bear market where there were more sellers than buyers. As prices fell, day after day, investors who had mortgaged property and borrowed money to speculate on promising stocks panicked. Then on October 29, 1929, sixteen million sales—a record number—were transacted in one frantic day.[20] Estimates of financial losses during the following days of October and November range from twenty million to hundreds of millions of dollars. Yet, few financiers suffered most of the losses, and a majority of observers regarded the crash as only a temporary, albeit sharp, downturn. The larger Kentucky newspapers reported the plummeting stock market averages as major stories, but only a small fraction of the state's population had been directly involved in the stock market speculation of the past few months. Less than 5 percent of Kentucky's total income that year came from dividends on investments.[21] A syndicated column by humorist Will Rogers that appeared on the front page of the *Lexington Herald* probably captured the attitude of most Kentuckians toward the financial turmoil. "What does the sensational collapse of Wall Street mean? Nothin. Why, if the cows of this country failed to come up and get milked one night it would be more of a panic . . . an old sow and litter of pigs make more people a living than all the steel and General Motors stock combined."[22] Not until the following year did the reverberations of the crash make themselves felt in the commonwealth.

Shock waves from the collapse on Wall Street moved outward first to American main streets and then to rural areas. The stock market's failure to recover as it always had after a downturn revealed the unhealthy condition of the nation's economy. Stock prices remained depressed, speculators declared bankruptcy, and banks closed when their outstanding obligations could not be met. By early 1933, approximately fifty-five hundred American banks had closed their doors, leaving most of their depositors without cash.[23] Many of these closings were temporary and the banks reopened after consumer confidence returned or the banks reorganized their finances, but some never reopened. In the years prior to the crash, ten or so bank failures per year were not unusual in Kentucky and did not cause undue concern among financial leaders. By 1930, however, as the fear of economic instability affected more people, anxious depositors withdrew large portions of their accounts, leaving many banks with shortages of operating capital. Several banks had overextended themselves in unwise loans or poor investments, and this wave of depositor distrust thinned their reserves even more. In 1930 twenty banks, twice the usual number, closed and among them was the largest and oldest bank in Louisville, the National Bank of Kentucky.[24] Its president, James B. Brown, announced on November 17 that the closing was "due to withdrawals in the past week and constantly increasing rumors on the streets."[25] His grim announcement promised a bleak Christmas and an uncertain economic future for thousands of Kentuckians. As an act of seasonal philanthropy, the *Courier-Journal*'s publisher, Robert W. Bingham, from his personal resources, guaranteed a 50 percent return of all Christmas savings accounts, thus alleviating the gloom for a few depositors at least.[26]

One of the largest depositors in this stricken financial giant was the Commonwealth of Kentucky, with an account of more than three million dollars. State Treasurer Emma G. Cromwell later recalled her reaction to the news of the bank closing. "A great wave of such despair as I had never felt before rolled over me."[27] Luckily for taxpayers, state deposits were bonded, and Cromwell eventually retrieved them, but not until she had spent six anxious weeks negotiating with the insurance firm.[28] The following year more than forty Kentucky banks closed. They ranged in size from the large Ashland National to the small Amsden Bank in Woodford County. More than fifty banks in the commonwealth folded in 1932, taking with them the savings of thousands of Kentuckians.[29] Many depositors later retrieved their assets when some of the banks reopened; many others suffered a permanent financial loss.

In the wake of bank closures came the collapse of many industries and businesses. Some companies closed immediately because their operating funds were frozen by the bank failures. Others failed later, when the effect of diminished payrolls cut back the demand for their products. Nationally, this cutback would be seen in reduced working shifts, cooling blast furnaces, and smokestacks that no longer belched smoke. In Kentucky the predominantly rural base of the state softened the blow of this decline, but the effects were still obvious. In 1929 there were 2,246 industries operating with approximately seventy-seven thousand production workers. By 1933 almost one-half of those industries were closed, and twenty-one thousand of their workers idled.[30] These industrial collapses gradually took down with them retail and commercial businesses; 245 Kentucky firms declared insolvency in 1930, a larger number the following year, and in 1932, 356 businesses failed.[31] The United States Department of Labor published a monthly bulletin that chronicled this decline state by state. In May 1932 the bulletin described the Kentucky situation as one of slowly falling productivity. It found that most steel plants in Ashland were operating on a reduced schedule, as were most industries around Lexington, Covington, Paducah, and Hopkinsville. Two furniture factories near Owensboro had recently suspended operations. One of the few encouraging notes for that month was the continued good health of the cigar and cigarette factories, especially in Louisville.[32] Two of the tobacco companies there, Axton-Fisher and Brown and Williamson, had actually profited from the Depression. They had successfully marketed packs of cigarettes for ten cents, a full one-third less than the usual price. Even with little advertising fanfare, they had difficulty meeting the demand from smokers of reduced means.[33]

Perhaps the most traumatic examples of business failures and their social consequences were in the coal-mining communities of eastern Kentucky, many of which depended almost entirely on the mines for their livelihoods. Coal production in the area had peaked in 1927. Of the 622 mines that had operated that year, only 380 survived by the end of 1932, and twenty-four thousand of the sixty-four thousand miners employed during 1927 had lost their jobs.[34] Among the hardest hit areas were Harlan and Bell counties, which captured national attention as their plight worsened. Union recruitment, violent strikes, state military intervention, and investigations by writers, professors, and theologians—all added to the confusion. The phrase "Bloody Harlan" became familiar to millions of Americans as the *New York Times, New Masses, New Republic,* a lengthy Senate hearing, and the controversial Theodore Dreiser "report" publicized the turmoil. The notoriety helped to document problems of this troubled area but did little to solve them; if anything, it exacerbated them. The increasing poverty was real enough, as was the violence and polarization between miners and coal operators. What could not be fully substantiated was the extent of Communist influence among various labor organizations.[35] Governor Sampson's administration took a united, if somewhat paranoid, stand in its support of management and fear of outside agitation. The governor warned that Harlan County must be "ridded" of the "Red" outlaws when he ordered national guardsmen into the area in the spring of 1931.[36] His commissioner of mines subsequently attacked the radical elements who he felt had been intent on "the destroying of property and lives and the upheaval of our government."[37]

As the economic situation worsened, human suffering increased. Reduced inventories, declining profits, and violence told one part of the story, but unemployed workers and their dependent families told another, more poignant one. The federal census of 1930 estimated that as many as twenty-nine thousand Kentuckians were without jobs and actively seeking work.[38] A special presidential study the following year discovered that the number of unemployed Kentuckians had risen to forty-two thousand. These rising numbers of jobless in the state paralleled the national statistics in which an estimated fifteen million workers were unemployed by early 1933, the highest number in American history.[39] Kentucky's commissioner of labor summarized the sequence of events: "Industry and business sank to new levels of impotence . . . new projects were abandoned; old established enterprises were suspended. . . . The period of inactivity lengthened. . . . Leaders were without plans. . . . Financial paralysis deadened initiative. . . . The mass of wage earners, after three years of enforced unemployment were soon reduced to a state not far from beggary. It does not take long to exhaust the resources of a wage earner."[40] A report from the U.S. Children's Bureau indicated that in the Louisville Public Health district one thousand more children in 1932 than in 1929 were too underweight to meet its Blue Ribbon health standard.[41] Not as well publicized but just as stark in its implications was the annual index of suicides. The number of Kentuckians who took their own lives in 1929 was 211; the statistics then rose as the economy fell and exceeded 300 in both 1931 and 1932.[42]

The largest sector of Kentucky's population—the agricultural—suffered less dramatically than did the urban wage earners, but it suffered nonetheless. Its economic decline had begun with glutted markets shortly after the Great War, and it had not shared in the general prosperity of the 1920s. Market prices continued their decline in the 1930s, and income from corn, livestock, and dairy products fell from $69 million in 1930 to $38 million in 1932. Even the perennially prosperous tobacco farmers joined the ranks of the distressed as their incomes fell by half between 1930 and 1932.[43] Overbountiful crops and reluctant consumers combined to punish farmers during the growing Depression, but they were not the only enemies. A drought of serious proportions and duration struck the lower Mississippi Valley in 1930 and created problems for men, beasts, and crops. Governor Sampson described drought conditions in August 1930 as the "most severe" in the history of the state and reported that Kentucky farmers were selling cattle and sheep on a glutted market for 10 percent of their value because the parched fields could not produce enough winter feed. A few days later he issued an emergency proclamation directing farmers to conserve remaining supplies by not selling grain outside the state and by making silage from barren stalks in the unproductive fields.[44] By early 1933 thousands of farmers, unable to sustain the losses and pay mortgages and property taxes, were selling their land, by choice or in forced sales.[45] The farmers, most of them reluctantly, were abandoning the soil in record numbers.

In the early spring of 1933 the profile of Kentucky was not the romantic one found in song and verse. Before the economic crash of 1929, Kentucky's per capita income of $371 had been only slightly more than half the national average; by the start of 1933, it had fallen to $198, still approximately half the national average.[46] Considering that a used late-model Chevrolet might cost $495 in Fayette County in 1933, this diminished average income of $198 would not stretch far.[47] The automobile, that symbol of the past decade's progress and prosperity, now reflected the new decade's inability to indulge its former love affair with technology and the highway. Fewer cars and trucks were registered in the state in 1930 than in 1929, and even fewer in 1931 and 1932.[48] Fewer people purchased new automobiles, more old cars stopped running as tires and engines wore out, and owners increasingly neglected to renew their licenses for lack of funds.

Because the origins of the Depression were so diverse and its effects so widespread, no community or state could have understood, let alone solved, all the problems it posed. Unemployment, agricultural market prices, and world trade were all beyond the power of Kentucky to control. By most reckoning of the time it seemed that the federal government alone had the wherewithal to mobilize the nation's resources against the hard times. After all, many still remembered the success of American efforts during the Great War to produce goods, conserve supplies, and defeat Germany. More recent was the effective government action against the ravages of the 1927 Mississippi River flood. In both instances, the federal government had been able to coordinate private and public efforts efficiently toward a common goal. During both crusades, one man shone brightly: Herbert C. Hoover. As director of the Food Administration during the war and secretary of commerce during the flood, he had displayed organizational skills and an ability to inspire confidence.[49] Now, as president of the United States, he seemed to have the credentials to lead another successful fight, this time against the Great Depression.

Commission and his fear of communism in labor organizations testified to his essential conservatism. Like Hoover, he had overcome youthful adversity to achieve wealth and political prominence. In addition to his public record as successful lawyer, businessman, and judge in the mountain town of Barbourville, Sampson treasured memories of the log cabin home and rustic schoolhouse of his youth. The two executives shared and endured another political condition: Kentucky voters had given the Republican governor a Democratic legislature to work with just as American voters had taken from Hoover his solid Republican Congress in the 1930 elections.

Two demons beset Sampson's term as governor—the failing economy, over which he had no control, and relentless political struggles, which proved once again the validity of James Milligan's much-quoted line that politics were "the damnedest in Kentucky." While many Americans watched the dramatic market on Wall Street in late 1929, most Kentuckians focused instead on the Franklin County circuit court, where Governor Sampson was on trial on charges of conflict of interest.[56] Although he won his case easily, he lost a subsequent fight to allow private utility development at Cumberland Falls rather than include the area in the state park system.[57] The estrangement between the governor and the Democrats became so severe that the general assembly removed the powerful State Highway Commission from Sampson's control and then censured the governor for a highly partisan speech.[58] Had these political battles come at any time other than in the midst of the deepening Depression, they might not have caused concern; under the circumstances they were divisive and debilitating.

Whatever the political fallout, Sampson followed the president's lead in responding to the unemployment crisis. He proclaimed Business Confidence Week to combat the "obsession" with economic distress.[59] Later he appointed several committees to study the problems of joblessness, to help coordinate local charitable activities, and to cooperate with the president's committees. Like Hoover, Sampson believed the crisis would prove transitory, and his creation of the Unemployment Relief Agency in December 1930 reflected that attitude. He appointed

Wiley Davis to the unpaid position of state director of this committee and gave him free rein to organize dances and other entertainments to raise funds for the Salvation Army.[60] A member of Hoover's POUR survey, following an interview with Sampson, reported that the governor had no plans formulated for state relief of the unemployed and that the appropriate state officials "had no knowledge of the relief activities of the counties."[61] POUR officials found Kentucky's executives to be more the rule than the exception among state governments.

At length, during his final month as governor, Sampson did recognize the growing severity of the Depression and created the Kentucky State Welfare Committee. This group, which had more authority than the previous ad hoc groups, worked closely with POUR to supply information and recommend solutions. The governor apparently intended that this committee would serve as a clearinghouse for contributions of money, clothes, and canned goods for distribution to the needy by the Red Cross.[62] After a few weeks as chairman of this new committee, Harry Bullock supplied a mixed verdict on the Kentucky situation. He was pleased that many communities, such as Lexington, had been generous with contributions, and he was convinced that most of the Kentucky counties would be able to cope with the crisis by working with emergency aid from the Red Cross. Unemployment in approximately twenty counties, however, was so great that occasional gifts were insufficient, and county government resources inadequate to supply the requisite assistance. Bullock recognized that those counties "must have help in order to prevent not only suffering, but a possible social upheaval." Could that help come from the federal government? he asked.[63]

Senator Robert M. LaFollette, Jr., of Wisconsin had been asking the same question for several weeks. He cited statistics from 810 cities around the country which had responded to his questionnaire and determined that the cities could not meet the needs of the unemployed. If things continued at the current rate, he predicted the bankruptcy of "practically every municipality in the U.S."[64] Ten Kentucky cities were among the 810 respondents, and although their plight was not as severe as that of other cities, the conditions they described were alarming enough. From Earlington's mayor came the message that "we are certainly in need of help . . . our finance is exhausted." Madisonville's estimate was that fifteen hundred people in the county "are now in actual immediate need of food and clothing; many of them are practically on starvation."[65] LaFollette's answer to these conditions was a massive program of public works funded by the federal government. His proposal drew little favorable response, however, since many legislators agreed with the president that government initiatives of this sort were not yet necessary or proper.

Federal assistance finally arrived in February 1932, although not the kind Bullock and many local relief agencies had requested. With Hoover's encouragement, Congress in January had established the Reconstruction Finance Corporation (RFC) giving it the responsibility to lend money to banks, other finan cial institutions, and railroads. In the prevailing wisdom, the solvency these loans would guarantee to the beneficiaries would then "trickle down" to other smaller institutions and, in turn, to individuals. This unprecedented, if limited, intervention by the government, it was hoped, would halt the downward economic momentum and restore public confidence. As two of Hoover's sympathetic biographers have pointed out, the RFC was "a symbol of the idea that, when the private sector cannot or will not meet critical public needs, government may well have to move to fill the void."[66]

Kentucky's new governor, Ruby Laffoon, who was inaugurated in the month preceding the creation of the RFC, faced the same grim economic situation his predecessor had endured, but he could anticipate RFC aid to help fight it. Nor was Laffoon one to retreat from a fight. He had suffered years of ridicule for his unusual first name, a name he had selected for himself during childhood. He had also struggled most of his life with a crippled leg.[67] Always a Democrat but frequently a loser in local and state elections, Laffoon seldom backed away from confrontation or retreated from his partisan loyalties. This Madisonville attorney and judge had won election as governor in November 1931 despite the opposition of the state's largest newspaper, the

*Courier-Journal.* He began his governorship with a shortfall of state revenues exceeding $11 million. Griffenhagen and Associates, public administration consultants, had been making recommendations to the state government for several years, and in February they reiterated the "unquestioned gravity of the fiscal problem that faced the commonwealth."[68] The RFC loans would come as a partial solution to Kentucky's economic distress, and a timely one at that. Fourteen Kentucky banks received emergency loans during the RFC's first two months of operation, and more than two hundred others throughout the remainder of 1932. The Kentucky Bankers Association applauded this federal generosity at its annual convention that year, and endangered financial institutions began to stabilize their operations, some with surprisingly little money. Barbourville's First State Bank, for instance, needed only five thousand dollars in RFC aid, whereas, the First National in Murray received a loan of twenty-nine thousand dollars to guarantee its solvency.[69] As helpful as these rescue loans were to the private sector, however, other measures would be needed to give the state government operating and relief revenues.

Laffoon's solution to Kentucky's fiscal problems was as simple as it was controversial. His message to the general assembly on February 23 proposed a 2 percent sales tax as a fair and relatively painless source of revenue. This proposal aroused heated debate. Particularly vehement in opposition to the proposal were businessmen who would have to collect the tax. Thousands of merchants staged a protest rally in Frankfort in early March, and more than a hundred people stormed the executive mansion during the rally, frightening the staff and damaging a carpet.[70] The governor then offered a 1 percent tax as a compromise but the proposal failed to pass the Senate, in part because of the opposition of Lieutenant Governor Albert B. Chandler. The defeat of the tax delighted many merchants, alienated Chandler from the governor, and created new political alignments, but it did not resolve the state's financial dilemma. Determined to save money where he could, Laffoon threatened to start pardoning and paroling state prisoners.[71]

The RFC spared Kentucky this dubious means of prison cost

reduction when it received additional funds and responsibilities in July 1932. The Emergency Relief and Construction Act, which Congress passed that month, advanced funds through the RFC for highway construction and limited public works and provided $300 million in specific loans for relief activities in financially embarrassed states. The very day Hoover signed this legislation, Laffoon sent a telegram to the RFC director requesting proper forms with which to apply for $15 million. He reported that "the resources of this state including all money available are inadequate to meet its relief needs."[72] Harry Bullock, chairman of the State Welfare Committee, wired the RFC the following day, however, that Laffoon's request had been hasty and that the governor was "floundering around on the relief matter." Bullock said that Laffoon had told him earlier that he intended to apply for only $5 million.[73] Later Bullock reported that a survey of state needs indicated that $3 million from the RFC would be sufficient.[74]

This initial confusion surrounding the RFC loans was a harbinger of the controversy that clouded Kentucky's first experience in borrowing from the federal government. The *Courier-Journal* immediately labeled Laffoon a "mendicant" and "panhandler" for his admission that the state's cupboard was bare.[75] The RFC privately questioned the governor's motives inasmuch as his main purpose seemed to be to pay off state debts rather than to supply relief to the needy. RFC officials also feared that Laffoon would be politically partisan in his administration of the loans.[76] As the application process developed and specific uses for the funds emerged, additional controversy arose. The United Trades and Labor Association of Louisville protested the potential use of RFC money by the Kentucky Highway Commission, charging that the commission would hire unemployed men to work for only twenty cents per hour, or six dollars per week, wages that would produce what amounted to "a condition of involuntary servitude." The Louisville group petitioned the RFC to prevent the state of Kentucky from imposing this bondage on the unemployed.[77]

In late September 1932 the RFC made its first loan to Kentucky public and also chastised the state for carelessness and lack of initiative. The loan covered only 41 of the 108 counties included in the state's application and amounted to only $672,550 of the $1,107,093 requested. Washington officials indicated that Kentucky had not given adequate data to prove a real need in the other counties and declared that the state had "taken no action toward meeting the relief needs of its own people."[78] Later, when additional loans arrived, the RFC continued to berate the governor about "the responsibility of the local communities and the State of Kentucky to make every effort to develop their resources to provide relief."[79] Laffoon's choice of Harper Gatton to be the Kentucky relief commissioner reinforced the doubts in the RFC of the governor's ability to rise above politics. A hometown friend and political ally of the governor, Gatton was superintendent of public schools in Madisonville and a well-known Democrat in the western part of the state. To ensure that the new Kentucky Relief Commission would comply with federal guidelines, an official from the U.S. Children's Bureau assisted Gatton in the early days of the program, and Laffoon attempted to reduce fears of partisanship when he insisted that "no poor man, woman or child goes hungry or cold."[80]

The Relief Commission worked with local, county, and charitable agencies to devise work projects for the unemployed. It also secured agreement with merchants and retailers to accept the vouchers, or scrip, that recipients would receive either for their labor or as direct relief; Gatton had decided not to pay cash. Although there was some predictable criticism of the scrip payments, especially from some merchants in Louisville who complained of slow redemption of the vouchers by the Relief Commission, Gatton stayed with the scrip system and reported early in 1933 that "work in Kentucky is progressing splendidly."[81] The mayor of Bowling Green agreed with this assessment. He recounted later in 1933 that RFC funds had enabled the city to undertake construction of tennis courts, a rustic dam, and road improvements in its park system—all work it could not have done otherwise. The mayor was also pleased that the grants had allowed men to work and "maintain their self respect" instead of being subjected to a dole.[82]

Gatton could take justifiable pride in Kentucky's increased credibility in Washington; the RFC by March 1933 had rewarded the state's new application efforts and forwarded loans for use in 112 of the state's 120 counties. Gatton had overseen scores of public works projects similar to the park improvement in Bowling Green, in addition to other less-publicized projects with the U.S. Public Health staff, school feeding programs in conjunction with the American Friends Service Committee, direct relief for the indigent, and the popular garden projects.[83] This last activity supplied seed and fertilizer to as many as 177,000 families for cultivating crops on their own land or on plots provided by local benefactors. According to Gatton, there had been a "general clamor" of approval about these gardens.[84] From the initial loan through the spring of 1933, the RFC had granted Kentucky more than six million dollars for emergency activities.[85] Gatton also took pleasure from the RFC report that he had run the least costly state office in the nation, with administrative expenses of only $5.09 per $100.00.[86] Laffoon's original request had been somewhat grandiose, and bureaucratic confusion and bickering had characterized the early stages of the program in both Kentucky and Washington, but subsequent developments had proved that a federally financed relief system could be administered with relative efficiency, popularity, and beneficial results for many. The Hoover administration, intentionally or not, had established a major precedent.

This precedent of federal welfare assistance notwithstanding, prosperity refused to return. In spite of RFC loans to more than 7,000 financial institutions, including 287 in Kentucky, in the first year of its operation and in spite of its loans exceeding $240 million for relief and public works, the Depression lingered.[87] President Hoover's chances of reelection in November 1932 fell with each new factory closing and bank failure. Many of Kentucky's leading Democrats had endorsed New York governor Franklin D. Roosevelt for the party nomination for president, including Governor Laffoon, Robert Bingham, and Senator Alben W. Barkley, who delivered a rousing keynote address at the party's convention that summer.[88] Candidate Roosevelt received a warm reception when he campaigned in Kentucky, and even though his promised New Deal was vague on details, it was more attractive than four more years of Hoover.[89] Roosevelt and the Democrats swept the election in Kentucky and across the nation, although the results were probably as much a repudiation of Hoover as an affirmation of Roosevelt.

The four months of waiting that ensued between Roosevelt's election and his inauguration as president were characterized by an absence of cooperation between the incoming and outgoing administrations. The resultant anxiety plagued the financial community and provoked a new wave of bank failures that could be slowed only by desperate, last-minute "holidays." Kentucky joined the nation in March 1933 in mourning the illusory prosperity of the past decade and in anticipating Franklin Roosevelt's New Deal and the answers it might bring.

# 2. Banks, Homes, and the Indigent

Among the forty acres of spectators awaiting Franklin Roosevelt's inauguration as president, March 4, 1933, were Governor Ruby Laffoon and several members of his administration. Because the Kentucky bank holiday, which started March 1, denied them access to their private accounts, the governor and his party had to borrow money from friends in Frankfort in order to travel to Washington.[1] Other governors suffered the same embarrassment; Pennsylvania's Gifford Pinchot watched the ceremony with only ninety-five cents in his pocket.[2] This inadvertent poverty among state chief executives created an enforced, although temporary, equality among the multitudes gathered at the Capitol's east front. Governors joined other distressed Americans in the cold while most of the nation's banks remained closed, symbolizing the most immediate problems confronting America. How would the new administration go about restoring the nation's confidence in its government and banking institutions and guarantee financial security for its people?

Roosevelt stood before the expectant throng that day, metal braces supporting his polio-withered legs, and repeated the oath of office after Chief Justice Charles Evans Hughes. Later, in his inaugural address, he promised that the stricken American spirit and economy "will prosper" again, just as he had overcome his own crippling adversity, he might have added. Referring to the banking crisis and the disarray within the financial community, he declared that the "moneychangers stand indicted in the court of public opinion" and that they had "fled from their high seats in the temple." The new president pledged bold, swift action by the federal government and demanded "broad executive power to wage a war against the emergency, as great as the power that would be given to me if we were in fact invaded by a foreign foe."[3] The rousing applause that followed served as a figurative declaration of war, and the following week Governor Laffoon issued marching orders in a proclamation asking all Kentuckians to unite behind their "intrepid leader," to cooperate to prevent the economic collapse of the nation.[4]

On his first day as president Roosevelt set his New Deal in motion. Invoking powers of dubious legality left over from the Great War, he declared a national bank holiday, making uniform and total what many governors had been putting together piecemeal for several weeks. All American banks were to suspend normal operations during this moratorium until Congress met in special session. Until then the nation's economy would have to coast for several days. As in other states, a few banks in Kentucky remained open to receive deposits, transact minor business, and redeem the vouchers that circulated in some areas in lieu of cash. The city of Covington began paying its employees official scrip as did the State Highway Department in all areas of the state. Department stores such as Wolf Wiles and Purcells in Lexington ran advertisements encouraging their customers to use their charge accounts in anticipation of a quick return to normal banking. Theater owners in Winchester, Corbin, and Frankfort announced that moviegoers could present IOU's for admission tickets.[5]

When Congress convened in special session on March 9, it was prepared to follow the lead of the president. Heavily Democratic, with many freshmen members who owed their election to Roosevelt's 1932 sweep, Congress knew that America needed swift and bold action and that the president held the initiative. The newly elected John Young Brown from Lexington characterized the mood of the House with only slight exaggeration when he said, "I had as soon start a mutiny in the face of a foreign foe as to start a mutiny today against the program of the President of the United States."[6] What Roosevelt wanted was a measure to rescue the country's banking system, legislation that would, in the words of one historian, "save" the banking system, not change it.[7] The Emergency Banking Bill provided for the governmental licensing and gradual reopening of banks, presidential control over gold to prevent hoarding, and circulation of a new issue of reserve notes. In an almost unprecedented display of activity, Congress passed the bill after less than one day of deliberation.

The following Sunday night, March 12, Roosevelt delivered the first of his "fireside chats" from the White House. He explained to a national radio audience what the legislation meant to them and their money. The president delivered an "elemental recital" on the history of banking practices in simple language. Most banks, he pointed out, had invested their depositors' assets "to keep the wheels of industry and of agriculture turning around"; only a few "had shown themselves either incompetent or dishonest in their handling of the people's funds." He promised that the next day only trustworthy banks—those whose soundness had been guaranteed by appropriate officials in the Federal Reserve System, Treasury Department, RFC, and state governments—would reopen. The federal government had done all that was necessary, and now it was the people's responsibility to return that trust and not resume their panic withdrawals. "You people must have faith. . . . We have provided the machinery to restore our financial system; it is up to you to support and make it work."[8]

Roosevelt and his advisers, the so-called Brains Trust, then waited for the reaction to his talk and to the end of the holiday the following day. Banks reopened first in the twelve Federal Reserve district cities; then more banks resumed normal services during the week. The response in Kentucky was similar to that across the nation. Panic had dissipated; people returned to their banks with previously hoarded cash, and very few tried to close out their accounts. Kentucky's bank commissioner James Dorman commented that after the first full day of banking in the state deposits exceeded withdrawals, and a "high degree of confidence prevailed."[9] Four days following the end of the moratorium, Federal Reserve authorities and state banking officials had cleared 362 of Kentucky's 458 banks for normal business.[10] The Emergency Banking Act, the New Deal's first move against the Depression, had succeeded. And if Roosevelt had harbored any doubts about the impact of a fireside chat on public behavior, this victory on the banking front should have dispelled them. Several months later, a federal field agent reported that many indigent Kentuckians listened intently to the president's radio talks and "learned by heart" his advice and admonitions.[11]

Having gained the psychological advantage by restoring faith in government and banks, the New Deal then proceeded to sustain the recovery with concrete reforms. Several pieces of legislation in 1933 and later in 1935 would complete the federal government's efforts to revamp the banking system and remove some of the threats to America's financial security. Between March 9 and June 16, when Congress adjourned its extraordinary "100 days" session, the government began a multitude of new initiatives, one of the most enduring of which was authorized by the Glass-Steagall Act. Named for Senator Carter Glass of Virginia and Congressman Henry Steagall of Alabama, the law attempted to simplify and stabilize parts of the nation's banking system. Of importance to the greatest number of people was the creation of the Federal Deposit Insurance Corporation (FDIC), which initially protected individual deposits up to $2,500. This insurance would take effect on January 1, 1934, for all member banks of the Federal Reserve System and any other bank approved for the program and willing to pay the required fee. The law also gave the Federal Reserve System new powers to regulate investments of member banks and forced a separation of commercial and investment activities.

Earnestly but vainly, the American Bankers Association fought this government intrusion into banking activity and labeled the premise of the legislation "fallacious" and a "substitute for good banking."[12] But by the time the FDIC had been in effect for a few months, the American Bankers Association conceded that "in the long run the changes will be for the better, both for the public and for the banks."[13] Roosevelt's comptroller of the currency recalled that bankers soon found that the new public confidence the FDIC generated offset the fees banks had to pay, and "bankers and depositors alike recognize that it has eliminated the danger of runs occasioned by hysteria."[14] By the end of the 1930s more than 91 percent of America's banks were participants in the FDIC, either because they approved of the reforms or because they accepted the inevitable. In Kentucky, 401 banks, more than 93 percent of the total, subscribed to the program.[15] The stabilizing effect of this system was soon evident in the commonwealth. The number of bank failures in the state during 1933 was only half that of 1932, and the rate of closings fell by half again in 1934 and 1935. The restored faith, the virtual cessation of panic and bank failure, that came during the first two years of the New Deal prompted Kentucky bankers to express their appreciation. At their annual convention in late 1935 they passed a resolution paying tribute to Senator Glass and Representative Steagall as the "patron saints" of the banking recovery and reforms.[16] The Banking Act of 1935 further refined the earlier reforms, gave the Federal Reserve System greater control over member banks, and increased both stability and centralization of the financial community.

Meanwhile, thousands of families were facing eviction from their homes because of their inability to meet mortgage and tax payments. News stories of sheriffs' sales and auctions that left families with no place to live had become common since 1929. The normal rate of nonfarm foreclosures across the country had been 78,000 per year prior to the crash; that rate had swollen to 273,000 in 1932, and by the spring of 1933, foreclosures were occurring at a rate of approximately 1,000 per day.[17] A potential victim of foreclosure in eastern Kentucky wrote to Congressman Fred M. Vinson asking if any government funds were available to prevent his eviction and pleading, "This is my only chance to save my home."[18] President Hoover had earlier recognized the problem, but his administration's attempts to offer assistance had had little effect. The Federal Home Loan Bank began operations in July 1932 but did not make substantial loans until December of that year. Very few loans were made to distressed Kentuckians during the bank's first months of operations; hence, Congressman Vinson's constituent asked for assistance beyond what Hoover had been able to provide.[19] In his inaugural address in March 1933 Roosevelt, calling the situation a "tragedy," committed the federal government to find solutions.[20] The sanctity of a person's home, like the soundness of that person's bank, depended on the creative concern of the New Deal.

The Home Owners Loan Corporation was one of the first of several agencies the New Deal created to aid Americans in preventing the loss of their property. Established on June 13 by the passage of the Home Owners Loan Act, the HOLC had authority to purchase delinquent or endangered nonfarm mortgages from lending institutions and to rewrite them at reduced interest rates and longer terms. Some controversy arose over this activity because the HOLC gave as much relief to lending institutions as to homeowners; by purchasing the mortgages, the HOLC saved the mortgager from having to absorb uncollectable debts and to foreclose on unwanted properties. Whatever the primary motive, the HOLC had a mandate to perform rescue loan missions at an emergency pace. The maximum loan was $14,000 and the HOLC had disbursed more than $3 billion to approximately one million homeowners by the time it stopped taking new applications in 1936.[21]

In Kentucky the rush for HOLC assistance was as frantic as in other states. The HOLC manager for Kentucky, William T. Beckham, reported that people assembled two hours before the doors opened for the first day of business at the state's main office on South Fifth Street in Louisville. Two patrolmen had to marshal the crowd into lines.[22] The HOLC office in Covington was the second busiest in the state, and federal officials had to hire additional staff to process applications from eager clients. Other branch offices soon opened in Lexington, Ashland, and Paducah, and within a year, the HOLC had aided more than seven thousand Kentuckians with approximately $20 million.[23] By the end of 1934, Beckham noted that the volume of applications had declined, in part because of improvement in the economy, the ability of homeowners to deal with private lending firms, and the diminishing number of distressed homeowners needing help.[24] When the HOLC stopped receiving applications and granting assistance in April 1936, it had rewritten more than nine thousand Kentucky mortgages valued at $25 million.[25]

Beyond the obvious benefits of keeping homeowners and their property together during hard times, the HOLC publicized the fact that many other people and institutions were its beneficiaries. These property owners were once again able to pay taxes to state and local governments, making possible the enhancement of government services. In the three years of its active operation until it ceased absorbing new mortgage cases, the HOLC reported that its approximately one million clients had been able to pay almost $225 million in state and local taxes, most of which would not have been paid if homeowners had suffered foreclosure. More than $1 million in tax payments went to local and state treasuries in Kentucky.[26]

By the end of the decade, the HOLC acted as a receiver of payments for past accounts, foreclosed on delinquent accounts, and rented or sold properties it had acquired. These transactions—normal business for private institutions—were innovative activities for the federal government and established a new relationship between citizens and the state. Kentuckians seemingly bore this altered relationship with the government better than citizens in other states. In January 1940 Kentucky clients of HOLC were repaying obligations at a rate much faster than the national average, and the rate of foreclosures and evictions in the state was lower than that around the country.[27] The program directly affected only nine thousand urban homeowners in a state of 2.6 million people, a relatively small proportion of the population, but the concept of federal responsibility for protecting the security of the home was a large and significant one that would be expressed in many other parts of the state during the course of the New Deal.

Rural homeowners benefited even more than urban Americans from New Deal protection of property. Roosevelt's gentleman farmer image was not just an affectation; he was genuinely sympathetic to and knowledgeable about the needs of farmers in 1933. On March 27 he issued an executive order establishing the Farm Credit Administration. Headed initially by his friend Henry Morgenthau, Jr., the FCA would consolidate the several federal agencies and bureaus dealing with agricultural assistance, some of them carried over from Hoover's administration. It was hoped that a single clearinghouse would be more efficient in getting aid to distressed areas.[28] The most immediate concern was farm foreclosures. Faced with eviction or sheriffs' sales for nonpayment of taxes, farmers had become increasingly militant in late 1932 and early 1933. Organized groups threatened to strike, withheld crops from markets, and flooded the White House with demands for assistance. Roosevelt related that in one week early in his administration twenty-two hundred letters and telegrams came in from angry farmers threatened by foreclosures.[29] In May and June of 1933 Congress granted the FCA emergency funds to come to their aid. The Emergency Farm Mortgage Act and the Farm Credit Act set into motion federal machinery that allowed refinancing of farm mortgages with longer terms and lower rates. Similar in concept to the HOLC, the FCA would lend directly to farmers through private institutions such as co-ops and Federal Land Banks. During its first seven months, the FCA lent more than $100 million which testified both to the extent of the crisis and to the willingness to the New Deal to be the answer for it.[30]

Just as homeowners in Louisville and Covington had crowded around HOLC offices for assistance, Kentucky farmers flooded co-ops and land banks with applications for loans. The rush was so great in all sections of the state that many farmers had to wait several months while officials processed their requests. Several impatient farmers in the Western Purchase area implored their Congressman to intercede in their behalf. Representative William Gregory complained to Henry Morgenthau about delays and bureaucratic bottlenecks that were keeping the New Deal from helping people who needed help.[31] By early 1936, the FCA had eliminated most of the delays and weathered the storm of applicants. Judge Lorenzo K. Wood, Kentucky's director of the National Emergency Council (a coordinating committee for federal agencies), reported that by the end of February more than seventeen thousand Kentucky farmers had refinanced their mortgages through loans from the FCA. These loans, according to Wood, were at "the lowest rate of interest ever charged" (generally 5 percent or less) and they allowed "practically every distressed farmer in Kentucky to prevent foreclosure."[32] Senator Marvel Logan appeared before Wood's Emergency Council later that year with a less effusive and more specific breakdown of the FCA largess. The rewritten mortgages in Kentucky amounted to almost $40 million in property value, much of which might have been lost if not for FCA action. Logan reviewed the rural situation since 1933 and recalled that Kentucky farmers had "believed that they were without hope; but that belief was soon changed when the FCA . . . commenced its efforts."[33] By 1938 the number of applicants for FCA aid had fallen off dramatically, indicating that the emergency had passed. This rural rescue effort had cost approximately $43 million in long-term loans in the state.[34] The eighteen thousand Kentucky farmers and nine thousand urban dwellers who escaped foreclosure were doubtless grateful for the New Deal's willingness to establish precedents regarding property ownership.

The National Housing Act of June 1934 added a new dimension to the federal government's interest in home ownership. Going beyond mere emergency protection of the family shelter, this law promoted home ownership, construction, and repair as catalysts for economic recovery and expansion. It established the Federal National Mortgage Association (frequently called Fanny May) to work with the RFC to get additional revenues into mortgage markets, and it created the Federal Housing Administration to expedite these mortgages for homeonwers. The FHA would underwrite loans granted by private lending institutions to people wishing to build or remodel a home, making it easier for people with weak credit histories to obtain loans. FHA officials advertised the potential benefits of new construction work, explaining that additional loans would multiply outward as carpenters, plumbers, electricians, and other workers returned to their jobs. Consciously or not, the FHA had adopted the theories of the British economist John Maynard Keynes; they saw the new agency as a Keynesian pump primer to get the stalled economy going again. Federal and state officials began arranging financial marriages between homeowners and lending institutions, and judging by results, the FHA efforts were successful. Between 1934 and 1940, the FHA insured 3 million loans for home repairs, amounting to $1.2 billion, and 711,000 loans for new home construction, totaling more than $3 billion.[35] FHA pump priming and matchmaking in Kentucky were equally extensive. By the end of 1940, more than thirty-eight thousand Kentuckians had negotiated FHA-backed loans for home construction and repair, and the $39 million had multiplied outward through the hands of various tradesmen and retailers.[36] Several factors contributed to the special popularity of these loans in Kentucky. The FHA set up "clinics" in several towns to generate enthusiasm for home remodeling and sent "flying squadrons" of advisors to expedite the loan process.[37] Governor Laffoon also joined in the spirit of the FHA ballyhoo. He declared October 1935 "Better-Housing Month," and urged Kentuckians to "take advantage of the programme of insured mortgage . . . in order that our people may thereby enjoy an increase in contentment and prosperity."[38] The state associate director of FHA, Judge Roscoe Dalton, reported that these loans were in fact restoring prosperity to the state. By his calculations, every dollar lent generated an additional fifteen dollars of business in related enterprises, a return he found "phenomenal."[39]

The following year, 1936, the FHA modified its regulations to make it easier to get loans approved, and the pace of Kentucky applications accelerated. In Owensboro a development firm announced plans to construct and sell thirty-nine small homes for less than two thousand dollars each. These homes qualified for FHA financing and required a down payment of only a hundred dollars. Within one day of the initial announcement, the developer had sold all of the homes, and Daviess County received considerable press attention for its inexpensive housing boom. Unfortunately some Kentuckians overextended themselves financially under the relaxed FHA rules. By the end of the 1930s, the percentage of Kentuckians who had become delinquent in their payments or who had been foreclosed on ranked far above the national average and roughly double the rate for the neighboring states of Tennessee, Virginia, and Indiana.[40] For these few people, the New Deal had made the carrot at the end of the stick too easy to reach, and they found themselves not with better homes but with none.

Meanwhile, the New Deal was experimenting with a concept far more dramatic, even radical, in scope. The Wagner-Steagall Housing Act of September 1, 1937, made the federal government an active agent in slum clearance and the construction of low-cost housing for the urban poor. The act created the United States Housing Authority within the Department of the Interior to oversee the lending of funds to municipal housing authorities. New York Senator Robert F. Wagner sponsored the original bill and drew support from urban politicians and social workers. Many rural and southern politicians fought the bill, in part because of its "socialistic" overtones and in part because they perceived that very few of its activities would benefit white southerners. Still, none of the Kentucky delegation opposed the measure. In its final form the Housing Authority would lend up to 90 percent of the necessary funds on sixty-year terms and set guidelines for affordable rental schedules. Local officials would retain authority to select the sites for housing projects and would administer them with continuing federal subsidies. Unlike previous public works projects that undertook ad hoc home construction as a temporary stimulant for the economy, the USHA was a systematic attempt to improve the urban landscape and the lives of slum dwellers.

Because the USHA appeared in the latter part of the 1930s, its accomplishments before World War II are hard to assess. One authority on government housing summed up the early USHA projects in uncomplimentary terms. They were, he wrote, "almost universally ugly and depressing developments, segregated, stigmatized by origin and by residency requirements, resented by local citizens and located in the worst sections of town."[41] In Kentucky, the Housing Authority by 1940 had committed more than nineteen million dollars to six cities for slum clearance. Like cities elsewhere, Louisville, Lexington, Covington, Paducah, Frankfort, and Newport had to demonstrate their need, an ability to supply the remaining 10 percent of the costs, and the capacity to administer the housing units according to federal criteria. The USHA projects in these six cities eliminated approximately one thousand housing units that were in serious stages of disrepair and replaced them with a comparable number of modern units.[42]

Two Lexington projects, although not necessarily typical of USHA activity, illustrated several features common to most. Bluegrass Park and Aspendale were begun earlier as Public Works Administration construction projects and then transferred to USHA prior to completion. Bluegrass Park contained 142 apartments for white occupants and Aspendale had 144 for blacks. Both projects encircled large oval drives, and each apartment had its own lawn. All units had gas ranges, electric refrigerators, and hot and cold water in kitchens and bathrooms. Rents averaged $6.75 per room per month, considerably lower than normal rents. Before their opening, there were long lists of applicants for the apartments.[43] Although both projects were segregated by race and income, sequestered in blighted areas, stigmatized by purpose and appearance, the apartments were nonetheless more desirable than what applicants had been accustomed to. The immediate and affordable comforts of Bluegrass Park and Aspendale were more compelling than criticism about aesthetics and ideology.

When Roosevelt signed the Social Security Act in August 1935, he culminated a long rancorous debate and stretched the Constitution's "general welfare" clause further than the Founding Fathers could possibly have dreamed. FDR later called the law the "supreme achievement" of Congress.[44] It gave legitimacy to the controversial idea that the government has a responsibility to guarantee a minimum of economic security for its citizens. The Social Security Act authorized the federal government to provide pensions for the elderly and to assist the states in providing aid for the elderly indigent, handicapped, temporarily unemployed, and other needy. Neither as radical nor as conservative as its various critics charged, this legislation did present a sharp departure from the American tradition of private and local welfare organizations.

Kentucky's Senator Alben Barkley helped draft and guide the

Social Security Act through its long passage, and it received strong majorities in both houses despite the rancorous debate that preceded the vote. It offered to Americans a wide variety of new services—already available in many European countries—and to state governments a partnership arrangement to administer them. For the retirement pension fund, which would begin payments in 1942, the federal government would supervise withholding a small percentage of employee paychecks that would be matched by employers. Beginning much sooner, in 1936, was the Old Age Assistance program, which provided a maximum grant of thirty dollars per month to the elderly, half of which would be paid by state governments. Similar, but optional state-federal matching grants would be available for the blind, the crippled, dependent children, and public health agencies. Finally, the federal government would assist states in setting up unemployment compensation plans. These plans were optional too, but all states quickly participated, for they stood to lose considerable revenues if they failed to set up appropriate programs. The federal-state partnerships allowed wide diversity in payments, depending on the state's ability and willingness to raise its own matching funds and on its local criteria for benefit eligibility.[45] Like many New Deal measures, the Social Security Act was a patchwork stitched together with emergency thread.

Of first and most immediate concern, the program filled a painfully documented void left by state and local welfare agencies. In 1934 only twenty-four states had assistance programs for the needy blind, and thirty states gave aid to the destitute elderly, but the largess from these programs amounted to "tiny sums to insignificant numbers." Only Wisconsin had adopted an unemployment compensation system, but it had yet to provide any benefits.[46]

Prior to passage of the Social Security Act, the Kentucky charitable situation was no better and frequently worse than that found in other places. State government had long provided some facilities for dependent children and some assistance or housing for the deaf, dumb, blind, and feebleminded; local and county governments however, had to absorb all responsibility for the elderly and indigent. Kentucky still clung to its 1909

statute, which held children legally responsible for the care of
their elderly parents, and in 1935, 98 of the state's 120 counties
still concentrated most of their charitable energies into alms-
houses or poor farms. Only 12 counties provided old-age pensions, and their benefits averaged only forty dollars per year per
recipient.[47] With neither jobs nor state assistance, many elderly
Kentuckians pleaded with federal leaders for help. One wrote to
Eleanor Roosevelt that he had no source of income and was
"destitute of food and raiment"; another informed Senator Barkley that "bad luck has overtaken me in my old days."[48] Following passage of Social Security but prior to its first benefit payments other down-and-out Kentuckians pleaded with state officials to be generous with the new program. One seventy-seven-
year-old man said that he and his family "have not got enough to
eate half of the time . . . [are] in a mity bade shape . . . and have
not got eney way to earn a living." Another elderly woman,
trying to raise a small boy, said she felt like "a toad under a
harrow."[49]

With such testimonials, representing a large constituency, it
should have come as no surprise to state and federal politicians
that the illusory promises of Francis E. Townsend and Huey
Long were finding a large audience. Townsend, a California
doctor, had become a champion of the elderly, and his scheme
for paying everyone over the age of sixty a pension of two
hundred dollars per month had gained millions of supporters.
Huey Long, the flamboyant senator from Louisiana, was publicizing his "Share our Wealth" program, which promised a
minimum income for all families. Neither the Roosevelt administration nor the Kentucky state government could ignore
these schemes. A Louisville contractor warned the lieutenant
governor in 1935 that "every carpenter and laborer I work has
some of the literature of one or the other."[50] Even after passage
of the Social Security Act, there remained much confusion as to
the level of benefits. An Owensboro publisher wrote to a friend
in Washington that many of the poor people in Kentucky "were
led to believe that Dr. Townsend's plan would be put into immediate effect."[51] Potential beneficiaries of Social Security payments anticipated these utopian alternatives with such

enthusiasm that the forthcoming piecemeal benefits from state and federal funds would pale beside them.

State governments, no matter how conservative, quickly adhered to the federal guidelines of Social Security in order to qualify for millions of dollars in matching funds. Arguments about damage to individual initiative and the dangers of the welfare state won few listeners when the elderly and indigent demanded their share of the available funding. Governor Laffoon, now in the last months of his administration, appointed a citizens committee to study and recommend to the state what should be done to expedite the Social Security program in Kentucky. Chaired by Dr. Arthur T. McCormack, chief executive officer of the State Board of Health, this committee was to plan the appropriate strategy to put Kentucky "in a position to accept all the benefits provided in the Federal Act."[52] Within a month, McCormack and his committee reported that if the state pursued all available options, Kentuckians could receive as much as $3,651,000 during 1936. Of course, before Kentucky's citizens could receive a penny, the commonwealth would have to raise almost that much in matching funds, to pass a constitutional amendment, and to establish the required agencies for disbursing the new benefits.[53] Considering the enthusiasm for Social Security, the constitutional amendment would be easy to accomplish; the other two tasks would depend on the outcome of the 1935 gubernatorial election.

One of the main planks in Lieutenant Governor Chandler's campaign platform when he ran for governor in 1935 addressed this need for Kentucky to work closely with the federal Social Security machinery. His campaign posters showed Roosevelt's spectral presence hovering over Chandler, and his brochures promised to assist the president "in his efforts to bring about greater prosperity and greater social security for the masses."[54] Chandler's ability to charm voters with his singing and joking earned him his nickname, Happy, and helped rally support. A political science professor at Transylvania College estimated that by November of that year voters had at least 816 times heard Happy's dramatic account of his rise from poverty in Corydon to success in college and law practice in Versailles.[55]

His almost total recall of the names of his past acquaintances on baseball diamonds, football fields, oil-drilling jobs, and Optimist Club meetings enhanced his popularity. Youthful and energetic at age thirty-seven, he had enormous ambition, and he chose to direct much of this drive into getting as many benefits from the New Deal as possible. At his rain-soaked inaugural ceremony in December, Chandler pledged "to cooperate with the great program of the president of the U.S. . . . [for] old age pension and social security for the benefit of the aged people of this state."[56]

Governor Chandler addressed the regular session of the Kentucky General Assembly in January 1936 and asked that the lawmakers pass enabling legislation to permit proper administration of the Old Age Assistance Program.[57] Federal officials wanted these benefits to start as early as possible, and Chandler had pledged during his recent campaign to work for the swift implementation of the program in Kentucky. He had conferred with the special citizens committee, his financial advisers, and others and had determined to pursue only a few of the available Social Security options, and some of those to less than their maximum benefits. These modest goals, seemingly out of character for the ambitious young governor, sprang from necessity. The required matching funds would be difficult to raise, because he had also promised to repeal the sales tax and alternative sources of revenue were uncertain. His proposed program, called the McCarthy-Ramey Old Age Assistance Plan, would permit a maximum payment of fifteen dollars per month to each eligible recipient. Chandler lobbied hard for the legislation, and it passed with only one dissenting vote. One of its sponsors boasted that the enabling law would "drive the wolf away from the door of many poor people," and the lone negative was a protest against the low amount of the pensions.[58] These initial benefits to Kentucky's elderly fell far below the amount to be paid in most other states and indicated the commonwealth's current financial embarrassment, parsimony, or both. Kentucky politicians could take some brief consolation however, from the fact that, although they would be paying less than eight dollars per month, on the average, to their aged and indi-

gent, the elderly in Virginia and Tennessee would receive nothing at all because their states were so slow to enter the program.[59]

In quick succession during the spring months of 1936 the
general assembly rushed through its regular session and three
additional special sessions, during which Chandler dominated a
process reminiscent of Roosevelt's hundred days of 1933. Laffoon's unpopular sales tax, passed in 1934, gave way to new
income and inheritance taxes and a variety of luxury taxes on
such consumer items as cigarettes and liquor. Compulsory primary elections replaced optional ones, and the entire state
government system was reorganized.[60] The governor reduced
state agencies and offices, consolidated some of them for efficiency, and made them more accountable to him in a manner
similar to what his political mentor, Harry F. Byrd, had done in
Virginia. The reforms would serve several purposes: they would
save money, increase the governor's power, and in some instances allow the state to work in tandem with the New Deal.
One department in particular, the restructured Department of
Welfare, became "the agent of the federal government in welfare
matters . . . and in the administration of any federal funds
granted to the state."[61] Lieutenant Governor Keen Johnson,
who presided over this welter of activity in the senate, commented, "It is the purpose of the state administration to syn-
chronize its efforts with the national administration so that the
varied humanitarian and economic activities it has sponsored
may reach maximum efficiency in this state."[62]

The Social Security Board informed Kentucky's commissioner of welfare, Frederick Wallis, in early May that it had
approved the state's version of the Old Age Assistance Plan.[63]
Later that spring, Washington officials expressed disappointment with Kentucky's refusal to pursue some of the other
welfare options and with Wallis's apparent inefficiency in man-
aging office and personnel matters. They recommended that
Kentucky hire "a Director of Public Assistance with experience
in social welfare administration."[64] Chandler and Wallis contacted Chicago public administration consultants for advice,
and they offered several organizational suggestions "to avoid

controversies with the Social Security Board."[65] By the end of August, the department had worked out most of the administrative problems to everyone's satisfaction and Chandler announced that "the employees are working night and day to put this difficult department in operation."[66]

To celebrate the issuing of the first Kentucky Old Age Assistance checks on August 24 the director of the new Division of Public Assistance, Dr. A.Y. Lloyd, organized a festive ceremony at the state capital. Recipients from around the state came to Frankfort, and Governor Chandler personally handed them their payments. Seventy-year-old James Raisor from Carrollton accepted his ten-dollar check and declared that "the hills don't seem quite so steep, . . . and shucks, it won't be near so cold this coming winter."[67] Warm applause and favorable press reactions followed the occasion. One critic, however, found the ceremony distasteful and accused the governor of staging a cheap political sideshow to advertise himself as "the great God of Charity and Mercy."[68] The critic missed the point; only 238 Kentuckians received benefits during the first month of the program, and their average payment was a mere $7.43.[69]

Within the next few months, Kentucky availed itself of additional options in the Social Security program and increased the number of elderly receiving assistance. By 1937 the commonwealth was receiving grants and providing matching funds for a variety of benefits covering crippled children, public health services, maternal and child health programs. It had also set into motion the state unemployment compensation machinery. Unfortunately, these expanded programs soon began to threaten Kentucky's financial resources. By October 1937 the state was sending Old Age Assistance checks worth more than $400,000 to slightly more than forty thousand elderly Kentuckians.[70] This amount was far more than state officials had budgeted, and it did not include the matching funds for additional Social Security programs. Commissioner of Welfare Wallis told the governor that the funds would run out soon if spending continued at the same level.[71] Consequently, Wallis started emergency measures to bring expenses into line with revenues. His office terminated some of the 395 employees of the division, enacted strict operating economics, and dropped some recipients from the eligibility lists. Director of the Division of Public Assistance Lloyd informed one recipient that Kentucky officials had anticipated twenty-five thousand participants and had instead received more than seventy-six thousand applicants. Accordingly, the state could afford to support only the most indigent until more revenues were available.[72] Many elderly who had received no assistance until Social Security began in 1936 regarded it as salvation; now they faced the prospect of doing without once again. By May 1938 the Division of Assistance had pared approximately seven thousand names from its list, and then in June, in an extraordinary instance of belt tightening, it dispensed with payments altogether for one month.[73]

As better estimates and more regular tax revenues coincided, the situation stabilized, and by the end of the decade, more than fifty-seven thousand elderly Kentuckians were receiving monthly checks averaging almost nine dollars. This amount was less than half the national average and considerably less than what was paid in the neighboring states of Virginia, Tennessee and Indiana.[74] Nevertheless, a small monthly check was better than none at all, and by this time, Kentucky officials had accustomed themselves to criticism about stinginess. Despite its limited participation in the Old Age Assistance program, the commonwealth took on other responsibilities, and by the onset of World War II, Kentucky had added aid for dependent children and the needy blind to its other Social Security obligations.

While Kentucky citizens took advantage of the new welfare benefits and clamored for more, state officials did their share of chafing over burgeoning stipulations from Washington. Governor Chandler fought a losing battle with the Social Security Board about standards for hiring and paying personnel. This running controversy resulted in a five-page letter to the chairman of the board in 1938 in which Chandler defended his political prerogatives within the state. He vowed "to resist all attempts by the Federal authorities to dictate . . . in the matter of selection, tenure of office and compensation."[75] Nothing came of this protest, which was typical of similar protests from other governors. Only Ohio carried its fight to the point of temporarily losing federal revenues.[76] Washington had become the source of money and the center of power as a result of the Great Depression. Although states could modify details, they had to adapt to New Deal operations.

The Social Security program, entrenched at the end of the decade, symbolized many of the New Deal measures that protected the security of millions of Americans. Arthur M. Schlesinger, Jr., has written: "No government bureau ever directly touched the lives of so many millions of Americans. . . . For all the defects of the Act, it still meant a tremendous break with the inhibitions of the past. The federal government was at last charged with the obligation to provide its citizens a measure of protection from the hazards and vicissitudes of life."[77] If Kentuckians had been hurt by bank closings and the loss of their savings or were threatened by foreclosures on their property or lacked a decent home in which to live or worried about unemployment and retirement, the New Deal provided some escape from those fears and problems. FDIC, HOLC, FCA, FHA, and Social Security now protected, insured, eased, and alleviated. In many cases such protection meant a diminished role for the family, private sector, and local and state government and an expanded role for national government. In most cases it meant additional taxes and bureaucracy and a new partnership between state and federal officials. Social Security taxes, in particular, drained considerable money from both employees and employers and contributed to the economic recession of 1937-1938. But in all cases it meant great change. As the New Deal faded into World War II, Kentuckians who looked for security for their savings, homes, and creature comforts looked to Washington, not to Frankfort.

# 3. Relief and Public Works

In the half century since its inception, the WPA has endured in the American memory perhaps more vividly than any other aspect of the New Deal. The largest of the depression-era programs, the Works Progress Administration (later renamed Work Projects Administration) came to symbolize the various "alphabet soup" agencies that provided relief and jobs for the unemployed. The WPA also came to symbolize the "boondoggling" of workers paid to loaf on the job who made WPA synonymous with We Piddle Around. Because of its size and duration, this agency became, for much of the public, a representative of the federal government's new role in securing the general welfare for unfortunate citizens. The WPA took on legendary status and mythic proportions as the New Deal's exemplar of both Christian charity andoalistic meddling.

The WPA did not begin until 1935, well into the third year of the New Deal, and it built on several already well established precedents. Thus, it does not deserve its reputation as a revolutionary agent of the welfare state. President Hoover's administration experimented in 1932 with RFC loans to states and municipalities to provide direct relief and public works appropriations, and like most of Hoover's programs to combat the depression, they were designed as expedients. These RFC monies avoided the connotation of "dole" relief since they usually reached their beneficiaries in the form of vouchers or scrip rather than cash. Of limited impact in stopping the economic decline, these RFC grants did, nevertheless, help establish the concept of government intervention in the economy with pump-priming techniques. Roosevelt's administration built on this beginning in early 1933. New Deal planners considered relief for the approximately fifteen million unemployed an immediate imperative. What direction the new relief measures would take and who would administer them—federal, state, or local officials—were questions that received several answers during the next decade. The Federal Emergency Relief Administration (FERA), the Civil Works Administration (CWA), the WPA, and the Public Works Administration (PWA) all provided different approaches to the question of relief, and they combined to establish a new relationship between individuals and the state.

Roosevelt perceived the problem of destitute American families as a genuine emergency that required swift attention, and in mid-May of 1933 he signed the legislation that established the FERA. Given an initial appropriation of $500 million to channel into state relief activities, the FERA was to provide relief for the hungry and jobless as quickly as possible. The federal government granted one-half of the funds to states on a matching basis, one dollar of federal money for each three dollars raised by the states. The other half of the funds would go directly for crisis situations regardless of whether states had supplied matching funds.[1] Each state had to establish suitable government machinery to apply for and to administer the funds, which were outright gifts, unlike the previous RFC loans. States also had to devise means of raising the matching funds.

The president's friend, Harry Hopkins, became federal relief administrator, head of the FERA, the first of several agencies that Hopkins would lead during the next ten years. The son of an Iowa harness maker, Hopkins had become a professional social worker and had been the relief administrator in New York during Roosevelt's governorship. There was a mutual trust and friendship between the two despite Hopkins's brusque and cynical personality. Because of his closeness to the White House, Hopkins's remarks frequently took on an importance beyond their worth. The remark attributed to him, summing up his administrative philosophy—"spend and spend and spend"—is probably apocryphal, although his critics never doubted that it expressed his view. During the life of the FERA, until it expired in late 1935, Hopkins presided over the spending of approximately three billion dollars of federal money to combat the economic emergency.[2]

Considerable tension arose over the relationship between federal and state officials in the administration of FERA funds. Federal officials continued to refer to the dual system as a partnership in which states applied for federal funds and disbursed them as they saw fit within certain safeguard guidelines.[3] Louisville's mayor, Neville Miller, to the contrary, described the relationship as more of a contest than a partnership. "The whole program," he later wrote, could "be characterized as a 'poker-playing' program—with the Federal Government engaged in a game with 48 individual governors. And the sad part of it was, the position of any state or community largely depended on what kind of a contestant the Governor happened to be."[4] As far as Kentucky was concerned, Miller's description seemed closer to the mark than the federal version. Governor Laffoon proved to be, as usual, a willing combatant if not a very effective one, and the result of the battles was a bruised chief executive. FERA money did arrive in Kentucky but not without public wrangling and damage to state pride.

In the early stages Laffoon borrowed from the established RFC organization for FERA administrative personnel. Harper Gatton made, in effect, a lateral shift from his job as director of the Kentucky RFC program to become Kentucky relief administrator. Gatton's job would be to document the level of need in the state, apply for federal funds, oversee the appointment of local relief workers, devise work projects, and recommend ways for the state to raise matching funds. Gatton had been successful with recent RFC projects, and he carried with him several predilections about administrative policies that were to clash with those of FERA officials. Among them was the desire to continue paying recipients with scrip rather than cash.[5]

With the lure of federal money dangling before them, Gatton and Laffoon did what several state governments did in early 1933; they exaggerated the level of need in Kentucky and overestimated the state's ability to raise matching funds.[6] Perhaps

the overestimation was intentional, since FERA had promised
additional nonmatching funds for states lacking sufficient revenues. In any case, such miscalculation was common and caused
frequent headaches for Hopkins and his staff in Washington. He
dispatched field agents to investigate state conditions and check
administrations and statistics.[7] When conflicts arose, as they
constantly did, Hopkins tended to agree with his field agents
instead of state officials. Howard Hunter, an agent assigned to
the Kentucky area, waged a running battle with Gatton and
Laffoon, disagreeing with them on most major decisions. Despite these conflicts and disagreements, FERA grants flowed
rapidly into Kentucky since the rationale behind the program
called primarily for speedy relief for the distressed and sec-
ondarily for an efficiently run organization. Within weeks of the
agency's inception, Kentucky was disbursing federal dollars in
the form of direct doles for the unemployed, surplus food distribution to needy families, and a number of municipal and
county work projects.

By July, Hopkins began to tighten FERA purse strings in
Kentucky and other states that he believed had not carried a fair
share of the financial burden. Laffoon received word that the
state would have to raise approximately $3 million in order to
keep FERA funds flowing into the state. When Laffoon did not
respond with sufficient speed or detailed plans for raising
matching funds, Hopkins sent a public telegram on July 11 to
the governor. "No state funds have been appropriated directly
for unemployment. . . . All relief in Kentucky at this date is
financed from Federal grants. I wish to make it perfectly clear to
you that the FERA will not continue to finance relief work
beyond August 15."[8] Laffoon made a hurried trip to Washington
to confer with Hopkins and suggested that some money from
the state highway fund could be transferred to relief activities
but not before April of the following year. Hopkins indicated
that this means was not satisfactory and told Laffoon what he
told other governors in the same predicament: He should call a
special session of the state legislature to raise relief revenues or
face the loss of FERA grants.[9]

The seriousness of Hopkins's threat was clear and Kentucky

responded accordingly. Gatton informed social workers around the state that all relief funds might dry up shortly and that relief offices would then have to close.[10] Laffoon called a special session of the general assembly to convene August 15. He listed several housekeeping items on the agenda, such as authorizing state banks to participate in the FDIC and setting up procedures for repealing the Eighteenth Amendment, but the major item for consideration was finding funds for relief programs. The governor indicated in his proclamation that the federal government was working hard to relieve economic miseries, "but our state must do its part."[11]

To address the situation directly, Laffoon invited Harry Hopkins to talk to a joint session of the general assembly, and the FERA chief did so on August 22. Many state legislators could only have regarded his appearance there as a form of blackmail, because, prior to his arrival in Frankfort, all federal money had in fact ceased to flow into Kentucky relief offices for a brief period. When he spoke to the assembled senators and representatives in the state capitol, Hopkins denied that he was trying to dictate policies to the state but insisted that revenues did have to be generated to prevent further suffering by "our fellow citizens who, through no fault of their own, are now without food or clothing." He also suggested that Kentucky observe how other states had met the challenge by raising taxes, diverting other state revenues to relief, or selling bonds.[12] Hundreds of unemployed Kentuckians marched to Frankfort in the days following Hopkins's speech, and their presence placed additional pressure on the state government to find matching funds. Laffoon did not follow the precedent of the previous year when President Hoover evicted the "bonus army" that had marched to Washington. Instead, he allowed the throng to camp out in state warehouses, and the state prison kitchens prepared meals for them.[13]

A sales tax, once again, was Governor Laffoon's answer to the problem. He had failed to gain passage of a similar proposal in 1932, but now he felt more confident about its chances. He was still cautious about the controversial proposal, however, and used the phrase "emergency gross receipts tax" rather than sales tax. Euphemism notwithstanding, Kentucky legislators refused to pass the measure, and again one of the opposition leaders was Lieutenant Governor Chandler. Instead, the general assembly passed a consumer tax on the sale of beer and liquor with all receipts earmarked for relief. One observer of Kentucky politics recalled that the general feeling then was that the liquor tax would raise sufficient revenues, and Chandler asserted that the relief needs of the state were exaggerated anyway.[14]

Lorena Hickok would have argued that point with Chandler if given an opportunity, for she had been touring eastern Kentucky that same month observing the relief situation. One of the FERA's roving agents, Hickok had a keen journalist's eye and a mandate from Hopkins to "tell me what you see and hear. All of it. Don't ever pull your punches."[15] She admitted that her reports describing conditions in Bell, Harlan, Clay, Knox, Leslie, Perry, and Whitley counties sounded "sobby" but insisted that they were "all true." She told of hungry and tattered people appearing at relief offices to be told of the "moratorium" on relief. They listened dumbly as social workers read them accounts of the special legislative session in Frankfort where nothing was happening. Her reports also described starvation deaths near Pineville, although she confessed that this information was secondhand. She witnessed for herself, however, a barefoot elderly woman begging for food in Knox County.[16] Much of Hickok's report was corroborated in reports from other field agents. In the following months FERA investigations revealed that the incidence of rickets was increasing in Jefferson County and that as much as 62 percent of the population of Jackson County needed assistance.[17]

Whether Kentucky was more to blame for its foot dragging on matching funds or Washington for its abrupt discontinuation of aid, the result was renewed distress among the needy. Harry Hopkins did not enjoy his role as hard-hearted administrator, and he told a conference of state directors of the National Emergency Council a few months later: "I tell you it isn't any fun, but what can you do? Here's the state of Kentucky. It would not put up any money and you say, 'You put up some money or we won't give you any.' What happens? They do not put it up.

Who gets licked? The unemployed. They always get licked. . . .
Believe me that is a tough order to give. It is going to be a long
time before I give another one. There will have to be somebody
else here to cut this food off from the unemployed."[18] Conservative officials in Virginia had been playing the same stall-and-
bluff game with Hopkins, but unlike their counterparts in Kentucky, they won. Hopkins had threatened to cut off their FERA
funds as well until a variety of political forces interceded on
their behalf.[19]

Fortunately, the promise of state matching funds from the
new tax on liquor sales lured federal money back into Kentucky.
The conflicts between Frankfort and Washington nonetheless
continued to roil the relief waters. It was soon apparent that
relief needs had not been greatly exaggerated and that forthcoming state revenues would not be adequate to meet them. Governor Laffoon made another hurried trip to confer with Hopkins
and found the FERA staff uncompromising in its demand for
more Kentucky matching funds than were anticipated.[20] The
governor sent a telegram to President Roosevelt and Hopkins on
November 5, asking that the federal government take over all
relief activities in the state. Kentucky was hereby abdicating
responsibility and, by default, declaring itself a pauper state in
order to qualify for further aid. Laffoon's wire blamed the shortfall of revenues on misguided members of the general assembly
who refused to follow his leadership. On behalf of the "unemployed men and their hungry and cold dependents," the governor dissolved the state partnership in the FERA. Harper Gatton
submitted his resignation as Kentucky relief administrator at
the same time, saying "there was nothing else to do. The money
failed to come in."[21] Behind the scenes of this public abdication
by the governor and the resignation of his administrator was a
skillful power play by one of the FERA field agents. Howard
Hunter had discovered a succession of careless—perhaps criminal—mistakes in the KERA bookkeeping and used them to force
Laffoon and Gatton to relinquish control.[22] Hopkins quickly
nationalized all relief programs for the state's 510,000 destitute,
and blamed their plight on "neglect on the part of State authorities." To replace Gatton as head of the restructured KERA,

he appointed Thornton Wilcox, who had been director of Louisville's public welfare program. Hopkins also enlarged the advisory body, the Kentucky Relief Commission.[23]

Even this nationalization did not stop FERA pressure on Kentucky to find some funds to help support federal relief programs in the state. Field agent Howard Hunter reported on his attempts to push state officials into greater self-sufficiency. "I put the screws on. . . . We have been suckers on the money business for relief long enough. . . . Frankly most of them . . . think we are kidding and if they hold out long enough, we will never stop paying the bill."[24] In March the FERA again imposed a freeze—this time only partial—on payments to Kentucky. Not wanting to get blamed for more starvation reports, Laffoon responded by ordering the state auditor to release $300,000 from the liquor tax fund.[25] In June 1934, facing the threat of losing all federal relief money again, another special session of the state legislature finally passed Laffoon's perennial sales tax proposal. This 3 percent tax would supposedly supply enough revenues for the FERA, and the state pledged $2.4 million to that effect.[26]

Kentucky's destitute escaped being the victims of further bickering between Washington and Frankfort, but the state endured several more months of political wrangling before Laffoon and federal relief officials declared a truce. Laffoon did not get along well with either field agent Howard Hunter or the federally appointed director of KERA, Thornton Wilcox. The governor charged in September that inefficiency, politics, and corruption were rampant in the relief operations and declared that these problems would have to be corrected before he would turn over any more state funds to federal officials. "Everyone knows there is something out of joint," he said. "Many are receiving relief who shouldn't and many don't get it who are entitled to it."[27] Despite investigations by federal officials and assurances from the Kentucky Relief Commission that politics and costs were being kept minimal, the governor suspecting a "whitewash," remained obstinate, and state funds trickled out fitfully. The *Courier-Journal* regretted that the poor had neither bread nor cake to eat while Laffoon played Marie Antoinette.[28] This embarrassing war of words ended in late October when members of the Kentucky Relief Commission resigned en masse, and Harry Hopkins replaced Wilcox with the Paducah newspaper publisher and businessman George Goodman. Although a Democrat and supporter of Laffoon, Goodman was more of an administrator than a politician, and the KERA under his guidance made peace with both Frankfort and Washington. Following the purge, relief activities proceeded at a less volatile and more effective pace until the FERA expired in late 1935.

During its two-and-one-half-year existence the FERA poured more than $35 million into programs for Kentucky's destitute, and state government added approximately $2.5 million—hardly the three-to-one ratio established in the original legislation. Nevertheless, money was being circulated to the needy.[29] The number of Kentucky families that qualified for relief averaged a hundred thousand per month in 1933, then fell gradually through 1935. The most immediate assistance came in the form of direct dole payments, worth $5.99 per month during the lowest and $13.62 during the highest months. These payments were less than half the national average, but southern rural areas had lower allotments than did northern cities.[30] The destitute unemployables were the only recipients of direct payments, and until the nationalization of the FERA in Kentucky, Gatton paid them with scrip to be redeemed at designated stores for merchandise.

Other forms of assistance consumed large parts of the FERA money. Almost half of the expenses went for distribution of commodities made available from other departments of the federal government. For instance, in November 1934 each relief family received twenty-four pounds of cabbage, and the following month, seven and a half pounds of canned beef.[31] These commodities were generally surplus goods the U.S. Department of Agriculture had removed from normal markets to stabilize farm prices. Available for distribution at other times were potatoes, flour, butter, oranges, cod-liver oil, and Milkwheato, a food mixture of milk and cereal especially adapted for children. Federal and state headquarters established precise guidelines as to who would receive what, depending on the number and ages of family members. County social workers and home visitors had to certify which families could receive which commodities. Some of the commodities also went to school lunch programs in those areas not able to afford their own.[32] Although many relief officials from Harry Hopkins down to county workers asserted that work-relief was preferable to direct handouts, jobs for the employable needy consumed only a quarter of the FERA funds in Kentucky.[33] The rapid planning of the program and its precarious financial status, particularly in Kentucky, did not allow for an extensive work program. Most of the work projects were swiftly conceived and took place on public property or produced items for public benefit. Some workers repaired community streets, sidewalks, sewers, and playgrounds. Others made blankets and mattresses from surplus cotton and materials supplied by the Department of Agriculture and then distributed them to needy families. The KERA devised a few jobs for about one thousand teachers whose regular county salaries had dried up and for unemployed clerks to index county records.[34] Otherwise, little effort went into matching unemployed people with suitable employment. These were emergency projects with few precedents. Few relief officials, moreover, were experienced in creating worthwhile programs. Perhaps the most productive of the work activities was the canning project. KERA officials set up at least twelve canning factories around the state to process harvests from relief gardens, like the earlier RFC gardens for which hundreds of relief workers received seeds and supplies for cultivating crops. Approximately fifty women worked at each cannery, and the KERA kept much of the canned harvest for later distribution. In November 1935, when the FERA was phasing out most of its activity, KERA offices had 3.5 million cans of beans and tomatoes for winter use.[35]

When all FERA programs had terminated in 1935, those Kentuckians still unable to support themselves were not without relief. Other agencies, both federal and state, had evolved to absorb most of the economic dislocation of the Great Depression. The FERA, by the federal government's admission, had been a stopgap to alleviate suffering. "It had given the time necessary to plan other measures."[36] Implementation of the program had introduced a new dimension of federal-state relations—sometimes poker game, sometimes partnership, but with Washington holding the advantage. One historian says the crisis nature of the situation forced Harry Hopkins to become a Simon Legree figure.[37] Ruby Laffoon would certainly have agreed with that description. The governor had felt the federal lash when Kentucky would not or could not carry its share of the relief burden. Several other states, including Ohio, Georgia, and Massachusetts also endured public humiliation when the FERA chief nationalized relief programs in their states.[38] Hopkins had certainly not made many friends among politicians.

Meanwhile, the New Deal experimented briefly with another emergency program, the Civil Works Administration (CWA). With eleven million people still unemployed in the fall of 1933, federal officials decided that the economy was not recovering as quickly as they had hoped. The CWA, hence, began operations in November to supplement, not compete with the FERA. Harry Hopkins also headed this agency, and he used many FERA personnel to implement this rapidly created jobs program.[39] Planned to last no more than six months and to hire as many as four million workers during the winter of 1933-1934, the CWA was to give "a quick shot in the arm to aid recovery."[40] It was almost exclusively a federal program, for which Washington provided 90 percent of the funding and state and local governments provided services, equipment, and occasional cash. All of the administrative personnel were federal; the rationale of officials in Washington was that an emergency program would gather momentum faster if its administrators did not have to negotiate with forty-eight state governments. In most states this created a dual system under which states administered the FERA and federal officials administered CWA work projects. Since the FERA had already nationalized relief efforts in Kentucky, both programs worked as one, sharing office space, personnel, and lists of needy families. Thornton Wilcox, the Kentucky Relief Commission, and county relief workers shuffled the qualified families and workers from one program to another as the situation seemed appropriate.

During its peak month, the CWA served as many as four million unemployed Americans, and in its brief tenure, it spent almost a billion dollars.[41] The jobs ranged from the temporary and trivial to the worthwhile and inspiring. Hopkins was more interested in getting people to work than in the quality of their activity. He once remarked about CWA employees, "Don't ask me what they are doing."[42] The largest number of them were, in fact, constructing or repairing highways and public buildings. Across the nation CWA workers earned money for improving 255,000 miles of roadways and 30,000 schools.[43] A great variety of other short-term projects, including archeological digs and musical performances, proliferated briefly, setting the precedent for larger, more substantial federal work projects to follow. The CWA aroused predictable criticism of the make-work quality of such projects as needless construction, leaf raking, and chasing rats from Chicago stockyards.[44]

Kentucky CWA activity followed the national pattern rather closely. More than a hundred thousand Kentuckians found work through CWA projects, and every county of the state was involved. Road construction and repair was the most common activity, but CWA crews also built or repaired schools in eighty-one counties.[45] A flurry of airport and airfield construction in nineteen Kentucky communities resulted from the often illogical hiring plans in Washington. CWA workers refurbished the existing facility at Owensboro and graded a landing strip near Beattyville, but the results of this feverish work were, inevitably, mixed. Some of the projects were never completed, some of the completed airfields never hosted an airplane.[46] Other projects across the state showed some imagination but employed only a few people and lasted only briefly. An unemployed artist in Lexington painted a mural for the University of Kentucky Library; a new sewage system was begun in Ashland; Kenton County undertook many bridge repairs; and unemployed residents of the Purchase built an amphitheater at Murray.[47] Some complaints about the CWA concerned its success. Although CWA wages in Kentucky rarely exceeded a dollar an hour, several farmers in the western sections "complained that they could not hire help because the CWA was paying such high wages for unskilled labor."[48]

One CWA project of particular interest to historians was the Historic American Buildings Survey, which took place in every state to greater or lesser degrees. Supervised by the Department of the Interior and designed to give meaningful employment to jobless architects and draftsmen, the HABS was to photograph, measure, and render scale drawings of buildings of unusual artistic or historical merit. The CWA would then deposit these accomplishments in the Library of Congress for reference purposes. Louisville architect G.M. Grimes led the Kentucky HABS and supervised a staff of twenty-one who selected sites from lists prepared by a committee of state historians and architects. Limited time and money prevented them from including all the suggested buildings in their survey, but they completed work on seventeen Kentucky structures before the CWA expired.[49] Frankfort's Old Statehouse, Bardstown's St. Joseph's Cathedral, and Shakertown Inn near Harrodsburg were among those included in the study. Patrons of Danville's Ephraim McDowell home and Transylvania College's Old Morrison protested the omission of these buildings from the survey, as did people in other cities who were proud of their structures, and so Grimes spent more time apologizing than he had bargained for.[50] The merits of this project were so obvious that other sponsors absorbed and continued it later.

As brief as its life was, the CWA accomplished several of its goals. It took millions of Americans off the dole and put them to work, pumped millions of dollars into the sluggish economy, showed that a federal program could be implemented quickly and efficiently with a minimum of state participation, and set many precedents for future work projects, especially in white-collar classifications. For all of its haste, expense, and occasional silliness, the CWA received a favorable public response. When Congress failed to renew the CWA in the spring of 1934, some fifty-seven thousand letters and telegrams of protest arrived in Washington in one week.[51] Until another works program began in 1935, former CWA employees had to be reabsorbed into the private sector, into makeshift FERA projects, or onto relief rolls again.

President Roosevelt agreed with Hopkins that work relief was preferable to the dole and that the CWA, despite its expense, had been a better program than the FERA. The WPA, created by his executive order in May 1935 to supersede these two agencies,[52] incorporated these beliefs and set into motion the nation's largest and most expensive relief program ever. By the time it closed out operations in 1943, the WPA had spent approximately eleven billion dollars and employed as many as three million workers at one time.[53] An estimated nine million Americans were on its payroll at some time during its existence. The WPA established a dichotomy between federal and state responsibility. National work projects would absorb the needy employable, and state direct relief would take care of the unemployable. This clear demarcation would prevent the unpleasant bickering over authority, matching funds, and political favoritism. A.B. Chandler's election and inauguration as governor took place during the initial stages of the WPA, and he helped make the transition into the new program as smooth as possible. Federal officials informed him of the new state responsibilities, and he was aware that the Laffoon administration had fallen behind as much as two million dollars in relief payments.[54] The new governor was more receptive to working with Washington than his predecessor had been, and Kentucky funding for its share of relief came in larger amounts and with more regularity than previously.[55] Hopkins took control of this third relief program, making him one of the best known of all New Deal personalities.

Like Hopkins, George Goodman moved from control of the KERA to the state WPA operations. He was compatible with Washington officials and Frankfort authorities alike, and his relations with Governors Laffoon, Chandler and, finally, Keen Johnson, remained cordial and professional. Even though the WPA was federally financed and its officials on the state and local levels were independent of Kentucky politics, several aspects of the program had to function in tandem with state and local systems, so Goodman's tact was important. Local relief offices had to certify all WPA employees, and city and county governments sponsored most of the work projects and supplied materials and equipment. The WPA would sustain much criticism both nationally and in Kentucky, but Goodman remained more or less immune from attack. The University of Kentucky awarded him a public service medallion in 1936, and Grayson County named one of its new schools in his honor.[56] He and Hopkins shared political longevity, but the Kentucky administrator escaped controversy better than his boss in Washington. The WPA headquarters in Kentucky occupied the fourth floor of an office building in downtown Louisville and became almost a small government in itself. Seemingly endless rows of file cabinets and desks—each with a gooseneck lamp—might have given the impression of orderliness and discipline, but brief observation would have proved otherwise.[57] Frenetic activity characterized the office day and night. The staff had to approve requests for new projects from 120 county relief offices, and had to prepare frequent news releases and "narrative reports" for local papers and national WPA officials. Washington authorities reorganized district and regional offices several times between 1935 and 1943, and Congress frequently reduced and increased WPA funding, causing multiple problems at the state level. Nature, the national economy, politics, and World War II also forced the Kentucky headquarters to adjust its priorities and hiring practices. For instance, the 1936 drought prompted new jobs for rural workers, and the 1937 floods created emergency opportunities for WPA projects along the banks of the Ohio and Kentucky Rivers.[58] An economic recession in 1938 and the elections of that year also caused a surge of pump-priming activities by the New Deal. Because of its scope and duration the WPA became a familiar force in Kentucky in the late 1930s and early 1940s, and its economic impact was substantial. The Louisville office channeled more than $162 million through thousands of state projects and had as many as seventy-two thousand Kentuckians on the payroll in the September 1938 peak.[59]

Heavy construction projects consumed a great deal of WPA money in Kentucky, making the state typical of national endeavors. The WPA undertook work on more than fourteen thousand miles of roads; seventy-three thousand bridges, culverts, and viaducts; and more than nine hundred public buildings, such as schools, jails, and fire stations.[60] Pineville's new city hall, Princeton's courthouse, Hopkinsville's stadium, and Morgan County's new school—all provided unemployed workers with jobs, put money into circulation, and produced needed facilities.[61] Whether from need or for lack of better inspiration, the WPA also constructed sixty-five thousand outdoor toilets around the state to serve country schools, recreation areas, and other rural sites.[62] These too, were typical of millions of WPA sanitary privies that dotted the national landscape and gave rise to many questions about extravagance and boondoggling. On rare occasion the WPA would single out one of its projects for special publicity, as was the case with the new high school in Morgan County. Federal officials, newspaper reporters and photographers, and assorted dignitaries descended on tiny West Liberty for lunch when Mrs. Roosevelt laid the cornerstone for the new building in May 1937. Senator Barkley and Governor Chandler both travelled long distances to pay tribute to their constituents and to the benefits of education and the federal government.[63]

Such construction projects constituted the bulk of WPA activity both in Kentucky and across the United States. Future generations would use the highways and facilities with little thought of the thousands of relief workers and millions of dollars that had made them possible. These WPA "memorials" were so numerous as to be ubiquitous and so standardized as to become almost interchangeable from state to state. Other, more distinctive, projects occupied a smaller portion of the WPA budget but deserve more analysis because of the uniqueness of their missions and the quality of their accomplishments. Among them were activities for women, white-collar workers, writers, and artists.

Sewing projects, usually reserved for needy women, appeared around the state to fill a variety of needs. Sponsored by the Kentucky Department of Welfare, these "sewing rooms" hired women to make clothing for their own families and for distribution to other needy families. The WPA paid the wages of the employees and their instructors and usually supplied fabric for their use. Local relief offices furnished space, heat, and light for the operations and arranged for local women to teach and supervise.[64] At times of peak employment, sewing rooms operated in 118 counties and hired as many as thirty-one hundred women at a time. Originally the project concentrated on teaching women to sew for self-improvement while they were supplementing family incomes. Later, mass production of garments for state-wide distribution became more prevalent and heavy-duty cutting and stitching machines gave an aura of factory life to several of these rooms. Some of the instructors also delivered health and sanitation lessons to their students; WPA handbooks supplied hints on how to encourage the women to shampoo their hair and use deodorants.[65] Statistics demonstrated the eagerness of the women to work, learn, and produce; by the time these sewing centers had ceased operations in 1943, they had produced more than eight million articles, including personal garments and those intended for statewide distribution.[66] The benefits extended beyond the workrooms as well. Louisville headquarters estimated that "a large percent of the children in the nearly destitute rural and mining sections . . . could not have attended school" had it not been for these projects providing basic clothing to needy families.[67] A small sideline in seven of the county sewing rooms was the production of mattresses, made from surplus cotton that the Department of Agriculture had purchased and released to the WPA. The mattresses, too, were distributed by the State Department of Welfare to needy families.[68]

The WPA's role as wholesale grocer helped dispose of some of the agricultural surpluses that plagued American farmers, supplemented some of the state's relief activities, and enhanced school lunch programs throughout the state. The Surplus Commodity Distribution Project continued a service begun under the FERA and allowed the Department of Agriculture to dispose of such commodities as potatoes, grapefruit, prunes, butter, cheese, and powdered milk.[69] State officials initially had only to furnish warehouses for storage in each county, but in 1937 the WPA insisted that the states assume a larger share of the costs for this program, including salaries and trucks for distribution. Governor Chandler protested the new burden but managed to find the funds for this project, which provided food to approximately ninety thousand Kentucky families.[70] Some Kentuckians in remote eastern communities tasted grapefruit for the first time as a result of the commodity program. Starting in 1939 these surplus foods were available for school lunch programs, to be served free to students of relief families. The WPA hired additional workers for school cafeterias, and by 1941, schools in 101 counties were participating. WPA dieticians, sometimes called vitamin girls, created new, balanced, and inexpensive menus making use of the ever-changing supply of commodities. The appearance of prune pudding, potato soup, and bean loaf on school lunch trays reflected the current USDA purchase of farm surpluses.[71] Local sponsors of school lunch programs also started garden and canning projects, both of which had proved successful previously. By 1941 there were 193 units using WPA equipment operating around the state and putting up 195,000 quarts of canned vegetables for future school lunches.[72]

More than two hundred WPA recreation centers sprang up around the state, providing various activities for local communities and employing as many as 825 teachers, coaches, and social workers. This project was one of several that hired white-collar workers to develop cultural and recreational programs to fill increased leisure time, according to Kentucky's Recreation Project head, Austin Welch.[73] Sponsored statewide by the Department of Education, and coordinated locally by schools, churches, YMCAs, and civic clubs, the project emphasized recreational activities primarily for rural areas. The University of Kentucky held training sessions for center directors, who developed a variety of brochures on craft and game activities. They also received copies of *Leisure Leader*, the newsletter that the state project published "now and then."[74] By 1939 these leaders were directing activities in 134 towns and providing leisure programs for as many as 584,000 children and adults per month.[75] Center athletic teams took advantage of many of the new parks and gymnasiums built by the WPA, and they also joined statewide competitive leagues. Craft and dancing classes, puppet performances, nature hikes, and camping proliferated in assorted local facilities and nearby state parks. The Lexington center conducted a Negro Song Festival, and Hollywood movie actress Jane Withers showed up at the Shively center for a game session. Henderson's center occupied a renovated tobacco warehouse, which included a woodworking shop, Ping-Pong tables, and a three-hundred-seat theater. Corbin and Mayfield produced successful boxing teams, which competed in matches throughout the Midwest.[76] Louisville band director Jacob J. Schilling worked as one of the Jefferson County recreation leaders and wrote the official Kentucky WPA marching song, which appeared in the *Leisure Leader.*

WPA of the USA, we take our hats off to you.
You proved yourself faithful, that is true
to the colors of the Red, White and Blue.
Your recreation sure makes us happy;
Brings happiness to everyone.
Three cheers for the WPA; your work is well, well done.[77]

This exaltation of leisure activity summed up one of the contradictions within the WPA. These centers were only a small part of the WPA effort and they promoted beneficial social activities, but even so, they often appeared nonessential. Could the federal government have found better means of revitalizing the economy than these recreational pursuits?

Most states had a WPA Library Project, but Kentucky may have been the only one that included horses and mules in the program. This distinctive equine dimension not only allowed more people to get books, it also attracted national attention. The State Library Extension Service sponsored the usual library activities in cooperation with local churches, schools, and civic groups. Together they enhanced old libraries and established new ones in about sixty counties, employed hundreds of workers, collected, mended, and circulated thousands of books and magazines to people who had never enjoyed library services.[78] Few of the services or employees were as unusual, however, as the packhorse book women who carried their wares in saddlebags and wound their way up creek beds and mountain paths to isolated families. Similar, short-lived experiments had begun in 1913 in Paintsville and in 1935 with a FERA project. The memory of these prompted several mountain communities to suggest their revival.[79] Elizabeth Fullerton, state WPA director of women's and professional projects, implemented the suggestion, and by late 1938 there were 274 women on horseback delivering reading materials to remote areas of twenty-nine counties miles from the nearest libraries and highways. The counties provided a central repository for donated books and magazines, and carriers then traveled assigned routes. They suggested appropriate books to new readers, filled requests from earlier visits, encouraged reluctant bystanders to borrow for the first time, and sometimes stopped to read to blind or illiterate patrons. In one year alone, these packhorse libraries circulated an estimated 100,000 books and 150,000 magazines.[80] Whitley County had twenty carriers riding routes out from Williamsburg, and Breathitt County had eleven routes and a demand for eleven more. In Harlan County, Ann Richards and five assistants delivered their books by mule, departing somewhat from the horseback norm.[81] State library supervisors approached Louisville, Lexington, and New York newspapers with appeals for book donations as the popularity of these services grew. Washington WPA officials used the term "famous" when referring to the Kentucky packhorse project, and one national library journal published an article about it, illustrated with a photo of an elderly mountain woman enjoying her pipe and a newly delivered book.[82] Many WPA libraries and most of the packhorse routes ceased operation during World War II, but with the coming of better highways in rural Kentucky, bookmobiles soon served the same readers as the former four-legged libraries.

Federal One was a unique public works project of great diversity and some controversy, which employed artists, actors, writers, and musicians to work and perform at federal expense. Employees of Federal One never constituted more than 2 percent of WPA payrolls, but the program generated disproportionate publicity.[83] Theater productions, musical concerts, murals and statues, and hundreds of books—all resulted from this group of unemployed creative artists. Many critics questioned the propriety of government subsidies for creative activity, just as they questioned the recreation projects. Harry Hopkins responded with one of his much-quoted aphorisms, "They've got to eat just like other people."[84] Many congressmen also had reservations about Federal One. They had never been comfortable with its separate administrative setup or with the left-wing ideology that seems to have invaded parts of the program, prompting a complete reorganization in 1939. The WPA jettisoned the theater project and transferred other parts to the state WPA offices where they went their diverse ways, no longer under unified national guidance or funding.[85] Kentucky spent less than 2 percent of its WPA funds in Federal One enterprises, but several distinctive and worthwhile projects emerged from the experience. Like several other rural and southern states, Kentucky had no theater project at all because it had so few unemployed theater personnel.

One of the aims of Federal One's music projects was to encourage an appreciation for American composers and folk music. Several larger cities formed WPA symphony orchestras, which toured extensively and often performed in radio studios for recording and broadcasting. Kentucky's involvement in this program was consistent with the national goals but on a less ambitious scale. From the start, the Kentucky music project sponsored a Folk Song Festival near Ashland that may have been the only one of its kind. Musicians and minstrels from many mountain communities showed up at the festival site, the cabin of Kentucky's well known "traipsin' woman," Jean Thomas. They sang and played ancient ballads and old folk tunes on handmade instruments. Thousands of visitors from as far away as Philadelphia and Washington attended this "spectacular and unique event" in June 1936, and WPA employees from Louisville were on the scene to record the music and transcribe the songs.[86] Jean Thomas later recalled that as a result of these festivals new and spontaneous folk songs came from the mountain musicians. The "Singing Fiddler of Lost Hope Hollow" created this New Deal quatrain:

> Uncle Sam was very kind
> He gave the people aid

The WPA is working hard
Good roads will soon be made.[87]

Less spectacular, although no less significant, was the contest sponsored by the WPA and the Columbia Broadcasting System in 1937 to elicit new choral works. Bowling Green's John Vincent, Jr., was one of the winners, and the New York City Madrigal Singers performed his composition *Three Grecian Songs* on a CBS broadcast the following year.[88]

Kentucky responded in several ways when federal officials turned the national music project over to the states in 1939. Both the adult education and the recreation projects hired music teachers to conduct classes and present community concerts and recitals. The University of Kentucky sponsored an assortment of activities around the state: music therapy classes at Central State Hospital, for example, and the *Kentucky Harmony* newsletters, which offered advice to teachers on such subjects as how to make a music stand from wire coat hangers. A small but energetic Kentucky WPA orchestra of five members toured the state doing an average of thirty-five performances per month. According to the state music supervisor the group "made good music available in communities theretofore without it."[89]

Probably the two most memorable accomplishments of Federal One's Federal Art Project (FAP) were the murals that graced more than twenty-five hundred public buildings and the Index of American Design, a collection of illustrations, or "plates," that documented the history of American decorative and applied arts.[90] Although there were never more than thirty Kentucky artists per year employed in the FAP, they participated in both projects and others as well. The WPA hired unemployed artists to design and paint murals depicting scenes of local heritage in several public buildings around the state, such as the Hopkins County Courthouse, the Harrodsburg Post Office, and the Kentucky Children's Home. On a smaller scale, it commissioned artists to paint or copy old portraits of local dignitaries for display in other courthouses. Illustrators produced directional and commemorative signs for other WPA work projects, and sculptors executed pieces for the University of Louisville campus.[91] The Index of American Design was to be a collection of visual records of American folk art and design from every state. Several Kentucky artists worked on this project. Charles Epperson painted meticulous replicas of quilt blocks from Brandenburg, Kentucky; Thomas Joyce copied the design of a copper powder flask owned by the Filson Club; and Orville Carroll and others photographed and painted likenesses of furniture, textiles, and household accessories traced to the old Shaker community at Pleasant Hill. Adele Brandeis, a WPA state supervisor, reported that one of the Kentucky artists had done so well with the intricate copy work for the design project that an aircraft plant hired him for similar employment.[92] The WPA exhibited the thousands of completed plates in several galleries and museums before finding a home for them in the National Gallery of Art in Washington.[93] This aspect of Federal One, by itself, contributed a priceless cache of Americana and kept many artists pursuing their craft during hard times.

The Federal Writers Project (FWP) performed the same dual function of recording part of the nation's heritage and putting idle writers on the payroll. One Kentucky author, Irvin S. Cobb, whose reputation insulated him from the ravages of the Depression, told the state office of the FWP that "to give a helping hand to needy writers, and at the same time to perpetuate the real story of our state in the printed word, seems to me to be about as fine a double-barreled idea as I, off-hand, can think of."[94] Dr. Urban Bell directed the project in Kentucky and at any given time supervised an average of fifty unemployed researchers, writers, editors, and photographers. Bell was a resident of Cobb's hometown of Paducah, where he had recently been president of the local junior college. He was also acquainted with another son of this Purchase city, George Goodman, the new state WPA director. Under Bell's guidance, the Kentucky FWP produced a number of books for national series and additional works inspired by local sponsors. Some of these studies were substantial books in hard bindings and were published by major houses; others never made it beyond the stage of mimeographed and stapled pages. The writers' efforts were of mixed quality, but the results of their activity have assisted students of Kentucky's history ever since.

The most ambitious project of the FWP, both nationally and in Kentucky, was the American Guide series, a comprehensive set of books for each state that included discussions of state history, geography, economics, and the arts and provided unusual guided tours through sites of local interest. Directives from Washington dictated the dimensions of these books, and Dr. Bell modified his staff and altered course with each new order. At one point he had more than a hundred workers gathering information from every county.[95] From its inception in 1935 until its completion in 1939, *Kentucky: A Guide to the Bluegrass State*, went through many revisions as the national project coordinator solicited editorial comments from many sources. The director of the Ohio FWP read the Kentucky manuscript and awarded it a "B − or C + " because he thought it lacked individuality and contained too much fuzzy writing. Several professors from the University of Kentucky thereupon offered suggestions for improving the sections on literature, art, and folklore. Shortly before its publication, historian Thomas D. Clark gave the WPA office a mixed review of the book. He congratulated the staff for compiling "a vast amount of local history which is not to be found elsewhere" but worried about some of the factual errors and regional stereotypes, especially regarding dialects and horses.[96] A reviewer for the *Journal of Southern History* repeated this ambivalent estimate of the book when it was released. He found it worthy but flawed, interesting but uneven.[97] The review was a typical response to the guide series, and the problem lay within its premise. A scholarly project undertaken by unemployed writers and aimed at a popular audience could only have a schizophrenic offspring. Dr. Bell seemed to flourish in these confused circumstances, however, and federal officials trusted him to revive and assist the Missouri Guide, which was foundering.[98]

Other publications by the Kentucky FWP followed the same pattern of group research, committee writing, and mixed results. Several cities and counties sponsored local histories, and the results included *Henderson: A Guide to Audubon's Hometown in Kentucky, In the Land of Breathitt, Lexington and the*

*Bluegrass Country, Old Capitol and Frankfort,* and *Louisville: A Guide to the Falls City.* Topical studies that crossed geographical lines also appeared. There were books on fairs, libraries, and colleges. *Southern Harmony,* a publication of particular distinction, was a facsimile edition of a collection of songs for group singing that had been published in 1854. Frederick Eichelberger produced a massive *Military History of Kentucky* for the state government in 1939, and the following year the FWP published *Medicine and Its Development in Kentucky.* The *Filson Club History Quarterly* offered tepid praise of the latter, saying only that it was better than most of the other WPA literary efforts.[99]

Like many other WPA activities, the FWP failed to complete some of its undertakings because of policy shifts, funding cutbacks, and termination of the program in 1943. One of the fascinating unfinished projects was "America Eats," an attempt to collect regional recipes and dining traditions. The Kentucky staff compiled stories about state culinary customs and deliberated over the correct ways of making burgoo, spoon bread, and mint juleps, but very little came of their efforts.[100] Another national project that never bore fruit in Kentucky was "These Are Our Lives," interviews with rural southerners transcribed for inclusion in books of folklore. Dr. Bell employed about thirty people to interview Kentuckians and write their biographies for this series. He instructed them on the types of people to interview, how to work quotations and local color into the narratives, and other writing techniques. Some of the finished vignettes were creative and revealing, others were prosaic at best, and none ever achieved publication.[101] Approximately a thousand such interviews were conducted in the states that participated in the project, and most met the same fate as those in Kentucky; the FWP laid the brief biographies to rest in manila folders and file cases. Only a few made their way into a small collection that W.T. Couch edited and published in 1939, entitled, appropriately enough, *These Are Our Lives.* Many years later, other historians have unearthed selections of the original interviews and published them posthumously, as it were. None of these anthologies has included any of the Kentucky selections, however.[102]

Another unfinished project, similar both in technique and

disposition, was the interviewing of former slaves still living in the South. Lawrence D. Reddick, a historian at Kentucky State College in Frankfort, had suggested to Harry Hopkins during the earlier days of FERA that such interviews were worth pursuing, and by 1936 the idea blossomed.[103] The Washington staff prepared standard questionnaires for interviewers to facilitate the gathering of information common to all the subjects. They also prepared guidelines on how to elicit information without influencing responses from elderly blacks and included instructions about transcribing dialect. Interviewers subsequently compiled more than two thousand narrative interviews from seventeen states, and the FWP deposited them in the Library of Congress.[104] The narratives have since been edited and published in whole or part. Dr. Bell assigned several of his Kentucky workers to this project, and they conducted approximately thirty interviews with former slaves still living in the state. The federal project editors returned several of the Kentucky transcripts for clarification. For instance, they wanted a translation of "We uster cyt a nikasses warrek ubter ed dat."[105] Once the Kentucky staff developed more expertise at either typing or interpreting, the narratives made interesting and historically rich reading. One elderly man from Calloway County remembered: "I waz a slave befo de wa. My boss . . . he wuz a race hoss man . . . I'd rub de legs uv dem hosses and rode dem round to gib em exercise." And a woman from Clay County recalled slave auctions from her childhood. "The slave trader had a long whop that he hit them with to see if they could jump around and wuz strong."[106] Historians have used the collections of interviews with both enthusiasm and caution, because they contain material not available elsewhere but are replete with the errors that fill any human memory of distant events.

Before the WPA ended in 1943, dozens of other projects occupied hundreds of unemployed Kentuckians on tasks as diverse as repairing toys for underprivileged children, assisting museums in mounting displays, listing the sites of veterans' graves, cleaning artifacts from archeological digs, continuing the CWA's Historic American Buildings Survey, compiling health statistics, and microfilming old Kentucky newspapers.

One project of special interest to historians was the Historical Records Survey. A national project, initially, this survey sought to locate, organize, catalogue, and describe collections of important documents held in various repositories around the state. Under five successive state directors the employees prepared mimeographed inventories of these holdings that became "valuable data for students of political, social and economic history."[107] The records of this survey, now in the State Library, reveal the immensity of the undertaking, and the collection of inventories remains today as valuable to researchers as their compilers promised in 1940.

The results of a Gallup Poll in June 1939 revealed that Americans considered the WPA the worst agency of the New Deal.[108] Many Kentuckians shared the attitude. Constant criticism greeted "leaf-raking" projects and the allegedly boondoggling workers who got paid to loaf on the job. The *Kentucky City* magazine solicited opinions from local government officials across the state, and seventy-four respondents mentioned this aspect of the WPA frequently, especially in reference to the white-collar projects.[109] Another frequent criticism was that the projects often displayed shoddy craftsmanship and were of little public benefit. It was true, of course, that the WPA seldom used contract bidding, hired many unskilled workers, and offered no chance of advancement; hence, workers had little incentive to excel in their tasks.[110] Although WPA wages, which averaged twenty-one dollars per month in 1936, were preferable to the dole, they were not sufficient to inspire extra effort. George Goodman told Governor Chandler, "I do not believe that relief employment should ever be so attractive that people would be encouraged to leave normal profit employment for it."[111] One factor that added to the negative image of WPA was that it openly mixed politics with relief. The politics became a serious issue in 1938 (see Chapter 7).

That same 1939 Gallup Poll revealed that Americans also believed that the WPA was the New Deal's finest agency. Millions of Americans and thousands of Kentuckians owed much in the way of self-respect to this federal agency for creating jobs somewhat related to their skills and, thus, sparing them the indignity of asking for welfare. For some, these jobs were distinguished and productive activities. As a counterbalance to those government officials who criticized boondoggling, there were others who praised the WPA programs. John Sherman Cooper, a Republican county judge in Pulaski County in the 1930s, fondly recalled the construction work on schools and highways and even on the outhouses. "I don't care what they say about the WPA . . . it was a great help in our county . . . these people turned out; they worked hard. I was very proud of our program."[112] Louisville Mayor Joseph Scholtz also praised the "splendid job" done by the WPA in Jefferson County. Without it, he said, the city "would be far behind" in construction, health, and welfare programs.[113] The president of the University of Kentucky expressed these same sentiments to George Goodman about campus improvements that would not have been done without WPA.[114] The *Courier-Journal* admitted that it had done its share of picking at WPA "sore spots" but added that "in the long depression days when most Kentucky counties couldn't pay their public officers, WPA was building roads, school houses, court houses, bridges—works that put the State twenty-five years ahead by conservative estimate."[115]

The Public Works Administration (PWA) provided a sharp contrast to the WPA and, indeed, to most New Deal agencies. It was relatively quiet about its activities, planned its projects meticulously, and spent its money carefully, and it seldom received criticism for being frivolous, extravagant, or political. When World War II brought its work to an end, the PWA had spent six billion dollars on 34,500 projects, the majority of which were large durable public facilities such as Lincoln Tunnel in New York City, Grand Coulee Dam on the Columbia River, and the aircraft carrier *Enterprise*.[116] Congress created the PWA in June 1933 as part of the National Industrial Recovery Act, and its original purpose was to stimulate the economy by creating construction jobs. Secretary of the Interior Harold L. Ickes became its director, but his personality made it impossible for the agency to move as swiftly as New Deal planners had intended. For that reason the CWA and later the WPA became the agents for rapidly instigated public works projects under

Harry Hopkins. Ickes, a former Bull Moose Republican from Illinois, was one of the chief critics of Hopkins's propensity for haste and his often questionable expenditures.[117] The PWA chief demanded scrupulous accountability and infuriated local and state authorities who wanted faster action and more money for their special projects. Known as Honest Harold and the Old Curmudgeon, he filled his diary with his testy opinions about his associates and with his intention to keep his branch of the government completely "legitimate" and scandal free.[118]

PWA activity in Kentucky paralleled that of most states in that its projects began slowly, were under close federal supervision with minimal participation by the state government, and tended to be large. Initial planning began shortly after the PWA's creation in the summer of 1933; the major work did not begin until well into 1934, however. Most of the projects were finished, phased out, or absorbed into other municipal or federal programs by 1940. During its tenure, Ickes's agency had undertaken six hundred projects in the state, hired thousands of workers, and spent $49 million.[119] To oversee and coordinate state projects, the PWA appointed a state engineer (later called director). George Sager filled that role in Kentucky for most of PWA's active years. The federal appropriations in Kentucky, as elsewhere, usually covered only 45 percent of a project's costs; the remainder had to come from the public agency sponsoring it, such as a school system or municipal government. Most commonly, these nonfederal sponsors supplied their share by selling bonds, which the PWA frequently purchased itself or made arrangements for.[120] Kentucky and many other states had to pass special legislation to allow municipalities to enter into contracts with the PWA and to incur bonded indebtedness. With these legal barriers out of the way by late 1934, the pace of PWA activity increased. After 1935 many politicians preferred to have Hopkins's WPA undertake their local construction projects because it paid all the costs, thus freeing them from financial burdens. In one of their few areas of accord, Hopkins and Ickes agreed that the larger and more expensive projects rightfully fell within the PWA jurisdiction.

A few of the PWA projects in Kentucky were classified as

federal because they involved properties or functions of the national government and did not require state or local funding. Except for the hiring of local workers, the Washington office handled most of the details. For example, Hazard, Mayfield, and Owensboro all received new or enlarged post office facilities. The PWA assisted the Army Corps of Engineers in the state with a variety of river improvements valued at two million dollars.[121] Major construction, including the new gold depository, took place on the military post at Fort Knox. Under unusually tight security, workers fashioned the concrete, granite, and steel into a twenty-ton vault, and waited for the first trainload of gold to arrive in January 1937.[122] PWA crews also installed new water and sewage systems near Mammoth Cave, which was soon to become a part of the National Park System.

PWA grants made it possible for municipal governments to undertake new projects and to accomplish building goals far ahead of their normal schedules. For instance, Kentucky towns acquired 276 new schools, 6 hospitals, 24 sewage treatment plants, and more than 80 new waterworks. In addition, Newport got a new fire station, Middlesboro an electricity-generating plant, and Dundee an auditorium.[123] Lexington and Louisville sponsored PWA slum clearance projects and low-cost housing complexes that the USHA later absorbed. As a rule the municipal projects went smoothly, and most local governments repaid their loans and redeemed their bonds on schedule. Salyersville, unfortunately, was an exception. The tiny town contracted for a new water plant and sold bonds to the PWA as its share of the $41,000 cost. Construction on the plant ended in late 1934, but because of an accounting error, the contractor did not receive final payment despite his many inquiries and threats to sue. The PWA finally corrected the error and paid the contractor in late 1935. No sooner was that issue resolved than the town government fell behind in the interest payments on its bonded debt and became an object of new demands and threats.[124] No doubt there were many in Salyersville who regretted that their town had ever aspired to such civic improvements as purified water.

Governor Chandler's administration, which also benefited from PWA grants, accelerated building projects that had been postponed for lack of funds. Kentucky State Industrial College in Frankfort constructed a new student dormitory, Eastern State Teachers' College in Richmond enlarged its library, and the University of Kentucky built a new student union building—all under the aegis of the PWA.[125] Chandler discovered that not all state-sponsored projects could proceed swiftly or smoothly. For two years he tried unsuccessfully to convince reluctant Washington officials that they should fund a new prison facility for the state. In early 1937 he complained to Ickes that the PWA was discriminating against Kentucky in the matter of the proposed new penal institution; then he urged Senator Barkley to exert whatever pressure he could to persuade Ickes.[126] The disastrous flood of the Kentucky River in 1937 did more good than letters and politics. It almost destroyed the ancient Frankfort prison and made the construction of a new facility an emergency, thus helping the governor's case. Ickes finally changed his mind, and ground breaking for the new $2 million minimum security prison took place at La Grange in June with both Chandler and state PWA Director George Sager turning spades of soil.[127]

Another state-sponsored project revealed how exacting the PWA standards were and how local recipients could be both grateful for and frustrated with the results of the work. Western State Teachers' College in Bowling Green had contracted for a new classroom building (Cherry Hall), and the PWA had selected Indiana limestone as the basic material. A three-month battle of the mails ensued, which involved the limestone, the economy of the Pennyroyal, and the pride of the state. The secretary of the Bowling Green Chamber of Commerce indicated to Senator Barkley that "we are very much exercised about this" because the use of local Kentucky stone would help the area economy more than the use of limestone from out of state. Governor Chandler also complained about the Hoosier stone to Ickes, saying it would not match the darker local stone of most campus buildings. PWA officials determined that the substitution of local stone would raise the cost of the project by approximately twenty-one thousand dollars. If the state cared so much for aesthetics and local materials, the PWA would allow the substitution, but Kentucky would have to foot the bill.[128] The

PWA finally constructed Cherry Hall with Indiana limestone after state officials decided it was easier to surrender their cause than to pay the extra money. A Bowling Green newspaper understood the reasoning but found the decision "most regrettable" following such a "strong fight."[129]

Had Cherry Hall been a WPA rather than a PWA project the battle would probably have taken no longer than one phone call. The WPA would have used local stone and borne the extra cost with a shrug of Harry Hopkins's shoulders, and Ickes would have had additional evidence of WPA extravagance. Toward the end of the New Deal, the manager of the Louisville chapter of Associated General Contractors outlined the differences between the two agencies. He praised the PWA for high standards, using competitive bids, and employing trained professionals, contrasting these practices to those of the WPA where the use of available labor and convenient materials frequently produced unsatisfactory work.[130] Although oversimplified, the remarks highlight the diversity in goals and techniques of two major public works agencies of the New Deal.

Starting with the FERA in 1933 and running through the demise of the WPA in 1943, the New Deal experimented with several kinds of relief and public works to aid the unemployed. For the first time in American history the nation's capital provided funds for a dole. This function later became partly a state responsibility, but the concept of federal welfare had become permanent, as had the acceptance of a semipermanent unemployed class living on the edge of the economy. The New Deal never claimed to have ended the problem of joblessness; it claimed only the new machinery for dealing with it. Pump-priming—that Keynesian shibboleth—went through several transformations in the 1930s. Some were transitory with the CWA jobs, some were federally instigated with the WPA, and some came from a local-federal partnership in the PWA. In whatever form, the technique of government-created jobs for public benefit became ingrained in the political lexicon as a means of injecting new life into a sluggish economy. Whether temporary or permanent, the public works projects served their purpose reasonably well. Thousands of Kentuckians were able to enjoy a better life because of participation in these programs, and the next generation could take for granted the public facilities that came from their labor. Buildings, books, and ball games in the commonwealth—all provided jobs, restored some individual pride, and created a few enduring monuments to this fearless, albeit expensive government innovation.

# 4. Kentucky Youth and the New Deal

Emma G. Cromwell lived by numbers. As a librarian, Kentucky's secretary of state, treasurer, and state parks director, she had mastered tiny fractions and huge statistics. But when she tried to assess the effect of the Civilian Conservation Corps in Kentucky, numbers failed her. "There is no arithmetic adequate," she wrote, "to calculate the immense amount of good accomplished by this agency. In addition to material benefits there is no doubt that thousands of boys had their eyes opened to the beauties of nature and were convinced of the dignity of labor."[1] In contrast to this praise of impersonal statistics, an anonymous nineteen-year-old girl from Monroe County offered personal testimony to the effect of the National Youth Administration in her life. "I am a high school graduate as the result of N.Y.A. aid. . . . With my first check I paid off a debt for school books. Then with my next checks I began to wear better clothes. This made me hold my head up and feel that I was as good as anyone there, because I felt that I had really earned them. . . . I now believe that there is a job for me and some way to earn my own way in the world."[2] The difference between the CCC and NYA were as pronounced as the contrast between fighting fires in a state forest and grading papers for a high school physics teacher. But the common thread linking them was a determination to use one of the nation's most precious resources—youth. The federal government's goal in both agencies was to cultivate that resource by providing jobs and training for young people before the Great Depression destroyed their chances for a better future. Those efforts were probably the most inspiring and least controversial of all the New Deal activities. The establishment of the CCC came as a natural outgrowth of Franklin Roosevelt's experience and interest. This gentleman farmer of Dutchess County, New York, had an abiding concern for natural resources and estate management, and as governor of New York in 1932 he had put ten thousand jobless men to work in the state forest lands. By planting trees, fighting fires, and learning conservation skills, unemployed men improved both the land and themselves.[3] Early in his presidency Roosevelt discussed the desirability of using this concept on a national scale, and on March 21 he urged Congress to pass legislation to create the CCC. He emphasized not only that such a work program would reduce the national relief burden but that it would correct decades of neglect and misuse of land and forests. In addition to "the material gains will be the moral and spiritual value of such work. . . . We can take a vast army of these unemployed out into healthful surroundings" for essential work such as "forestry, the prevention of soil erosion, flood control, and similar projects."[4] He signed the resultant Emergency Conservation Work Act on March 31, then took a personal interest in its administration until its termination ten years later. The first camp, near Luray, Virginia, bore his name, and he visited it and other camps frequently. If the president had a favorite child in the prodigious New Deal brood, surely the CCC was it.

Goals for the CCC were simple, but administering the program was a bureaucratic nightmare because four separate federal departments were involved. The Labor Department recruited and selected the enrollees from lists of relief families in forty-eight states; the War Department supervised the camp sites and living quarters; and the Departments of Interior and Agriculture formulated work projects on hundreds of federal properties. Additional projects took place on land owned by state governments and private individuals.[5] Bringing order to this administrative confusion was the CCC director, Robert Fechner, who maintained an amazing degree of calm despite the array of federal and state agencies under his jurisdiction. Fechner was a

self-educated labor organizer from Tennessee who had worked
his way up from machinist apprentice to vice-president of the
American Federation of Labor by 1933. His selection as head of
the corps was wise on its own merits, but it also pacified some
labor unions who had initially been dubious about this new
government experiment.[6] Original plans specified that the CCC
would hire only unmarried men, aged eighteen to twenty-five,
from needy families and would place them in camps for six-
month terms. These men would get thirty dollars per month for
their training and work, twenty-five dollars of which went home
to their families.[7] For the most part, Fechner adhered to these
original plans, although some modifications did occur, notably
the establishment of camps for war veterans and Indians. By the
time of its demise, more than 2.5 million men had served time
in "Roosevelt's Army" at hundreds of camp sites and had,
among other things, planted approximately 2.3 billion trees, the
most memorable of their many achievements.[8]

More than eighty thousand young men from Kentucky served
as volunteers in this army in the woods. Most of them were
applicants from relief families, but several hundred were veterans from the Great War.[9] Enrollment quotas varied from year
to year, based on state populations, unemployment rates, and
other factors, and the largest number from Kentucky to be
enrolled at any time was during 1936-1937 when thirty thousand men worked in camps. At one point in 1938 Kentucky
ranked first in the nation in the number of men serving in the
CCC in proportion to population.[10] State relief officers selected
from among the relief applicants, and state Veterans Administration authorities filled their quotas from the unemployed
veterans' applications. There were generally more applicants
than openings in the CCC until the economic revival and the
coming of war in Europe in 1939, when private industry and the
military draft began to deplete the number of potential enrollees. Soon, there were "insufficient applicants" to staff the
already reduced number of camps, and the CCC began to phase
out the program, completing its task by mid-1943.[11]

The official CCC handbook for selecting enrollees specified
that "no discrimination shall be made on account of race, color,

or creed."[12] Because each state worked out its own method of selection, however, some racial problems did develop. One historian described the CCC treatment of minorities as "shabby," indicating that blacks did not receive a fair share of CCC appointments, according to either population or unemployment ratios. Fechner was a southerner who was passive about issues of racial equality, and the army was traditionally segregated and discriminatory in its practices. Both factors conspired to keep American blacks from participating as fully as they might.[13] Like other states, Kentucky established a black quota within its state allotment, usually around 10 percent of the total. Frank Linkenberg, state director of CCC selection in the KERA office, was sensitive about charges of discrimination and did not like to use the racial quota system, but the Louisville Urban League demanded that it be kept.[14] These quotas ended in July 1941; whereupon the number of Kentucky black enrollees increased 200 percent. Approximately one hundred blacks in Kentucky had been allowed in during the previous six-month enrollment term, and more than three hundred enrolled following the lifting of the race quota.[15] Most blacks who joined the CCC lived in segregated "Jim Crow" camps, the location of which caused tension and controversy in some areas, including Tennessee. Kentucky, however, escaped similar problems.[16] Black CCC camps were located around the state at different times. Morganfield had one, as did Russellville. Camp 510 at Mammoth Cave won several superior ratings for exemplary achievements and was the subject of a feature story in the national CCC newspaper, *Happy Days*.[17] There were also a few integrated camps, one of them for older veterans at Pine Ridge in Wolfe County.

Before CCC enrollees headed to their camps for conservation work, most had to endure two or three weeks of "hardening," usually at a military post. Men from the Fifth Corps area, which included Kentucky, Ohio, Indiana, and West Virginia, traveled to Fort Knox, where army personnel gave them haircuts, immunized them against various diseases, issued them olive drab uniforms, and introduced them to military discipline, strenuous work, and isolation from their normal social lives. Specially designed CCC uniforms of spruce green replaced the army

clothing in 1939.[18] One young enrollee from Carlisle County
recorded his impression of this conditioning routine in verse.

> I've raked most of Ft. Knox.
> I've cut down some stumps.
> I'm safe from typhoid,
> And even the mumps.
> I'm safe from the women,
> But that ain't no fun.[19]

This military regimen relaxed somewhat when enrollees traveled to their assignments, but because the army had supervision
over living facilities at each camp, a martial spirit prevailed
throughout the enlistment period.

Another part of the hardening process was the dislocation
that came with travel and living apart from home and family, a
new experience for many recruits. CCC officials tried whenever
possible to assign men to camps within their own states and,
ideally, not more than two hundred miles from their homes.[20]
Camp site availability influenced the decision, however, and so
many Kentuckians worked as far away as California while hundreds of enrollees from other states worked in Kentucky. For
instance, Arnold Rennie of Louisville worked on a reforestation
project in Maryland, Oscar Huffman of Denton planted trees in
Colorado, and Woodrow Bryan of Clinton built fences in Idaho.
Willie Himes of Jackson County had hoped for an assignment in
the West when he enrolled; instead, he traveled only to a camp
in McKee, within his home county. While working there, Himes
met corpsmen from at least three other states. Because reenlist-
ment was possible after the first six-month term, many recruits
traveled to several camps. Russell Stanford of Johnson County,
for example, worked first at a camp in Montana, later at a camp
near Paducah, and finished his service with the corps in Corbin.[21] Inadvertently, these recruits were gaining a new geographical education at the same time as they were losing some
of their regional provincialism.

Federal officials estimated that each CCC camp with its
approximately two hundred enrollees would spend between two

thousand and five thousand dollars per month in the surrounding area. These expenditures went for food, supplies, and salaries for personnel such as cooks and "LEMS"—Local Experienced Men—who served as guides and instructors at the work sites.[22] Local governments were quick to appreciate the economic stimulus as well as the long-term benefits of the projects, and they petitioned state and federal authorities to obtain camps for their area. Kentucky's chief forester said in 1936, "There isn't a county in Kentucky that hasn't sent a delegation to my office with the request for a CCC camp."[23] And whenever Washington announced reductions in the number of camps, local officials again lobbied to keep theirs for as long as possible. For example, the Newport Chamber of Commerce petitioned Congressman Brent Spence for assistance in keeping an installation near Fort Thomas, and the Harlan Kiwanis Club enlisted Governor Chandler's aid to get a time extension for a camp in their area.[24] These entreaties seldom succeeded because Fechner had to balance camps with national employment trends and congressional appropriations. The number of requests, however, did indicate the popularity of the CCC and the desire of communities to take advantage of the opportunities it provided. Kentucky had its largest number of camps during 1935 when fifty-nine projects were located around the state.[25] Some of the camps were "portable"; the men lived in temporary tent facilities, and the sites changed upon completion of the work project. Others remained in one place for several years and saw several classes of enrollees pass through the wooden barracks and landscaped grounds.

The Department of Agriculture supervised roughly 75 percent of the CCC camps through the Soil Conservation Service and Forest Service. From these hundreds of camps devoted to reforestation and erosion control came legendary stories of the youthful armies marching across the American landscape like Johnny Appleseeds dressed in army surplus. In their wake rose new forests, brush dams to repair gullies, lookout towers to reduce fire damage, and windbreaks to thwart the Dust Bowl. Kentucky shared in the prolific work. One Forest Service camp in Laurel County, near London, worked an area of thirty-five thousand acres of national forest land. In addition to planting the usual seedlings, these 203 men learned to do timber estimates for future lumber marketing and fire prevention landscaping. They also constructed a bridge across the Rockcastle River and stretched telephone lines through miles of countryside. Near Danville, a Soil Conservation Service camp sent its enrollees out to private farms by contract. They worked with individual farmers to improve their land and to learn estate management techniques with such projects as spring development, ditching, and hillside terracing. A similar camp near Paducah helped farmers with seed gathering and nursery tending.[26] The University of Kentucky's Agricultural Extension Service agents frequently served as instructors and liaisons between these CCC camps and local farmers. One such agent reported that the Russellville camp had been demonstrating contour plowing on hilly terrain. Following the demonstration, one farmer slowly surveyed the curving furrows and exclaimed, "How in the #!/* do you expect a man to follow these crooked rows when he is sober?"[27]

In contrast to the camps supervised by the Department of Agriculture, the Department of the Interior conducted work projects in national park lands. Mammoth Cave properties were in transition from state management to national park status, and the presence of the CCC there accelerated the progress. To facilitate this transition, the state turned over deeds for Mammoth Cave, and the Department of the Interior allotted $300,000 to acquire an additional nine thousand acres of surrounding land.[28] Four different CCC camps worked within the developing park, planting nearly one million trees, building miles of new roads and hiking trails, preparing topographical survey maps, and constructing rustic homes for park employees.[29]

When the Department of the Interior announced that special arrangements would permit CCC camps in state parks, state authorities pressured to get their shares. Because both Emma Cromwell and Bailey Wootton, successive directors of the Kentucky state park system, were aggressive about getting camps, most of the state parks that were large enough to support camps had them at some point. Cumberland Falls State Park and its camp received considerable publicity, largely because of the park's recent admission into the park system after being saved from a utilities development plan. In addition to building cabins and roads and trails within the park, CCC enrollees constructed the impressive Dupont Lodge, a rustic hotel with twenty-six rooms and a huge stone fireplace. A camp of junior enrollees had started work on the two-story lodge, and another camp of veteran recruits completed it. Park officials estimated its worth at sixty thousand dollars in the spring of 1940 when a fire destroyed it.[30] Another distinctive and ambitious project was at Pine Mountain, the site of the annual Mountain Laurel Festival. CCC corpsmen excavated an amphitheater from the hillside and constructed new seats and facilities for the thousands of visitors who made the yearly spring pilgrimage to see the governor crown a new queen among the blossoming laurels. More than $500,000 worth of CCC expenditures went into this park alone.[31] Emma Cromwell was especially proud of the work done in Henderson at Camp Cromwell, where work crews of both the CCC and WPA developed a new state park to commemorate Kentucky's premier ornithologist and wildlife artist, John James Audubon. The French Norman design of the park museum highlighted Audubon's ancestry while providing nesting places for birds in the stone tower. Nearby was a wildlife preserve, a lake, and hiking trails.[32] Bailey Wootton also appreciated the CCC contribution to the state, although he took umbrage over some federal decisions. Near the end of the CCC era, he admitted that without the camps, Kentucky's state park system would have gone without the improvements valued at approximately three million dollars.[33]

In addition to its goals of creating jobs and doing conservation work, the CCC insisted that it wanted to "build up" the minds and bodies of the young men at the camps. At the time of his induction, the average CCC junior enrollee was twenty years old, noticeably underweight, and with very little work experience outside the home.[34] Using this norm as the starting place, the CCC had much building to do. Hard work and three regular meals per day did put several pounds on most of the corpsmen, and the CCC boasted that the average enrollee gained from eight to fourteen pounds during his stay in the program. Kentucky's chief forester indicated that the average enrollee in the state matched or exceeded that gain.[35] If the menu for April 15, 1935, at the Pine Ridge camp was typical of other camp's food service, one can see why the body building occurred. Meat and bread, along with assorted fruits, vegetables, coffee, and milk, were available at all three meals that day, potatoes and dessert at two. Unlimited portions helped, too. Willie Himes later recalled that he had never tasted grapefruit until it was served at his camp in Jackson County. He enjoyed the fruit so much that he once ate seventeen halves during breakfast. When he left the corps, he had gained eighteen pounds.[36] One can also understand why wholesalers in nearby communities appreciated the presence of the camps.

Educational and vocational training were more complex issues than body building. CCC Director Robert Fechner was not hostile to education programs at the camps, but he regarded anything beyond skills related to the work projects as "incidental" at best.[37] Camp supervisors taught enrollees on the job and the young men became adept at forestry, erosion work, fire fighting, and drainage projects. Fechner also expected the army to conduct first aid classes and to teach illiterate men to read and write. During the first three years of the program, the CCC rescued about thirty-five thousand men from illiteracy during after-work classes, and as basic education programs continued, more enrollees mastered remedial skills. In the fiscal year 1939-1940 alone, nine thousand more corpsmen learned to read and write.[38] Beyond these basics, Fechner left education to military personnel. The army was apparently more interested in the bodies and morals than in the minds of the enrollees, for they gave far less attention to formal instruction than to other matters. Military officers saw to it that the camps had adequate recreational equipment, regular religious services, and periodic checkups for venereal diseases. They also inspected camp libraries to prevent "radical" books and magazines from infiltrating the collections. The regular inspection report of the CCC camp near London, Kentucky, gave the library there a clean evaluation since the officer had found "no communist literature."[39] Other than these exercises and precautions the army left intellectual development to the discretion of individual camp supervisors. Most educational and recreational programs, therefore, developed randomly and without clear direction. The district educational adviser stationed at Fort Thomas emphasized, "It is a voluntary enterprise; no curriculum is prescribed, and the program in each camp grows out of the needs and wishes of its men."[40] WPA administrators sometimes sent qualified teachers to receptive camps for formal classroom instruction in the evenings, and some nearby school systems and colleges offered classes to enrollees who wanted to complete a degree. At the Columbus-Belmont camp men could take algebra, typing, and public speaking. The offerings at McKee were more prosaic—quarrying, masonry, and truck driving.[41] If a general rule prevailed, it was that leisure activities were more popular than academic rigors. The men at a Dawson Springs camp arranged dances and invited women from nearby communities; movies were featured regularly for corpsmen in Whitley County; and men from one Corbin camp frequently relaxed at a skating rink after work. With the onset of the European war, more emphasis went to defense-related training in the camps. Kentucky Congressman Andrew J. May, chairman of the House Military Affairs Committee, discussed the possibility of making military training mandatory in the camps. Although nothing came of May's suggestion, many camps did shift their class offerings to include auto maintenance, radio communications, map reading, and explosives handling.[42]

The CCC had a high regard for its work and worth and enjoyed wide public agreement with its self-appraisal. Its annual reports touted the improvements of the national estate, the millions of dollars circulated within the economy, and the therapeutic effect on the enrollees. At the end of three years, the corps thought it had "provided new hope, new skills, renewed bodies, and renewed faith" to thousands of previously idle and depressed youth.[43] In 1939 and 1940 Washington headquarters asked state officers and relief workers to forward success stories about local men who had shown demonstrable progress because of their CCC experiences; many of these stories appeared in the *Happy Days* newspaper. Frank Linkenberg and George Goodman of Kentucky sent a dozen or so stories about corpsmen who had made good. One alumnus of a forestry camp had recently become manager of a lumber firm; another had married a girl who lived near his camp and now owned a grocery store in her hometown. One enrollee had learned to type and read blueprints in his camp classes and subsequently became a successful contractor. He credited the CCC with his new self-confidence and ability to meet people.[44] Kentucky officials had no difficulty finding such stories because newspapers printed frequent feature articles about nearby camps and hometown boys who sent news from distant sites. Many of the smaller weekly papers printed holiday editorials aimed at the camp residents, and some editors encouraged Kentucky enrollees who were stationed out of state to send letters for publication. Not even publicity about occasional incidents of theft, desertion, and venereal disease could diminish the popularity of the corps. No other New Deal activity received comparable adulation.

A few discordant notes from Frankfort did occasionally disturb the calm the CCC enjoyed, and these disagreements were the same sort that had strained federal-state relations regarding other New Deal programs. Fechner informed Governor Laffoon in 1935 that the state would have to assume responsibility for maintenance of CCC construction projects in state parks, and he wanted a commitment from Kentucky before the CCC undertook any more work on state property. Governors of many states received similar letters, and Laffoon's reply was probably typical. He affirmed his support of the CCC, acknowledged the agency's popularity in Kentucky, and hoped that the state legislature would appropriate more funds for the necessary maintenance in 1936.[45] The exchange of pressure and promises between Washington and Frankfort continued during the early days of the Chandler administration in 1936. By early 1937 Fechner informed Chandler that Kentucky would have to supply approximately twenty thousand dollars per year for park expenses, and if that sum were not soon forthcoming, all CCC work would cease and the camps would vacate state park sites.[46] Chandler managed to find some emergency funds to pacify the CCC but officials in the Department of the Interior ranked Kentucky near the bottom on its scale of "state cooperation" and accused the state of "poor administration" of its park system.[47]

This battle between Fechner and Chandler must have created a sense of déjà vu for Kentucky politicians since it was reminiscent of the fights between Hopkins and Laffoon over FERA funds in 1933. The private conflict became public in 1939 when the *Louisville Times* published one of Fechner's letters accusing the Chandler administration of not providing adequate revenues for park maintenance. Editor Tom Wallace, a long-time crusader for a larger and better state park system, used this as an opportunity to further his cause. He asserted that the CCC construction work was "rapidly going to wrack as a result of lack of proper direction and management." And he lamented that state park officials had no expertise or interest in caring for Kentucky's natural resources.[48] National Park Service inspectors visited several CCC camps following these charges, and the CCC headquarters announced in March that it would remove most of the camps from state park sites because "the Kentucky State Park System is being operated in a way that offers little promise of a very bright future." It specifically indicted the Division of State Parks under Bailey Wootton for not employing trained professional architects, engineers, foresters, or recreational planners.[49] A rushed meeting between Chandler and representatives from the Department of the Interior stalled the CCC departure without removing the basic conflicts. Newspaper editors in Henderson and Pineville, fearing the loss of camps in nearby Audubon and Pine Mountain parks, waged campaigns for compromise and blamed the dilemma mainly on the state administration.[50] Senator Barkley helped create a last-minute compromise when he arranged a meeting in Washington between Wootton and Fechner. They agreed that Kentucky would hire a National Park Service official to supervise park maintenance, and the camps would remain in the state parks to complete their projects.[51] Chandler had lost a similar battle over personnel matters with Social Security officials the year before, and the phrase "dictated to by Washington" reverberated in Frankfort during this squabble. In both cases, popular New Deal programs prevailed. Chandler chafed publicly at the loss of state power but surely realized that Kentucky had gained immense benefits despite his personal chagrin.

As impressive as the CCC was, even its most vocal defenders had to admit that it could not solve the problem of jobless youth. At its peak in 1935 it enrolled only 500,000 young men. That same year some estimates showed that as many as 7 million young Americans might still be in search of work, and they constituted as much as 30 percent of the total number of Americans between the ages of sixteen and twenty-four.[52] Many of these had dropped out of high school because of financial problems; many were not able to leave their homes for CCC camps, and none of the girls were eligible for the corps. College enrollments in America had dropped 10 percent between 1932 and 1934, indicating that thousands of the nation's potential leaders were postponing or forgoing their intended careers. These young people were entering their prime years for pursuing careers, starting families, and becoming productive members of their communities, but the Great Depression conspired against their chances of success and doomed much of their youthful idealism. According to two contemporary observers, they were "a potential deadweight on the nation for half a century to come."[53]

President Roosevelt was obviously mindful of this problem on June 26, 1935, when he issued an executive order establishing the National Youth Administration (NYA). He said, "We can ill afford to lose the skill and energy of these young men and women. They must have their chance in school, their turn as apprentices and their opportunity for jobs."[54] A part of WPA but an autonomous administrative unit, the NYA was to help high schools and colleges to find jobs for students so they could remain in school. It was also to provide part-time work and training for young people who were no longer in school and to establish vocational guidance and placement programs for this same group.[55] Even though the NYA fulfilled all these goals between 1935 and 1943, and served a much larger number of youth than did the CCC, it never captured the public imagination as did the corps. Thousands of students sitting in classrooms did not exude the drama of men in spruce green uniforms planting trees. And additional thousands of young men and women learning to be carpenters and seamstresses in NYA workshops did not command newspaper space the way CCC firefighters did. The NYA never developed a distinct personality; most Americans thought of it—if they thought of it at all—as just another branch of the verdant WPA relief tree.

The national director of NYA, Aubrey W. Williams, for all of his unique vision, did not help appreciably in giving the organization a clear focus or memorable direction. A onetime minister and social worker, Williams had previously held several federal posts related to relief and public works. As a field agent for the RFC, regional director with the FERA, and deputy administrator of both the CWA and WPA, he had become an aide and friend of Harry Hopkins, and he shared Hopkins's disdain for dole relief. Like many other New Dealers he was, according to his biographer, "young, idealistic, vaguely leftist."[56] His youthful crusades for labor unions and racial equality surprised and angered many of his Alabama kinsmen but made him sympathetic with other reformers who gravitated to Washington in the 1930s. One of his early enthusiasms developed shortly after he returned from service in the Great War. A Lutheran church in Dayton, Kentucky, hired him as a minister but did not anticipate the fervor with which he would lecture on the struggles of the working class. His sermons alienated some the the church's leaders, and Williams resigned under pressure. His departeure did not sever his Kentucky connections entirely. He had become an avid fan of horse racing and often found his way to Churchill Downs whenever NYA work brought him to Louisville headquarters.[57] Williams's crusading zeal soon attracted the attention and friendship of Eleanor Roosevelt, who shared many of his ideals. She became an advocate of the NYA as her husband was of the CCC. In fact, the president frequently referred to the NYA as the "Missus's organization."[58]

In Kentucky, Williams had two strong supporters. One of them, Frank Peterson, had held several positions in the Kentucky Department of Education for ten years before becoming state administrator of the NYA. Interested in both education and politics, he was conversant with the economic realities facing Kentucky youth. "It is a cold and unpromising world that our young people are entering," he said. "Like eggs, they will not keep unspoiled indefinitely."[59] Peterson later recalled that his political contacts with Senator Barkley were helpful in getting him the appointment as state NYA chief, and he spent some time in Washington with Aubrey Williams and Harry Hopkins learning the inside operations of the organization.[60] Assisting him in the Louisville headquarters was Robert K. Salyers, deputy administrator from 1935 through 1937, then state administrator following Peterson's resignation. Salyers had worked for the Kentucky Education Association and for the president of the University of Kentucky before joining the NYA. Both Peterson and Salyers regarded the NYA as a mission, and for this reason Williams held them in high regard. Their letters and reports to national headquarters read more like advertising circulars than office memos, and the Washington staff frequently responded with praise.

The largest segment of NYA activity was the creation of part-time jobs at high schools for students who were finding it difficult, if not impossible, to stay in school. Despite the myth of free public education and compulsory attendance laws for those under age sixteen, Peterson knew that there were thousands of young Kentuckians "whose parents cannot provide them with the clothing, books, school supplies and other things incidental to school attendance."[61] The youngsters had no choice but to drop out of school. NYA officials allotted job quotas to states based on populations and relief lists, and local school administrators were responsible for finding suitable work. According to the NYA the jobs should be "socially desirable" and not just janitorial duties or make-work.[62] Some school principals took their allotted quotas, found that many part-time jobs in their schools for needy students, and paid them the maximum six dollars per month for their work. Other principals stretched their quotas by creating additional jobs and paying all workers less for working fewer hours. In the first school year of NYA operations, 1935-1936, an average of seven thousand students per month worked in the program in Kentucky. The most common jobs were clerical—typing, grading papers, filing. Smaller numbers of students found jobs working in school libraries and cafeterias and as aides in laboratories and playgrounds.[63] At the end of the second school year of NYA, Peterson estimated that if additional funds had been available another five thousand Kentucky students might have been able to attend school that year. During the life-span of NYA until it expired early in World War II, the number of Kentucky students receiving work assistance never fell below seven thousand and sometimes exceeded ten thousand.[64]

Equally effective but smaller in scope was the NYA student aid program for college students. A short-lived attempt to aid college students, begun under the FERA in 1934-1935, had documented the need for such a program. The NYA allotted quotas to institutions of higher education, and campus administrators selected from needy applicants to fill the quotas. They then supervised the recipients, who were required to carry no less than three-fourths of a normal academic load with passing grades. For their part-time jobs they received a maximum of fifteen dollars per month. A small quota also existed for graduate students who could make as much as thirty dollars per month.[65] Nationally, 98 percent of the eligible colleges and universities participated in this program, and in Kentucky only one eligible school chose not to be involved. Louisville's Southern Baptist Theological Seminary, troubled by the potential conflict between church and state interests, did not accept NYA funds. Thirty-one, and at one time thirty-three, other schools in the state did participate, kept their enrollments higher than might have been the case, and slightly reduced the state's unemployment figures. In the first year of operation, approximately twenty-eight hundred students qualified for part-time work to defray their expenses.[66] As in the high school program, applications for the jobs exceeded the quotas, demonstrating that both schools and students were receptive and eager. The deans of men and women at the University of Kentucky, who supervised the largest number of NYA students in the state, reported in 1939,

"The desire for Government aid, the need and appreciation of it are as well established as the law of gravity."[67] An assortment of imaginative and relevant jobs appeared on Kentucky campuses, and both students and institutions harvested the NYA largess. At the University of Louisville one undergraduate biology major worked in the science laboratory slicing pollywogs for slide specimens. His work would later be used for instructional purposes to show "the development of a tadpole into a frog." Some students at Berea College worked as music accompanists for vocal instructors, and others developed new designs for decorative tea sugars in the college's unique confectionery. The historian of Barbourville's Union College recalled that NYA students enhanced the campus landscaping by planting additional hedges and lombardy poplars. Georgetown College had almost closed in 1931 because of financial problems and enrollment declines. NYA helped the college stay open, and this small Baptist school had no qualms about separation of church and state; "there was only the desperate need to keep students in school."[68] Aubrey Williams's zeal to guarantee that blacks got NYA educational opportunities also helped to stabilize Kentucky State College in Frankfort and Louisville Municipal College, both of which suffered financial and enrollment problems in the 1930s. Kentucky blacks received slightly larger quotas of student jobs than their percentage of the population seemed to warrant. These quotas reflected Williams's lifetime commitment to minority progress.[69]

Most Kentucky educators had praise for NYA programs, but a few national administrators found fault with aspects of Williams's activities. Some of the criticism was based on fears of educational nationalization, and some on disagreement with the NYA academic-vocational ratios. Kentucky NYA officials sent a questionnaire to school administrators after the student aid program had been in effect for several years. The questionnaire drew almost two hundred responses, only one of which was negative. Dr. James Richmond, president of the Kentucky Education Association and of Murray State Teachers College in 1943, assessed the program's benefits in terms that Aubrey Williams might have liked to use as an epitaph. He said that the

NYA had made "an outstanding contribution," that it had "fully justified its creation."[70]

The NYA went beyond merely helping students to stay in school with part-time jobs. It also sponsored guidance and counseling services to assist students in choosing careers and preparing for the job search once they were ready to start working. Kentucky's NYA staff compiled and published materials for dissemination to high school and college counselors as well as to placement bureaus and potential employers around the state.[71] These publications included descriptions of job opportunities in a variety of careers in the tobacco industry, sales, baking, clerical work, and other enterprises. They outlined the educational requirements for these jobs, pay scales, chances for advancement, and other pertinent information. Peterson spent much time publicizing these pamphlets to businesses, schools, and civic groups so that potential employees and employers could meet on common ground.[72] One pamphlet, *Which College Shall I Choose,* described every Kentucky college, its size, costs, degrees offered, and extracurricular activities. Every high school in the state received a copy of the brochure. Like other states, Kentucky established a placement service for young job seekers that worked in tandem with the state employment office and had its own offices in Louisville, Covington, and Ashland. During a single month the Louisville office found positions for fifty-two young people.[73]

For needy youths between the ages of eighteen and twenty-five who were not in school, the NYA devised work projects similar to those in the parent WPA organization. County relief agencies had to certify that applicants were from needy families. In fact, it was not uncommon to find the head of a needy family leaving home four days a week on a WPA assignment and the son or daughter departing twice a week for an NYA project. During its first year of operation, 1935-1936, the emphasis was on relief—simply creating jobs; after that, the emphasis shifted to teaching marketable skills in apprenticeship programs and workshops. Local governments or school systems frequently sponsored work projects, and the average Kentucky NYA youth worked fifty hours per month for about ten dollars.[74] NYA projects and workshops were located in practically every Kentucky county, and during the peak year 1936-1937, more than fourteen thousand young people were on its rolls.[75]

Local governments, schools, and civic groups were eager to sponsor NYA projects for the same reasons they competed for WPA activities: construction or repair work could be paid for with federal money, and the community would derive both immediate and long-term benefits. In eastern Kentucky the superintendent of schools of Morgan County praised the NYA boys who had repaired and painted a school building. "Our county is just too poor to do this work," he said, "and if it hadn't been for NYA, it never would have been done." The city of Owensboro had similar sentiments about the twenty-five NYA boys who refurbished Chautauqua Park by cleaning a lagoon, sodding the banks, building foot bridges, and generally sprucing up the area.[76] Henderson's city government sponsored projects for improving playground equipment. NYA youth constructed a bandstand for concerts in Barbourville and indexed city health records in Louisville. Princeton's Butler High School got two new tennis courts, and in Bowling Green 250 fire plugs received fresh coats of paint.[77] Most of the projects were not of sufficient substance to qualify for PWA construction grants or full-time WPA adult work programs. Nevertheless, they and hundreds like them offered needy youths part-time work and the towns an opportunity to undertake the projects at little or no cost to themselves.

NYA workshops and apprentice-training programs were more systematic than the locally sponsored construction and repair projects. State officials would contract for space and instructors to teach such skills as carpentry, sewing, and auto mechanics. The eligible youths got instruction and received wages for their work. Graduates of these workshops had little difficulty locating jobs in private enterprise, so NYA administrators actually considered a high rate of turnover in these programs a sign of success. In December 1937 there were thirty-five of these workshops established around the state, mostly in urban centers.[78] One of the largest workshops was located in Covington in a renovated old building. It employed 250 girls and boys to learn sewing, carpentry, radio repair, welding and several other skills. By 1941 the average youth at this facility was working eighty hours and making sixteen dollars per month. Among their marketable products were finished cabinets, which they could not produce fast enough to meet the demand from such public agencies as the Lexington Municipal Housing Commission and the University of Kentucky. Hence, the workshop hummed with activity like a factory in full production.[79] One national survey of NYA workshops reported that Kentucky had made "excellent use" of the concept and singled out two in Morgan and Wayne Counties for their carpentry apprenticeship projects in which students made furniture for local schools. The new WPA school in Morgan County was without furniture until the NYA workshop equipped it with desks, bookcases, lockers, and other items.[80]

State administrators were especially pleased when one workshop could supply another NYA project with materials for its activity. One of the girls' sewing workshops and a nearby construction project in Edmonson County had a complementary relationship of this nature. The sewing students designed and made work overalls for a young man employed on an NYA road crew who weighed 410 pounds and was unable to find suitable work clothes. Salyers sent a photograph of the "tremendous" results to NYA headquarters in Washington and got the congratulations he expected.[81] Students in another sewing project in Cannell City learned to make their own clothes and also decorated the rented room where they worked. When they produced surplus items, they gave them to local relief agencies for distribution to needy families.[82] The most publicized of such cross-fertilization efforts in Kentucky NYA workshops involved the making of wooden looms and handwoven cloth. Salyers told the Washington office, "We believe it is highly desirable to preserve this craft in our state." Boys constructed the looms, girls wove the fabric, and the Louisville staff published blueprints and instructions for other people wishing to follow the Kentuckians' example. These operating looms were the centerpiece of a highly popular exhibit at the Kentucky State Fair.[83]

The fervor of a missionary crusade permeated much of the
NYA administrative activity both in Washington and in Kentucky. One of the underlying assumptions of the program seems
to have been that the training and jobs could rescue young
people before they became shiftless adults. One Kentucky NYA
publicity circular argued that "it is reasonable to presume that
without this aid . . . many of the youth in this class would fall as
a burden on the shoulders of their fellow men. Our penal institutions are crowded with recruits from this group."[84] Periodic
NYA pamphlets publicized success stories about projects whose
redeeming work had saved young Kentuckians from saloons,
pool halls, and jails. Many of these stories were testimonials by
relief workers and project supervisors, who testified to previously sullen and antisocial girls and boys from destitute families for whom the NYA was a salvation. The money, comrade-
ship, discipline, and job opportunities provided by NYA work
transformed them into positive-thinking young adults ready to
become productive members of their families and communities.[85] Many NYA administrators wanted to give more to their
students than just a little vocational training and a few wages.
One Kentucky district official sent this directive to his project
leaders:

> No one expects you to play little tin God and re-order their
> whole lives but have you done any of the little things
> which may mean so much in their future? Do they come to
> work cleaner and with better clothes than they formerly
> did? Do they work harder at their job and take some pride
> in what they are doing? Have defeated outlooks on life
> changed to more optimistic ones? Do they read more than
> they did when you first knew them? . . . Do they feel like
> they are beginning to earn a living or do they still think
> that the government is playing Santa Claus?[86]

In addition to playing counselor and role model, many project
supervisors provided self-improvement classes for their wards,
especially those with limited educational backgrounds. On a
volunteer basis, after their work was finished, the youths could
take courses in health, basic reading skills, and first aid, to

enhance their personal growth. All this attention and group activity offered the stimulant that many troubled youths needed to get a fresh start. One gauge of its success, albeit an extreme one, was the testimony of local law enforcement officials. Several judges mentioned that they were seeing fewer juvenile cases in their courts, and they linked a general "reduction of crime and juvenile delinquency" to the presence of the NYA.[87] The *Courier-Journal* in an analytical series gave an even more comprehensive assessment of this sociological uplift: "When a representative student is graduated from an NYA work project, that student is definitely a better citizen, better trained, almost invariably in better health, with more self-confidence, more ability to get along with people, more desire for self-improvement and with a feeling of fitting into the world around himself or herself."[88] In a final self-analysis at the close of the NYA program, Kentucky administrators applauded themselves for helping the "unkempt, rebellious boys and girls who showed signs of becoming self- respecting workers."[89]

The NYA zeal for social uplift—its crusade to transform blighted youth into exemplary adults—can best be seen in the short-lived resident centers. Begun in 1936 in Louisiana, these experiments in communal living captured Aubrey Williams's fancy, and he pressed for their expansion. The first were intended to give poor rural youths a chance to live and learn with other people, to pick up remedial social and educational skills, and to taste, even if briefly, some urban amenities previously unknown to them.[90] For this segment of the population, members of which would rarely go away to college, the resident centers would be temporary substitutes; youths would return to their isolated homes after having made new friends, learned new skills, and raised their horizons. Without being condescending, although dangerously close to it, the rationale for the experiments gave the impression that rural life was in itself stifling, provincial, and limiting. The stated goal of the Kentucky centers followed that rationale in their attempt to introduce rural youth "into a fuller life." By the time the program ended in 1942, Kentucky had experimented with at least nine resident centers in different sections of the state.[91]

Kentucky's resident centers, started in 1938, varied considerably in goals and size but shared the common denominator of living and learning away from home. One of the centers for girls, located near London, used several cottages belonging to the National Park Service. Sixty girls from surrounding counties would spend two weeks living in these cottages and learning social graces while refining their techniques of farm and domestic chores. Sixty different girls would then replace them while the original group returned to their homes for two weeks. These staggered shifts would continue for a year so each group received six months of communal experience. Chaperons assisted them in planning and preparing meals, raising gardens and small livestock, canning produce, and sewing and weaving. For each two-week stint a girl received room, board, eleven dollars, exposure to new concepts, and "some of the niceties of life."[92] At this Laurel County center and one similar to it at Levi Jackson State Park, the girls also enjoyed cultural enrichment trips and programs. Many had never ridden in a train or seen a motion picture before living in the NYA centers, and these experiences alone probably convinced NYA planners that the center rationale was valid.[93]

Several other resident centers experimented with different forms of cultural uplift. At Carrollton, a center housed as many as 125 boys, who not only received training in woodworking, metal-working, auto mechanics, and radio repair but also participated in group sports and took recreational trips to nearby Butler State Park. Another boys center located in Richmond taught similar skills and encouraged the boys to attend classes at Madison High School or Eastern State Teachers' College.[94] The largest resident center in the state was coeducational. It used the facilities of Murray State College during the summer months, where 170 NYA youth confronted a variety of new social and educational challenges, including the publication of a monthly newspaper complete with editorials and sports columns.[95] Lincoln Institute in Shelby County allowed young black men from Kentucky to live away from home for a time, and their training in carpentry produced several items of dormitory furniture for Kentucky State College. Likewise, black women could live and study practical nursing, among other things, at Paducah's Western Kentucky Industrial College.[96]

By 1942 America was at war, and all NYA activities ceased except those training programs that were geared to defense work. Some of these were workshops such as the one in Louisville that taught metal-work and welding in conjunction with Ahrens Trade School. Others had been resident centers, such as one in Carrollton, which now became merely a dormitory for vocational trainees. And the NYA created others expressly for the war effort, including one for nurses' training at Lexington's Saint Joseph Hospital.[97] So great was the need for trained defense plant workers that by the end of 1942 some five hundred youth from Kentucky had found full-time positions in war production as far away as Rhode Island, making as much as a dollar per hour.[98] From the early days in 1935 when idle youth painted fire plugs in Bowling Green to the last days in 1943 when NYA graduates produced war material for use against the Japanese, this New Deal program had traveled a long and changing course. The sequence of Great Depression, New Deal, and World War II brought many transformations to the economy, American life, and the young people who matured during all of it.

It is much easier to point out the contrasts between the CCC and the NYA than to show the likenesses. Although these were the only two New Deal agencies established exclusively for youth, and the Roosevelts took an intense interest in both of them, the two organizations were more different than similar. The CCC's major purpose was to take young men away from the scene of unemployment into rural pursuits. On the other hand, the NYA's major goal was to keep young men and women where they were, either in school or, failing that, on a part-time job near home. Only in a few instances—the resident centers, for example—did it attempt to remove them from their surroundings, and then the tacit and, in Kentucky, revolutionary goal was to urbanize them. The results of the CCC and NYA efforts, however, were the same; young people received job training and wages at the same time. The NYA's secondary motive—that of social and cultural uplift—was hardly present in the CCC. The corps limited its self-improvement activities, for the most part, to those related to conservation skills, literacy, and first aid. Aubrey Williams and the NYA made conscious and successful efforts to insure that blacks got a fair apportionment of funds and programs; Robert Fechner and the army did not regard racial quotas or civil rights as a major priority, and local pressures, such as those applied by Louisville civil rights groups, had to create whatever new policies prevailed.

The financial impact of these two agencies is also difficult to compare because of much overlapping and the inherent gap between full- and part- time activity. The average annual cost for training and maintaining a CCC youth was approximately $1,200; the most expensive NYA cost, excepting the rare resident centers, was $240 for an out-of-school work project.[99] Salaries for both provided an economic boon for local economies, although the major portion of CCC salaries went to families who frequently lived many miles from the camps. NYA wages, on the contrary, stayed at home, but were considerably smaller in amount and were spread among larger numbers. On several occasions, a NYA project or center would assume use and financial responsibility of a former CCC camp. This happened at Quicksand, Kentucky, and in several state parks. The construction and maintenance costs of these sites, therefore, were divided between the two groups, making a clear cost differentiation almost impossible. On other occasions, the NYA and CCC shared responsibility for a common site. For example, janitorial crews from a Corbin CCC camp provided regular maintenance service for the girl's NYA resident center near London, just a few minutes away.[100]

Franklin and Eleanor Roosevelt did not gravitate to these two agencies because of the drama or charm involved; they were genuinely concerned about salvaging youthful energy and idealism before the Depression drained it away. As parents, survivors of adversity, and compassionate liberals, the president and his wife knew the efforts necessary to keep hope ascendant. An independent study done in 1938 declared that the NYA had already proven itself of "profound social significance" in rescuing this potentially lost generation of young Americans.[101] The same assessment could just as easily have applied to the CCC. Little has happened in the half century since their inception to alter that evaluation. Millions of Americans owed their adult careers to the opportunities and training they received from those two programs. A few were doubly blessed by participating in both. The NYA assisted Russell Stanford with work and wages during his final year of high school near Paintsville; the CCC then offered travel and job training until the Depression ended.[102] Regardless of whether Kentuckians planted trees, stayed in school, or learned the welder's trade, their fresh start in life came from the New Deal's concern for youth. The presence today of CCC and NYA alumni groups, which meet and reminisce about projects that transformed their lives, pays tribute to the dual catalysts that also shaped much of the American future.

# 5. Newly Plowed Fields

If a case can be made that the New Deal revolutionized America, the strongest and most obvious evidence would be in the field of agriculture. The changes that occurred in rural life between 1933 and 1940 as a result of new federal policies, appear radical in retrospect. Significant transformations took place in farmers' attitudes, uses of the soil, farm productivity and marketing, and in the relationship of the individual farmer to the government. Prior to these New Deal innovations, the book *I'll Take My Stand: The South and the Agrarian Tradition*, published in 1930, caught much of the Kentucky state of mind. A somewhat Jeffersonian defense of the agricultural life, this collection of essays by twelve southerners lamented that recent urban, technological, and industrial incursions had eroded the South's traditions and identity. The authors extolled the virtues of agrarianism, regional autonomy, and self-reliance. Two Kentuckians, Robert Penn Warren and Allen Tate, were among these twelve writers. Although neither could be regarded as a farmer in 1930, both articulated views that approximated those of Kentucky. Still, the New Deal by 1940 had won wide acceptance in the state for federal policies that encouraged farmers to destroy cotton and pigs and paid them to not grow tobacco and corn. Kentucky had also welcomed New Deal measures that would submerge thousands of acres of rich bottomland along the Tennessee River, displace thousands of families from their farms, and change their lives by providing cheap electricity and modern appliances. Now more reliant on new technology and the federal government than on human toil and nature's kindness, the rural Kentuckian had either won or lost an attitudinal revolution, depending on one's ideological values. The New Deal did not have to force its agricultural policies on a reluctant population. On the contrary, the commodity surpluses of the 1920s, loss of foreign markets, and resultant price declines had already convinced many farmers that their situation called for radical measures. The onset of the Great Depression intensified their problems and made them even more receptive to new answers. Annual farm net income fell from $6.1 billion in 1929 to $2 billion in 1932, a drop of almost 68 percent in three years.[1] President Hoover's agricultural and economic policies had no appreciable effect on production or prices, and during his administration, one-fourth of the farms in America changed hands because of delinquent taxes or unpaid mortgages.[2] The national press paid close attention as militant farm organizations threatened to withhold crops from markets unless prices improved, and others destroyed produce rather than take losses at the marketplace. The presidential election campaign in 1932 coincided with the specter of rebellion and violence from previously docile farmers. Candidate Franklin Roosevelt acknowledged this "acute distress" in rural America and promised to find solutions.[3] His subsequent appointment of Henry A. Wallace as secretary of agriculture was a signal that unconventional answers would be forthcoming. This son of a former secretary of agriculture was well known as a publisher and scientific farmer in Iowa; he was also, according to one writer, "a humanist free from tradition and orthodox practices, receptive to new ideas and challenges." He dabbled with poetry, politics, and religious mysticism in addition to his agricultural interests.[4]

Unconventional and controversial, the Agricultural Adjustment Administration was the first of many New Deal attempts to correct the problems that had plagued America's farmers for many years. Established in May 1933 as a part of the Farm Relief Bill, the AAA experimented with production controls and marketing agreements to cut surpluses and raise prices. Roosevelt had warned Congress in March when he urged passage of the bill that "it is a new and untrod path, but I tell you with equal frankness that an unprecedented condition calls for the trial of new means to rescue agriculture."[5] Wallace and the AAA focused on seven commodities—wheat, cotton, tobacco, rice, corn, hogs, and milk—of which there were high current surpluses and low prices, which were considered easy to regulate, and which dominated American farm exports. If farmers volunteered to curtail production, the AAA would pay them subsidies based on projected harvests and price levels from good market years of 1909-1914 (for tobacco, 1919-29). Taxes levied on processors or handlers, such as gristmills and slaughterhouses, would produce the revenues for the benefits.[6] AAA officials would also arrange contracts between farmers and markets for mutually agreeable price elevations. These contracts would allow the markets to assume virtually monopolistic control over their areas and yet to avoid prosecution under prevailing antitrust legislation.[7] All in all, the AAA was the federal government's most ambitious rescue mission for farmers in American history.

Of the seven AAA commodity programs, cotton was the first to receive publicity. Since cotton farmers had already planted approximately half of their normal acreage prior to passage of the new legislation, AAA administrators knew that haste was necessary to stabilize the already glutted markets. They wanted to reduce the 1933 harvest by roughly three million bales; to do so it would be necessary to curtail additional planting or to plow under some of the land already planted.[8] Following several meetings with cotton farmers and marketing experts, the AAA announced on June 19 that America's cotton farmers would be asked to participate in a voluntary plow-up program to destroy approximately one-fourth of the potential harvest of 1933.[9] This unprecedented program aroused instant criticism among those who recoiled at the prospect of destroying a growing crop, but this seeming violation of nature, for all of its alleged radicalism, was merely the fruition of a plan put forth earlier by Hoover's Federal Farm Board. That plan had died of political ridicule at the time, and some observers recalled that Roosevelt himself had referred to the suggestion as a "cruel joke."[10]

Despite the predictable uproar from the public, cotton farmers greeted the plan with enthusiasm, knowing apparently that tough diseases required tough medicine. The editor of the *Hickman Courier*, whose readers included most of the cotton growers in Kentucky's Purchase section, stated pragmatically, "We are in an excellent position to profit from the recovery program."[11] By the time of the cutoff date for signing the emergency contracts, more than a million farmers across the south had voluntarily agreed to participate. During the following weeks in July and August, they proceeded to plow up entire fields of young cotton or alternating rows of immature plants. With tractors and mules they destroyed in a few hours what had taken many weeks to plant, germinate, and grow. At the completion of their work, they had plowed under more than ten million acres of cotton plants and been paid $110 million, an average of $10.60 per acre.[12] A total of eighty-seven farmers in western Kentucky signed the contracts and plowed under approximately twenty-three hundred acres of cotton in Fulton and Calloway counties. They played what was obviously a minor part of the national enterprise, but their participation meant $42,000 to the sparsely populated Purchase area, a fact duly noted by the local newspaper.[13] After observing the site of one plow-up operation, Henry Wallace commented: "It was too bad to have to turn all that product of wasted effort back into the ground. But it would have been a great deal more destructive and wasteful to have kept going on blindly."[14]

The results of this emergency program were mixed. Many farmers had proved their willingness to volunteer for a "radical" program; the government had helped prime the economic pumps by paying those farmers millions of dollars in benefits—money that came much earlier in the season than the harvest revenues they had been accustomed to receiving. And when marketing time arrived, their cotton sold for prices averaging three to four cents per pound higher than the year previously.[15] The federal government then enhanced its efforts to stabilize the cotton markets when in October it created the Commodity Credit Corporation. This body allowed farmers to store their surplus bales in return for government loans equal to or above the market price if they agreed to participate in the 1934 curtailment program.  To offset some of the criticism of the 1933 emergency destruction program, the Department of Agriculture transferred part of the stored surplus to relief agencies such as the FERA and, later, the WPA mattress factories. The Commodity Credit Corporation later expanded its operations to absorb storable surplus products other than cotton. Although the plow-up program was admittedly an emergency measure and was not repeated, it did reveal much about the AAA procedures. Involving farmers in the planning process, implementing programs hastily, using county agents and state extension services as arms of federal policy, and transferring surplus produce to relief agencies were all techniques that the AAA would employ in the coming years. As dean of the College of Agriculture at the University of Kentucky, Thomas Poe Cooper also directed the activities of the county agents and extension services. From Lexington Cooper could quickly dispatch new AAA directives to almost every rural area in the state.

Hogs, even more than cotton, provoked early controversy during the AAA's experiments with price stabilization. Similar to the emergency plow-up of cotton was the onetime slaughter of hogs that the AAA organized to reduce a glut of marketable pork and to raise prices for beleaguered hog producers. The slaughter was just as successful but much noisier than the cotton plow-ups. Unlike cotton, hogs were not limited to the South, and approximately 60 percent of all American farmers were involved with some aspect of pork production.[16] New scientific breeding and feeding practices during the 1920s had created larger and healthier litters and thus had also produced glutted markets, since foreign markets for American pork had been declining. The result was too many pigs, which ate expensive food and then drew low market prices. By July 1933 hog prices registered lower on the fair exchange value scale than any other agricultural commodity.[17] One official in the AAA later recalled that "train loads of little pigs began to come to market, but nobody would buy them. Nobody wanted them. . . . they were driving little pigs into the Mississippi River at St. Paul and just letting them drown."[18] Few Kentuckians were ready to drive their pigs into the Ohio River in despair over low prices, but the situation in the commonwealth was equally serious. Kentuckians had marketed more than 250 million pounds of pork in 1932, and the predictions for 1933 were for an even larger slaughter and lower prices.[19]

To combat the problem, the AAA worked with delegates from major hog-producing states to devise an emergency program. An Ohio delegate suggested an immediate slaughter to stop the impending glut on the market. The AAA could then distribute the pork to the needy, possibly through agencies such as the Red Cross. An Indiana delegate, Claude Wickard, later recalled the initial reaction at the meeting. "At first I could tell that several people were startled by it. It seemed to be a little drastic I guess."[20] Drastic or not, the AAA refined the suggestion, and Wallace announced the voluntary program on August 18 in Chicago, the nation's hog-slaughtering capital. He explained that removing five million hogs from the market prior to regular slaughtering time could allow the market price to rise 30 percent. If hog farmers would agree to sell their animals at designated sites, they would receive triple the going rate for small pigs and a bonus above the current price for sows.[21] Federal meat inspectors would work with these 139 licensed plants in eighty-two cities around the county to establish delivery schedules and quotas for farmers, grade the animals as they arrived, and arrange for payment. Authorized processors would then salt-cure edible meat for relief distribution, render lard and grease from the smaller pigs, and turn the remains into fertilizer tankage.[22] Emotional opposition to the slaughter arose even before it began. If destroying immature cotton plants seemed a violation of nature, the slaughter of little pigs and pregnant sows defied the vocabulary of outrage. Henry Wallace had by now become accustomed to such reactions to his revolutionary policies. "It was a foregone conclusion," he remembered, "that the public would not like the idea of slaughtering baby pigs. . . . To hear them talk, you would have thought that pigs are raised for pets."[23]

Critics to the contrary, hog farmers not only helped plan the program but flooded the slaughtering sites with their broods and competed with each other for available quota permits. Between the opening of the program on August 23 and its closing on September 29, more than six million pigs ran through the chutes for premature slaughter, a million more than Wallace had asked for. For their cooperation, the AAA paid out $30 million to farmers, slaughterers, and processors.[24] No licensed plants were open near Kentucky until the third day of the campaign, when the first Louisville site began accepting hogs. By the end of the program, most Kentucky hogs went to two sites in Louisville, two others in Cincinnati, and one in Henderson. At those plants more than fifty-eight thousand Kentucky hogs gave their lives for this New Deal glut reduction and earned for their owners approximately $276,000.[25] AAA officials in Louisville had allotted quotas carefully, and the slaughtering proceeded in an orderly fashion, but Henderson's Eckert Packing Company was not so fortunate. Hog raisers in the western part of the state "completely swamped" the Eckert plant on its first day because of a less disciplined quota and schedule system. The local newspaper thereafter ran front-page stories warning farmers not to deliver their hogs without advance booking.[26]

Undoubtedly, more Kentucky hog producers would have participated except for the administrative difficulties. Farmers in eastern Kentucky had to deliver their hogs long distances to Cincinnati or over the West Virginia mountains to Wheeling. Likewise, western and southern Kentucky farmers had to compete for quotas at Henderson and Louisville or travel south to equally crowded plants in Nashville, Tennessee. One Winchester farmer argued that traveling for many miles was not the only problem; he accused the Louisville and Cincinnati sites of granting slaughter permits to only their regular customers, thus eliminating "a large percentage of the farmers of central Kentucky."[27] Another farmer from the western part of the state had similar difficulties. After trying unsuccessfully to get his pigs on the slaughter docket in Henderson, Louisville, and Nashville, he complained to Henry Wallace, "I want to do my part" but added that he could not find a way. He wrote a similar protest to President Roosevelt, but his inquiries were to no avail. AAA officials responded to his letters with apologies and good wishes; solutions, however, were unavailable.[28] A few independent buyers readily exploited frustrated farmers who could not get slaughter permits. A farmer from Cynthiana wrote angrily to his congressman about having no alternative but to sell his hogs cheaply to an Indiana buyer who had managed to get extra permits at one of the Cincinnati plants. An irate hog raiser from Mays Lick sold his animals to a middleman who later sold them for a large profit with previously obtained permits at a Cleveland site.[29] These examples of scalping were, unfortunately, common enough to prompt several federal grand jury investigations, which produced seventeen indictments and several fines for guilty parties.[30]

Disposing of the slaughtered pork proved to be a dilemma for the AAA, as several unforeseen difficulties altered its plans. The larger pigs produced a hundred million pounds of salt-cured pork, which went to the FERA for relief distribution; the AAA also recouped some of its expenses on eight million pounds of lard, twenty-one million pounds of grease, and five thousand tons of dry fertilizer.[31] Unfortunately, packers found that their dehairing equipment would not work effectively on the smaller animals, and manual processing was slow and costly. Consequently, most of the piglets became fertilizer tankage or waste. Washington administrators allowed the individual plants to dispose of their waste as best they could, whether by burying it in pits, burning it, or giving it to farmers for livestock feed. Reports that a plant in Illinois had dumped its refuse into the Mississippi River may have been just rumor, but they fed public indignation. One Missourian wrote to express outrage that the government could "destroy food while many are starving."[32] Residue from the slaughtering of pigs in Louisville went up in smoke after municipal and plant officials decided that burning the waste in the city incinerator was the most efficient method of disposal.[33]

The immediate benefits of this emergency slaughter were obvious. Farmer purchasing power made a dramatic surge, increasing nationally by thirty million dollars in one month. And the reduced surplus helped raise market prices of pork during the following slaughtering season. The drastic quality of the program convinced many farmers that the federal government was serious about trying to ease some of their agricultural travails, and as a result, they were receptive to subsequent, less flamboyant production control measures. Politically, the pig slaughter continued to haunt the New Deal for many years. Senator Barkley tried to brush aside any memories of cruelty and waste when he delivered the keynote address at the Democratic National Convention in 1936. "They have wept over the slaughter of a few little pigs as if they had been tender human infants nestling at their mother's breasts. They have shed these tears over the premature death of pigs as if they had been born, educated and destined for the ministry."[34] Despite Barkley's humor, Henry Wallace bore the scars of the episode for many years. Campaigning for the vice-presidency in 1940 and the presidency in 1948, Wallace found himself branded as the candidate who "might run amok with the butcher knife again" and as the person most qualified to "slit a pig's throat."[35]

The two emergency programs out of the way, the AAA could concentrate on less volatile and longer-range measures to limit output of other commodities. Most of the domestic allotment contracts that farmers volunteered to sign did not go into effect until the following season, so farmers could negotiate contracts without the haste and embarrassing publicity that characterized the 1933 emergency cotton and hog programs. The usual procedure was for AAA officials to hold conferences with representative producers of a particular commodity, decide how much reduction they wanted to achieve to prevent further surpluses, determine the level of subsidies to be paid to participating farmers, and then rely on county agents to hold local meetings and oversee the signing of individual agreements. Each commodity had different goals, details, and payments, and each participating farmer had to adhere to individual quotas based on past production records. Kentucky domestic allotments included only four commodities: cotton, tobacco, wheat, and the combination of corn and hogs, usually grouped together because most corn eventually became pork. From late 1933 until the end of the program in early 1936, county agents and AAA officials presided over a kaleidoscope of activity as thousands of farmers negotiated contracts, curtailed production,

**Newly Plowed Fields** 113

realized greater profits, and became increasingly dependent on federal assistance. Annual reports of the Kentucky Extension Service indicated that throughout 1934 and 1935 county agents spent most of their time doing AAA work at the expense of their traditional educational and demonstration duties.[36] The era of rugged individualism in which the lonely farmer braved the whims of nature and the fluctuations of the marketplace had come to an end. Replacing it was a new era of cooperative enterprise in which the farmer and the government planned and negotiated for mutual benefit.

Since it was Kentucky's largest single cash crop, tobacco generated the most extensive AAA activity in the state. Kentuckians had sold more than 300 million pounds of tobacco in the 1932 winter auctions for $31 million, an amount that was less than one-half of their receipts prior to the crash of 1929. The Annual Outlook Report prepared by the University of Kentucky predicted that the coming year would be worse: a larger yield and lower market prices. Consequently most tobacco farmers were eager for the AAA to save them from this situation.[37] John B. Hutson, the head of the AAA's Tobacco Section, was particularly sensitive to Kentucky's plight because he was a native of the state and a former tobacco farmer. He had grown up near Murray and graduated from the University of Kentucky before becoming a researcher for the U.S. Department of Agriculture. In addition to studying tobacco cultivation in both America and Europe, he had earned a doctorate from Columbia University. Now he worked closely with his native state to devise corrective measures for its major source of revenue. Congressman Fred Vinson's district contained hundreds of tobacco farmers, and he labored with Hutson and other AAA officials to guarantee that his eastern mountain constituents received a fair share of benefits. Vinson later recalled making all-night automobile trips between Washington and Kentucky to attend crucial planning sessions that outlined contracts.[38] Representative Virgil Chapman also took an important part in convincing his Bluegrass constituents to cooperate with the AAA. A majority of Kentucky's tobacco farmers grew the burley leaf, though some produced fire-cured and dark air-cured strains, and the AAA program for burley was representative of the agreements for all growers. The basic plan was to reduce acreage for 1934 by one-half. Farmers who agreed to participate would get twenty dollars for each acre taken out of production, plus two additional benefit payments based on such factors as the market price.[39]

While AAA officials and Kentucky politicians spent the summer of 1933 devising the tobacco reduction plans for 1934, Kentucky farmers cultivated and harvested their current crop. As predicted, a bumper crop arrived at sale warehouses in December, and buyers and farmers alike were confused when sales began, for they did not know what to expect from the 1934 season. If only a few farmers signed curtailment contracts, then another bumper harvest would drive prices down; if most of the farmers participated, there would be a short crop in 1934, and bidders could feel confident about paying high prices for the present year's harvest. During the first week of sales, burley prices reflected this indecisiveness. Lexington sale prices were respectable, averaging more than twelve cents per pound, but at such locations as Maysville and Glasgow, bidders refused to pay more than ten cents. A few warehouses closed early on some days rather than continue the disappointing sales, and several distraught sellers pleaded with Governor Laffoon to declare a marketing holiday until confidence replaced the confusion.[40] Lackluster sales in North Carolina had preceded those in Kentucky, and the governor of the Tarheel State had declared a moratorium there until the new AAA program stabilized markets. John B. Hutson assured Laffoon that such a desperate measure was not warranted and that prices would improve early in the new year when the extent of the AAA contract sign-up became evident.[41] Laffoon disregarded Hutson's advice and proclaimed a holiday on December 16. Acknowledging the plight of the "considerably perturbed" farmers, he requested that warehouses suspend all tobacco sales until the "National Government may be able to perfect a plan" for crop reduction and price adjustment.[42]

Laffoon's tobacco holiday served the same purpose his banking moratorium had the past spring; it stopped the price decline for the moment and provided time for farmers, buyers, and state and federal officials to work out agreements that would prevent further panic. Before sales warehouses reopened in early January 1934, several meetings produced the necessary arrangements to restore confidence. The governor and Congressman Chapman held an open meeting for growers at the state capitol in late December, and representatives from all parts of the state filled the House Chamber. Following their discussions, they passsed a resolution urging Kentucky farmers to sign the AAA curtailment contracts. At the same time Senator Barkley and Representative Vinson were meeting with the major buyers to set a floor on prices once sales resumed.[43] Editors of the *Lexington Herald* assisted county agents in encouraging farmers to participate in the 1934 program by running a series of articles entitled "Why I Signed" that featured tobacco growers who had already agreed. They also printed an optimistic piece written by John Hutson, in which he announced that the predictions of a short crop in 1934 had convinced ten large tobacco purchasers to guarantee a floor price of no less than twelve cents per pound for the remainder of the 1933 crop sales.[44] The result of all this waiting, planning, and publicity was a Kentucky sign-up of approximately 90 percent of the burley growers and the stabilization of market prices when the warehouses resumed operations.[45] Congress solidified these gains in June 1934 when it passed the Kerr-Smith Tobacco Control Act, which made crop curtailment almost mandatory. The law imposed a special tax on crops marketed by noncontract farmers, thus transforming the voluntary program into a coercive one.

Despite the predictable bureaucratic problems that characterized this new program and the criticism that greeted the compulsory parts of the Kerr-Smith law, the AAA tobacco curtailment program worked with remarkable success for the two seasons it lasted. More than a hundred thousand Kentucky growers participated and received benefits exceeding fourteen million dollars, an amount second only to that paid to farmers in North Carolina.[46] The ultimate test of the program's worth was the warehouse auction price. By the end of 1935 Kentucky farmers had reduced their production by 28 percent and had raised their market income by seven million dollars, compared to pre-AAA years. When asked if they wanted to continue the curtailment contracts after the 1935 season, ninety-six thousand of them agreed, giving overwhelming affirmation to the experiment.[47]

Domestic allotment programs to bring cuts in the output of cotton, wheat, and corn-hog production were similar to that for tobacco. Regional and state meetings devised plans and quotas, county agents supervised contract sign-ups, and farmers then received AAA benefits to curtail production. In Kentucky considerably fewer farmers were involved with these commodities than with tobacco, so less time and money were expended. Cotton farmers in Hickman County overcame their reluctance of 1933 and joined their neighbors in Fulton and Calloway counties in reducing acreage. The Bankhead Cotton Control Act of 1934 actually made their compliance "semi-compulsory." Its tax on nonquota cotton was similar to the Kerr-Smith tobacco levy and punished those farmers who chose not to participate in the curtailment program.[48] As a result, the eighty-seven Kentucky cotton farmers who had joined the 1933 plow-up expanded to two thousand participants in 1935. Impressive as this increase was, Kentucky lagged behind the national average, because of the difficulty of arranging quotas for the small-acreage farms common in western Kentucky.[49] Nonparticipants had to pay the tax on their cotton and complained mightily to county agents about the inequity and hardship of the system.[50] Controls were not as stringent for wheat and corn-hog producers, but potential benefits persuaded twenty-seven thousand farmers in the state to sign curtailment contracts. By the end of 1935 participants in the cotton, wheat, and corn-hog programs had received more than six million dollars in AAA benefits, found their market revenues moving upward, and voted by large majorities to continue the domestic allotment system.[51] No one denied that frustrating delays, red tape, and confusion characterized the AAA programs, but the stabilized productivity and improved market prices seem to have made them acceptable. The editor of a Kentucky farmers' publication declared in 1935 that the AAA "has done more for the farmers of America" than anything seen in this generation.[52]

Regardless of its success or popularity, the AAA died a sudden death in January 1936, when the Supreme Court ruled that certain portions of the program were unconstitutional. The Court's ruling came as no real surprise to Kentuckians. AAA legal problems were well known, and the commonwealth played a role in its demise. Some processors, unhappy from the start that their taxes financed AAA benefits, had sought legal redress. Meanwhile, a federal judge in Louisville ruled the Kerr-Smith levy illegal. While these cases were under review, some of the production control contracts for 1936 hung in limbo. Kentuckian Stanley Reed had the responsibility in late 1935 of defending the AAA before the Supreme Court. Reed, who had risen from a log cabin near Maysville to his position of solicitor general, had marshaled legal arguments in favor of several beleaguered New Deal projects. While defending the contracts and taxes that were central to the AAA, Reed collapsed from exhaustion. Chief Justice Charles Evans Hughes adjourned court early to allow him time to recover, and some observers thought Reed had "become so enwrapped in the defense of the AAA he did not realize" how far he had overextended himself.[53] When the court handed down its ruling in *United States* vs. *Butler*, it was apparent that Reed's efforts had failed. The ruling held that the AAA processing tax had exceeded the federal government's jurisdiction in regulating agricultural commerce. The Department of Agriculture would either have to restructure the entire program or jettison it immediately.

Agricultural states and farm leaders protested this Supreme Court decision. The AAA was the New Deal's premier program for rural America, and judging from the 1935 referenda for its continuance, millions of farmers strongly supported it. A week after the six-to-three verdict, Henry Wallace said: "Thus far the farmers, like many of the rest of us, are a good bit like the man who had just had the breath knocked out of him. When he comes to, he doesn't know whether to laugh, cry, or cuss."[54] W. Vaughn Spencer, editor of the *Farmers Home Journal* in Louisville, did some of each, accusing the justices of being "9 cloistered old gentlemen who never ventured out of narrow academic society."[55] Governor Chandler expressed his "great shock and disappointment," and the Kentucky Senate passed a memorial requesting Congress to replace the AAA with a similar substitute. Senator Ralph Gilbert from Shelbyville supported the memorial, relating that he had lost money for years raising pigs until the AAA had taught him how to make money by using porcine birth control.[56] Somewhat later, the WPA's Federal Theater Project dramatized the situation in one of its social commentary plays, *The Triple A Plowed Under*. Therein farmers questioned how they would survive without their benefit payments, and the ghost of Thomas Jefferson wondered if a constitutional amendment might help.[57]

Although the Supreme Court may have plowed under the Agricultural Adjustment Act, that program proved to be a hardy plant. Congress gave it new life in February 1936, when it passed the Soil Conservation and Domestic Allotment Act. Provided with legislative appropriations to replace the invalidated processing tax revenues, the Department of Agriculture would encourage farmers to transfer land from soil-depleting crops to land-enriching crops. Farmers would now get benefit payments in the form of "rental checks" for reducing their acreage of tobacco, cotton, wheat, and corn and by replacing them with fields of clover and legumes. Instead of devising thousands of separate commodity reduction contracts, county agents would work with individual farms to arrange conservation programs appropriate to that property. With these new practices, farmers could receive cash benefits, curtail potential surpluses, and instill new life into marginal acres with scientific management.[58]

Kentucky farmers were quick to sign up for these revised contracts. In the first year and a half of the new program, more than 108,000 Kentuckians participated in the new soil-building programs and carried them out on about 2.5 million acres. For this activity they received more than $11 million.[59] These payments were comparable to what farmers had received for earlier commodity reduction contracts, although the money frequently went to different people and for different reasons. The new program had only minimal effects on surpluses, however, partly because ingenious farmers learned to increase yields per acre. Only the severe drought in 1936, prevented debilitating surpluses of corn and wheat; likewise, only Commodity Credit Corporation storage loans in 1937 kept cotton prices reasonable.[60]

In the autumn of 1937 Kentucky farmers joined farmers from other states in demanding a return to the greater security of the original AAA. The Senate Agricultural Committee brought one of its regional hearings to Louisville's Brown Hotel in mid-October to learn what American farmers wanted. More than three hundred Kentuckians attended, some traveling as far as two hundred miles to help educate the senators, and they cheered spontaneously when one county spokesman said, "The farmers of my county want another AAA." O.M. Farrington of the University of Kentucky explained that the burley tobacco farmers had approved so strongly of the original AAA production controls that they had tried to continue them on their own. The president of the Kentucky Farm Bureau Federation informed the federal officials that the Department of Agriculture not only should reinstate quotas and allotments but should make them more available to the small farmers who had previously had difficulty qualifying for benefits. By the end of the hearing it appeared that the gathering was also favorably disposed to Henry Wallace's plans for an "ever-normal granary" for which the government would offer price supports, purchase surplus produce, and store nonperishable commodities—all as insurance against future short harvests and low incomes.[61] If this hearing offered a message to Washington, it was that farmers wanted more, not less, federal assistance and control; their agenda did not include a return to the freedoms preceding the New Deal.

When Congress created the second AAA in February 1938, it tacitly responded to these requests from the Brown Hotel and retained the conservation programs of the past two years. The renewed AAA allowed the secretary of agriculture to set allotment quotas when a surplus of a particular commodity appeared imminent, but only if a two-thirds majority of the farmers producing the commodity approved the quota in a referendum. This system would give the farmers more of a voice in determining policies than under the previous programs. Wallace would implement his "ever-normal granary" by accelerating Commodity Credit Corporation loans for excess storable produce, which the Department of Agriculture could hold for lean years or could sell in foreign markets. These loans would help stabilize prices and act as parity payments so that farmers could receive the market prices designated as desirable levels.[62] Aside from the inclusion of a crop insurance plan, most of the new AAA ideas were reinstatements or modifications of those of 1933. There were, of course, no processing taxes. The renewed AAA strove for a balance of production control, democratic participation, price supports, surplus storage, loans, insurance, and soil conservation practices. In its efforts to satisfy farmers, conservationists, and the Supreme Court, it became a massive, expensive, and enduring government program with major impact on both domestic politics and foreign trade.

Kentucky farmers quickly endorsed the new AAA. Statistics give a good indication of Kentucky's receptivity to the variety of programs. The number of farmers who participated rose each year and exceeded 250,000 in 1941; those farmers reduced the acreage of soil-depleting crops by approximately 600,000 acres and experimented with greater use of pasturing and lime additives. By signing conservation and curtailment contracts, they received an average of ten million dollars in federal benefits each year, and in 1938 Kentucky ranked ninth in the nation among states receiving AAA benefits. Annual returns on what farmers sold increased almost uniformly during the New Deal years, with predictable drops during the recession of 1937-1938.[63] Not all agricultural prices were linked to government controls. So the AAA could not take full credit for this stabilization and improvement, but prices for major commodities were directly related to federal manipulation of production and marketing. Farmers sometimes exercised their option, rejected government quotas in scheduled referenda, and took their chances. Tobacco farmers, for example, accepted AAA quotas in 1938, but rejected them in 1939. Kentucky burley growers wanted to continue the quotas that year, but lost the election to farmers elsewhere. Overproduction in 1939 caused a sharp decline in tobacco prices and AAA quotas re-

Governor Ruby Laffoon, 1932. *Louisville Courier-Journal*

NRA's Blue Eagle in a Louisville parade, 1933. Caufield and Shook photo, courtesy University of Louisville Photographic Archives

The Fort Knox gold depository under construction by Public Works Administration, 1936. Courtesy University of Louisville Photographic Archives

Sublimity Farms, an experimental community of the Farm Security Administration, in Laurel County. *Louisville Courier-Journal*

Gubernatorial campaign poster, 1935. Courtesy Special Collections, University of Kentucky Library

WPA sewer construction project in Owensboro. Courtesy Special Collections, University of Kentucky Library

A CCC construction crew at Audubon State Park. Courtesy Kentucky Department of Libraries and Archives

Eleanor Roosevelt sees a weaving demonstration in NYA exhibit room, West Liberty, 1937. Courtesy Special Collections, University of Kentucky Library.

President Franklin D. Roosevelt, Governor A.B. Chandler, and Senator Alben Barkley, 1938. *Louisville Courier-Journal*

The kerosene lamp is buried at dedication of the Henderson County REA Cooperative, 1937. *Louisville Courier-Journal*

WPA packhorse librarians in Knott County. Courtesy Special
Collections, University of Kentucky Library

Birmingham, Kentucky,
before being submerged
in Kentucky Lake.
*Louisville Courier-
Journal*

Kentucky guardsmen escort miners as Harlan County mines reopen, 1939. John L. Carter photo, courtesy Special Collections, University of Kentucky Library

Looking south on Louisville's Fourth Street during the 1937 flood. Caufield and Shook photo, courtesy University of Louisville Photographic Archives

Governor-elect Keen Johnson prepares for his inauguration, 1939. *Louisville Courier-Journal*

TVA's Kentucky Dam under construction near Gilbertsville, 1938-1945. *Louisville Courier-Journal*

turned in 1940.[64] Henry Wallace was especially pleased with the results of his "ever-normal granary." The Department of Agriculture had absorbed sufficient surpluses from the commodity markets so that in the early days of World War II the United States could ship wheat, corn, and cotton to the embattled British without causing shortages for American consumers.[65]

Perhaps the severest indictment of the AAA programs was that they favored larger farms and sometimes hurt the smaller ones. Most AAA benefits were geared to stabilizing commodity prices rather than to helping individuals; consequently, those farmers who produced large harvests benefited more than those who did not. Farmers of small plots had difficulty qualifying for allotment quotas and frequently could not participate in the programs. Several AAA officials regarded small farms as inherently inefficient and ultimately doomed to extinction. By aiding larger farms, the AAA accelerated the natural process of consolidation. In addition, especially in the South, when farmers curtailed production they removed from cultivation those acres tilled by tenants or sharecroppers. The latter then either moved from the land or became day laborers.[66] A comparison of the 1930 and 1940 census reports reveals that this regional phenomenon was certainly occurring in Kentucky. During this decade farms containing a hundred acres or fewer decreased in number by four thousand, and those exceeding a hundred acres increased by nearly eight hundred. Numbers of Kentucky tenants and sharecroppers also diminished during the 1930s; there were twelve thousand fewer in 1940 than ten years earlier. Especially striking was the sharp decline in the number of black farmers; there were almost four thousand fewer than at the start of the Depression.[67]

AAA programs cannot be held exclusively responsible for this demographic shift, however. An exodus of people from small plots into urban areas had already begun prior to the New Deal. The consolidation of smaller farm holdings into larger ones had also commenced, as a part of the national trend toward agricultural mechanization. What the AAA did was to accelerate these gradual trends. As the major farm program of the decade, it favored bigness and created more of the same.

Although the AAA did little to assist the tenant, sharecrop-

per, and small farmer, other programs of the New Deal attempted to alleviate some of their problems. Often these attempts ran
counter to AAA policies, further compounding the contradictions inherent in the New Deal. Harry Hopkins's FERA included a small, short-lived project devoted to rural rehabilitation. When the FERA phased out in 1935, the new Resettlement
Administration absorbed its programs. The Resettlement Administration, in turn, merged into the Farm Security Administration in 1937. All three of these federal organizations tried to
help the small farmer become more nearly self-supporting by
extending loans or by moving him to better land elsewhere.
Eventually, these agencies tried other methods, such as cooperative marketing and collective communities. By the time World
War II brought all their activity to a close, several improvements
and a few revolutionary experiments had altered the face of rural
America.

Rural Rehabilitation was one part of the FERA in Kentucky
that got little attention or publicity. State director Earl Mayhew
avoided political battles and quietly built his agency around the
needs of its clients, 60 percent of whom were tenants. Mayhew
was a native of Knox County and had served as a county agent
there and in nearby Clay and Harlan Counties. He had, therefore, an intimate knowledge of the state's poorest section and
the problems of marginal land and subsistence farming. The
Kentucky Rural Rehabilitation Office granted small loans, averaging about three hundred dollars, to help farmers defray expenses and to educate them in better farming techniques and
soil improvement. Only about eleven hundred farmers received
these loans, and Mayhew was pleased that at the time of the
termination of his agency two-thirds of them were paying back
their debts. In his view, these borrowers showed a combination
of honesty and initiative that could lead them to real advances if
they were properly assisted.[68] When he was a county agent,
Mayhew's supervisor had been Dean Thomas P. Cooper of the
University of Kentucky. Cooper had initially doubted that any
assistance program could help these people because of their long
experience with poverty and declining soil conditions. At the
end of the brief loan experience, however, Cooper joined May-

hew in expressing delight that it had been not only "surprisingly satisfactory but also surprisingly successful."[69]

A more ambitious Rural Rehabilitation Program provided for the purchase of submarginal land from poor farmers and their relocation to better property or to new communities. The abandoned land would be added to state and national forests, and the new communities would introduce cooperative farming and marketing. This process would also help to break down some of the isolation that had characterized the small, remote farms, inhibiting individual progress. The national relocation project envisioned for at least twenty-nine sites barely got beyond the planning stage before the FERA expired.[70] One of these planned relocations was an eleven-thousand-acre site in Bell and Harlan counties in eastern Kentucky. Rural Rehabilitation officials decided that the sixty-four families living in this area were fighting a hopeless cause, trying to farm hillside land that had once been timbered and was now badly eroded. They recommended that the farms be purchased, the land reforested, and the families relocated. In 1935 the Resettlement Administration accepted these recommendations when it assumed the rural responsibilities of the defunct FERA.[71]

When President Roosevelt created the Resettlement Administration in May 1935, he was acknowledging that the problem of the rural poor demanded more than just a small agency within the FERA. His executive order empowered the new office to continue and accelerate the loan and grant programs and the projects for soil improvement, relocation, and community development planned by Rural Rehabilitation.[72] He chose Rexford Tugwell, undersecretary of agriculture, to administer this multifaceted agency. An urbane New Yorker who had taught economics at Columbia University, Tugwell pursued many reform visions that some friends called impulsive and unrealistic and some critics called utopian. Enemies of the New Deal took delight in quoting a poem he had written earlier in a burst of undergraduate enthusiasm. "I shall roll up my sleeves," he had vowed, and "make America over!"[73] This poem was proof enough of Tugwell's radicalism to make congressional conservatives view the Resettlement Administration with caution and treat it with fiscal restraint. Earl Mayhew had managed to avoid the political battles of his previous boss, Harry Hopkins, and he now succeeded in tempering the reform excesses of his new boss, Tugwell. He interpreted and implemented the changing priorities of rural uplift in Kentucky with the same quiet efficiency that characterized his earlier work. When Tugwell left the position in late 1936 and the agency got a new name in 1937, Mayhew carried on as usual.

The Resettlement Administration provided more loans and grants in larger amounts to farms it regarded as redeemable than had its predecessor. By the end of 1936 more than fifteen thousand Kentucky families had received approximately $1.7 million to help them rehabilitate their properties.[74] The typical recipient was a tenant who wanted to stay on his small plot of land and learn more effective methods. With the money came lessons and supervision by county agents; the goal was not just an economic boost, it was an educational advance. The farmer "is taught the latest farm methods," according to Tugwell, "so as to get the most out of his labor."[75] Additional loans assisted groups of farmers in forming small cooperatives for more efficient purchasing and marketing. In Kentucky at least fifty rural organizations obtained loans to purchase machinery or new breeding stock that none of the individual farmers could have afforded but now all could use.[76] When Congress changed the Resettlement Administration into the Farm Security Administration in 1937, it also changed the emphasis of its loan programs. Rehabilitation loans would continue, but now larger loans at low interest and for long terms would encourage tenants to purchase their farms. This new program incorporated the philosophy of the 1936 report from the President's Committee on Farm Tenancy, which revealed that most tenants, like most Americans, wanted to be owners rather than renters.

Purchase loans were apparently all the encouragement rural farmers needed. Their applications so exceeded available funds that it would have taken four hundred years for all of them to become homeowners at the rate the agency approved and granted the loans.[77] In Kentucky during the peak years of this activity, 1938-1941, almost eleven thousand tenants competed for the limited funds, and fewer than seven hundred were recipients.[78] A.H. Hall from Pendleton County was the first Kentuckian to make the transition from renter to owner with one of the coveted purchase loans. A committee of county farmers selected him as a prime candidate for success, and Earl Mayhew awarded him a loan of $5,000. Hall had been renting and sharecropping for seven years, and with the loan he purchased a 168-acre tract on which he started his new life with eleven cows, twenty-five ewes, and fields of tobacco, corn, and alfalfa.[79] Corby Huff of Hart County pursued a similar course. He received a $7,740 loan to purchase 103 acres near Munfordville and was so successful that he became the subject of a lengthy case study and national publicity by the USDA. He had followed the provisions of the loan so diligently—adhering to county agent advice, sending his children to school, testing his livestock regularly for diseases, using scientific farming methods—that federal officials touted him as model farmer in the program. Not only had the Huffs paid off their loan in six years and increased the farm's value to nearly $20,000, they had also "increased their initiative and raised their social standing" according to the case study.[80] This success story was certainly compatible with Tugwell's initial poetic vision even though he was no longer a part of the administration when it came true.

Early plans by the Rural Rehabilitation agency to relocate families from submarginal land to better farms turned into extensive social experiments by the Resettlement Administration. Tugwell visited several of the ravaged sites across the country that he wanted to return to forest land and wrote his assessment of the problem for the *Courier-Journal*: "Stop for a while on your trip through Kentucky and interrupt the man who hoes a barren patch of land. . . . He is in debt even for the shabby clothes in which he stands. . . . Follow his gaze, and there in great waves and processions march thousands upon thousands of stumps, hacked and cut that once were trees shading these now famished fields. This landscape is the result of overexploitation of the forest that once stood here."[81] Four such areas in Kentucky were the object of relocation plans. The Bell and Harlan county site, left over from previous FERA recommendations, doubled in size to twenty-five thousand acres and became the Kentucky Ridge Project. Resettlement Administration officials planned to turn it into a forest preserve and recreational center. An eight-thousand-acre tract of eroded land in Meade County, just west of Louisville, was to become Otter Creek Park in cooperation with the National Park Service. A game refuge near Princeton would replace twelve-thousand acres of submarginal farms. The largest of these four projects was located in western Kentucky between the Tennessee and Cumberland Rivers. There fifty thousand acres of denuded hillsides and abandoned homes and farms were destined for a new life as the Coalins Forest and Game Reservation, to be administered by the State Forest Service. These sites contained more than four hundred families to be relocated and ninety-five thousand acres to be purchased. The land's appraised value of $800,000 did not include cost for resettlement and development.[82]

Tugwell encountered many obstacles in the course of transforming rural blight into rustic charm. Some farmers set unexpectedly high prices on their farms; others were reluctant to leave land they had always farmed, regardless of price; and some farmers had already sold their mineral rights to coal companies, thus further complicating negotiations. A few local politicians in Trigg County lost their enthusiasm for the Coalins project when they calculated that the county would lose fifteen hundred dollars annually in property taxes once the land was in the hands of the federal or state governments.[83] In addition to escalating land acquisition costs, the Resettlement Administration and Farm Security Administration found development expenses for these properties much higher than anticipated. They then had to modify some of their plans and seek additional revenues elsewhere because Congress refused to appropriate any supplements. In several cases the PWA stepped in to complete unfinished projects, such as construction of roads, bridges, and fire towers. Harold Ickes's parsimonious staff and crews took charge of putting the finishing touches on several outdoor facilities at Kentucky Forest, Princeton, and Coalins.[84] By the beginning of World War II in 1939, the Farm Security Administration had either completed or turned over all its relocation projects to state or federal agencies for future development and administration. Finding new homes for displaced families was a challenge that the New Deal met in a variety of ways. Several agencies experimented with differrent forms of housing—urban and rural, single-family and communal—and the Resettlement Administration assumed the main responsibility for this activity. Kentucky had several examples of two types of Resettlement Administration housing. The "infiltration" type involved finding and purchasing a new farm and home for the family that had sold its submarginal property. The relocation usually was no more than a few miles from the original family farm, and in its role as real estate agent the Resettlement Administration worked quickly, efficiently, and with little publicity. "Farm communities," on the other hand, were more controversial and expensive, and they stirred up considerable public attention. Envisioned as totally new rural towns with modern amenities, these communities had to be planned, built, furnished, and supervised by federal officials, an entirely new responsibility for the government. Among the many critics of this experiment was Virginia's Senator Harry F. Byrd, who regarded the concept as radical, the cost as unreasonable, and the thought of introducing indoor toilets and electricity to poor rural families as extravagant.[85] The thirty-seven communities that resulted were fewer and less grand than originally projected but were intriguing experiments nonetheless. Two such communities—Sublimity Farms in Laurel County and Christian-Trigg Farms in Christian and Trigg counties—were constructed in Kentucky.

Resettlement Administration officials first announced the idea for Sublimity Farms in November 1935. Named for Sublimity Springs, near London, the new town was to be developed on land that the Forestry Service was buying to add to the Cumberland National Forest. The planners of this experimental community changed its premise several times, and it failed to achieve any of its goals before the government abandoned the project. The initial plans called for the development of a rural community of about four hundred people, most of whom had sold their land for relocation purposes. The town would be more than just a random collection of residences; it would be a planned community with paved streets and a central waterworks.[86] By the time WPA crews began construction in late 1936, the Sublimity plan had loosened considerably to a casual grouping of sixty-six small farms of three to ten acres, each with its own well and septic system and a four- or five-room house. One central building for group activities was all that remained of the original design for a unified community. Because the farms were so small as to preclude self-sufficiency, the relocated families would have to find supplementary jobs in nearby London or in neighboring lumber mills.[87] The nature of the community thus forced residents to become more interdependent, less reliant on individual farm productivity, and more diverse in their work efforts. Their new homes also had electricity, hot water, and indoor bathrooms, regardless of Harry Byrd's protestations. As long as this was an experiment in civic engineering, the end results might as well include higher levels of comfort and cleanliness. In sum, the government spent almost $500,000 to develop the physical facilities for this Kentucky laboratory.[88]

The new Farm Security Administration had no trouble in late 1937 finding applicants who wanted to move into the sixty-six neat white clapboard homes with dark shutters. The local newspaper had observed the early development of the community and featured an editorial cartoon attacking Tugwell and the resettlement concept. But when the new town became fully populated, the editors had little difficulty accepting it as a part of Laurel County's landscape.[89] Residents paid less than twelve dollars per month to live in Sublimity Farms and got for this sum not the title of owners but the status of students. The community was now a living demonstration school for families who would later move on to other areas, better equipped to handle the intricacies of property management. A resident agronomist and social worker taught farming techniques, nutrition, and budgeting, and the resident Forest Service ranger instructed classes in care of orchards and forest land. The ranger pointed out in 1939, "We are taking people who were defeated before they could ever start fighting, and turning them, we hope, into responsible intelligent tax-paying citizens. If we can hope to produce even as high an average as sixty such citizens and their families every five years we'll count ourselves lucky."[90] These predictions never came to pass, because outside pressures ended the living demonstration even before its first class had graduated. An increasingly cost-conscious Congress demanded that the communities be sold and allowed to revert to "traditional patterns of complete individual ownership, private enterprise and local control."[91] The experiment ended in its early stages, and Sublimity Farms gradually lost its collective identity as families purchased the homes and pursued their separate dreams. The NYA briefly occupied ten of the dwellings for a girls' residence center in 1941, and when the Federal Housing Administration assumed responsibility for all former Farm Security Administration housing enterprises in 1946, it quickly disposed of the remaining unsold homes at auctions.[92]

In contrast to the ever-evolving social experiment of Sublimity Farms, the other farm community in Kentucky, Christian-Trigg Farms, pursued a linear course from inception to dispersal. This development started out to be a community of inexpensive farms for sale to tenants and sharecroppers from the Pennyroyal area and to other displaced families from the nearby Coalins and Princeton relocation projects. It accomplished just that. The Resettlement Administration purchased about eight thousand acres of land, some of which had been parts of antebellum plantations. It thereupon built or renovated 106 houses in an area sixteen times the size of the Laurel County development and spent nearly a million dollars. Although most of the houses and farms were similar in acreage and appointments to Sublimity, the great distances between the units made the finished project a community in name only.[93] Still, the federal planners maintained a degree of social experimentation with Christian-Trigg Farms. A central office in Hopkinsville supervised the construction, accepted applications for purchase, and arranged loans for suitable clients. According to one amused reporter, "handsome college girls in boots and breeches" interviewed the prospective buyers and looked for "industry and sobriety and for evidence of their will to better their lot." Once selected, the future owners then chose their sites, and whenever possible, helped with the construction work on their new homes.[94] When the Farm Security Administration began to phase out its operations in 1943, half of the homes had been sold and the rest rented.[95] The Federal Housing Administration disposed of the latter following World War II, and Christian-Trigg Farms merged into the routine of life in south-central Kentucky with little to distinguish it as an unusual New Deal innovation.

Whatever the success of their relocation and housing efforts, the Resettlement and Farm Security Administrations did effective work in publicizing the plight of the American small farmer and the precarious state of the nation's rural resources. Both agencies commissioned writers, photographers, and film makers to document social and ecological problems, and the results of their work left a rich legacy for sociologists and historians. Pare Lorenz's 1936 documentary film, *The Plow That Broke the Plains,* with an original musical score by Virgil Thompson, dramatized the dust-bowl devastation on the prairies and played to commercial success and critical acclaim. *The River,* which appeared in late 1937 with script and music by the same two men, emphasized the effects of poor land use and flooding. During the filming of the latter, Lorenz allowed nature to become his coauthor by incorporating into the script the spring floods on the Ohio and Mississippi Rivers.[96] Roy Stryker followed his Columbia University colleague, Rexford Tugwell, to Washington and became chief of the Resettlement Administration's Historical Section. In that capacity he presided over a growing collection of photographs and books that showed urban Americans how their rural neighbors lived and sometimes suffered. Among the notable publications that originated in his office was Dorothea Lange and Paul Taylor's *An American Exodus* (1939) and, probably the most enduring of the lot, James Agee and Walker Evans's *Let Us Now Praise Famous Men* (1941). These collections of visual images with captions and commentary were poignant and often shocking juxtapositions of rustic charm and rural decay. And they frequently provoked angry reactions from reviewers who thought them exaggerated or oversimplified.

Stryker's roving photographers visited Kentucky on several occasions and recorded thousands of mountain and small-town scenes. Very few of these were ever published, however, and they reside today with thousands of other prints in the Library of Congress. Ben Shahn toured the state briefly in 1935, as did others in 1936, 1938, and 1940. Marion Post Wolcott stayed the longest and captured the most impressions. This young lady from New Jersey had worked for the Philadelphia *Evening Bulletin* before joining the Farm Security Administration in 1938. She recalled later that photography was merely a small part of her 1940 mission in Kentucky. "I was convinced that through our photographic interpretations and honest forceful documentation of the social scene and of F.S.A.'s efforts to improve living conditions . . . we were contributing to the education not only of the public, but also of the legislators and bureaucrats."[97] She drove on extended field trips from her headquarters in Louisville to mining camps in Virgie, creekside baptisms in Morehead, harness races in Shelbyville, funerals in Breathitt County, and other events and sites that were both culturally and geographically remote from her eastern, urban experience. Her letters to Stryker complained about fixing flat tires, walking up creek beds, and scratching chigger bites; they also spoke pleasantly of attending church picnics and riding a mule with a mailman.[98] The product of her camera work is a collection of approximately seven thousand photographs that depict great diversity among Kentucky people and places. Her work lacked the sensationalism often evident in that of her colleagues. She captured the images of unpainted homes, barefoot children, and eroded hillsides, but her compositions were more affectionate than condescending, and they revealed more dignity than depravity.[99]

The Farm Security Administration also conducted several sociological studies in Kentucky, which, like most of the photographs, did not appear in print. Agency researchers undertook a series of surveys and interviews to determine the depth of rural poverty and to make recommendations for its alleviation. They selected two Kentucky counties, Morgan and Magoffin, for comparison with two in North Carolina because all four counties contained high percentages of families on relief and had experienced recent population increases. The findings and recommendations of the studies appeared in mimeographed pamphlets, intended apparently for administrative rather than public consumption. L.S. Dodson's "Living Conditions and Population Migration in Four Appalachian Counties" (1937) and Dodson and C.P. Loomis's "Standards of Living in Four Appalachian Counties" (1938) bore the earmarks of rapid research and committee prose, accompanied by copious statistics and graphs. The two reviewed demographic shifts, family sizes, employment, income, literacy levels, the prevalence of electricity and plumbing, animals, and many other factors. For both Kentucky counties their evaluation was grim; Morgan and Magoffin needed better roads to overcome social isolation, greater emphasis on vocational education in their schools, and quick replacement of crops with livestock if the populations were to break their dependence on federal relief. The recommendations for Morgan County were startlingly candid. Part of the population quite simply needed to migrate out and find jobs elsewhere; the remainder needed to get rid of some of their dogs and take up sheep raising if they wanted a chance at success.[100] If these pamphlets had circulated widely at the time, local opinion would probably have forced the Farm Security Administration to recant or apologize for its derogatory statements, no matter how true they might have been. As it turned out, much of the visual and written documentation never became public, and it disappeared quietly when the agency changed its priorities and expired a few years later.

No other New Deal agency involved with the countryside aroused such emotions in Kentucky as did the Tennessee Valley Authority. From the moment of its announcement in 1933 until the dedication of Kentucky Dam in 1945, the TVA produced rancorous debate in the commonwealth. This massive undertaking in the Upper South pitted federal government planners against private enterprise, small farmers against utility corporations, and western land developers in Kentucky against eastern coal miners. Other New Deal experiments would deal singly with flood control, soil conservation, family resettlement, recreational development, social engineering, and inexpensive electricity, but the TVA incorporated all in one package. Arguments between Congressmen Andrew May of Prestonsburg and William and Noble Gregory of Mayfield were a microcosm of the differences that animated many Kentuckians. May was a conservative Democrat from Kentucky's eastern coal-mining district; William Gregory was a moderately liberal Democrat from the farm country of the Western Purchase. When he died in 1936, his younger brother Noble replaced him in Congress and continued to champion his causes.

William Gregory's congressional district included Paducah, the largest city in western Kentucky, located on the Ohio River just a few miles downstream from where the Tennessee River ended its meandering journey from the Smoky Mountains. Every year spring rains washed topsoil from the denuded hillsides of Tennessee, Mississippi, Alabama, and North Carolina and dumped it into tributaries of the Tennessee River. And each year this yellow flood pushed the Ohio River out of its banks into Paducah homes, businesses, and adjoining McCracken County farms. Gregory, who sympathized with the victims of uncontrolled nature, had supported the efforts of Nebraska Senator George W. Norris to harness the Tennessee. Several years of attempts to provide flood control through a series of dams culminated in May 1933 when President Roosevelt signed legislation authorizing the TVA. In the process of controlling the flood waters, TVA could also provide better stream navigation, thousands of construction jobs, inexpensive hydroelectric power, and recreational facilities.[101] The auxiliary effects of TVA were endless; it could attract new industry and tourists; provide phosphate and nitrate fertilizers for farmers; improve the tax base, allowing for better highways, bridges, and schools; and stanch of the outflow of population from the upper south. In short, the project could rejuvenate this depressed region. Congress and the press discussed these possibilities at length, and Representative Gregory enthusiastically supported this ambitious, innovative, and expensive project. He voted for the legislation that resulted in TVA, and campaigned to get one of the dams constructed in his home district near Aurora. A year later, he praised the work already done in other states and promised that if the system expanded into Kentucky his constituents would receive jobs, cheap fertilizer and electricity, better homes, and "greater security" from this "great experiment."[102] In his reelection campaign in 1936, he used as one of the leading issues his "gallant fight" to secure one of the TVA dams for his state.[103]

Andrew May knew about floods too. His mountainous district had suffered the rampages of the Big Sandy and the Levisa Fork for years. But the TVA would not correct these problems; indeed, it would take tax revenues from his constituents to spend on rivers several hundred miles away. If the TVA followed through on its plans the dams would destroy thousands of acres of rich bottomland, a commodity that mountain people prized because it was so rare to them. Congressman May argued that this covering and destruction of nature's dark alluvial soil by manmade lakes would be unforgivable. Most of May's opposition to TVA, however, derived from the fact that cheap electric power provided by the new dams could well mean economic disaster for the already depressed Kentucky coal industry. Coal from the eastern mountains had long been a staple fuel for electricity-generating plants. What right did the federal government have to create this competition for private utility companies? May argued that TVA would become "one of the most vicious competitors coal will ever have." He fought its expansion, declaring that "TVA is a steady, sure and unmistakable trend toward socialization" at its worst and a "reckless and unnecessary waste of public funds" by any reckoning.[104]

These debates were purely academic to most Kentuckians inasmuch as TVA was a distant abstraction to the majority of the state's population. All construction activity for the first five years took place in other states, mainly Tennessee and Alabama. Not until 1938 did Congress finally appropriate funds for a dam in Kentucky to be located just a few miles south of Paducah. Hence, between 1933 and 1938, Kentuckians had time to observe the progress of TVA and to consider problems that would affect them in the future. Their observations brought sufficient evidence to fuel the debate that continued.

As the TVA system expanded, advocates of its extension into

Kentucky could easily cite potential advantages. Had it not been for the dams already in place upstream, the 1937 floods would have caused even greater chaos. The Army Corps of Engineers estimated that the flood damage during January and February of that year amounted to twenty-five million dollars in Paducah alone, and the TVA featured pictures of the soggy city in its annual report for 1937. Representative Noble Gregory told a congressional hearing that the flood would have been one foot higher without the Tennessee dams "slowing the mad rush of water."[105] Dean Thomas Cooper reported that same year that the University of Kentucky and its extension agents were having great success with the TVA fertilizer experiments. AAA officials purchased the inexpensive phosphates from TVA plants and distributed them as a part of their soil conservation programs. Kentucky experiment stations and agents assisted as many as fifteen hundred farmers in forty-eight counties with the testing of these new fertilizers, and by 1937 crop yields had increased as much as 60 percent as a result of the additives.[106] If Kentucky had its own dam, the output of agriculture in the state would surely be increased.

The lure of inexpensive TVA electricity attracted more and more Kentucky municipalities. Congressman Gregory had predicted in 1934 that consumers could save as much as one-third on their electricity bills by switching from private utilities to TVA.[107] In October 1936 a delegation of officials from twelve Kentucky towns and cities traveled to Knoxville to discuss the possibility of transferring from their present sources of power. Citizens of Middlesboro voted by a two-to-one margin the following month for a bond issue to build a municipal power plant that would allow them to transmit TVA electricity and to terminate their existing arrangement with Kentucky Utilities. Middlesboro thus became the first Kentucky city to sign a contract with the TVA, and plans for the fifty-mile transmission lines were underway by July 1937.[108] Similar savings for consumers would result if there were a TVA dam within the state, instead of many miles away. The Lower Tennessee Valley Association, with headquarters in Murray, capitalized on this argument and lobbied to persuade Congress. TVA officials were a few steps ahead of Congress and had already tested several sites for a dam at Aurora, Shannon, or Gilbertsville. They had also begun tentative negotiations to purchase land, just in case Congress approved the expansion into Kentucky. It appeared by early 1938 that a dam might be built near Gilbertsville, a small community on the west bank of the Tennessee River a few miles south of Paducah.[109]

Opponents of TVA were able to thwart a dam project in Kentucky until 1938. Even after that, they managed to slow and occasionally halt its progress. Congressman May continued to argue that the TVA would destroy Kentucky coal mines. He finally had to accept the fact that the productivity and employment levels of Kentucky mines were increasing as the TVA expanded; by 1940 the state's mining industry was selling more coal than in any of the past ten years.[110] Gregory and his allies used such statistics to win a congressional victory in April 1938. By a mere seven votes, the House approved $2.6 million to begin construction at the Gilbertsville, Kentucky, site, and Gregory boasted that his "incessant" lobbying had convinced "a sufficient number to carry the measure."[111] May nonetheless persuaded an increasingly conservative House to kill an additional appropriation for work on the dam the following year. He pointed out that it was not too late for the TVA to relinquish land already purchased for the "socialistic" dam; jobless workers could then build homes and could farm on the soil. Congress later restored the funds, and construction work continued apace on the Kentucky Dam.[112]

Despite progress on the dam itself, other critics of the TVA stalled its electrical transmissions into the state. Shortly after the city of Middlesboro signed a TVA power contract in 1937, Kentucky Utilities filed suit to prevent the action. Until this legal conflict was resolved, the transmission of TVA electricity by municipal power plants hung in limbo. Not until late 1940, after several delays, did the Kentucky Court of Appeals rule that Middlesboro could not use TVA power. A contract between the city and TVA, according to the ruling, would infringe on municipal autonomy, and only the state legislature could grant authority for such agreements.[113] Tennessee, Alabama, and Mississippi had already passed such enabling laws, but the Kentucky General Assembly refused to do so; intense pressure from Kentucky Utilities and the coal industry was largely responsible for its refusal. Several farmers in western Kentucky found a loophole in this legal barrier and formed electrical cooperatives to obtain TVA power. Not bound by the state restriction on municipal contracts, rural co-ops developed during and after the Middlesboro test case; these independent farmers began receiving inexpensive electricity even while the state legislature was denying urban dwellers the same privilege.[114] Governor Keen Johnson tried to bring an end to these inconsistencies within the state in 1942. He urged the general assembly to listen to consumers rather than to the special interests who had blocked transmission of TVA power to urban areas. Kentuckians could have saved seven million dollars in one year alone, he argued, if they had been allowed to purchase power from TVA. The son of a Methodist minister, the governor told the legislators that the desire of the people on this matter was "as correct as the Ten Commandments" and hence that they should pass the enabling law.[115] Kentucky Utilities published its views in the Frankfort newspaper just before the vote. They stated that if Kentucky permitted municipal contracts with TVA, the price of Kentucky Utilities stock would plunge and the employees of the firm would be demoralized.[116] In late February 1942 the general assembly followed the lead of the governor and the rural co-ops and authorized city governments to proceed independently. Within four months Bowling Green, Hopkinsville, Mayfield, Murray, and Russellville had all signed TVA transmission contracts.[117]

While the debate about electricity raged on in Frankfort, the TVA proceeded to construct its largest dam ever in western Kentucky. Because the Kentucky Dam followed several other TVA dams, its construction was relatively uneventful. The controversies that had attended the construction of Wheeler in Alabama, Norris in Tennessee, and Hiwassee in North Carolina had taught TVA the best ways to acquire land, to displace families, and to alter the face of the earth. Therefore, similar actions in Kentucky between 1938 and 1945 moved smoothly for federal officials. But to thousands of Kentuckians who lived near the Tennessee River where it divides the Purchase from the rest of the state, the dam represented a revolution. It promised the destruction of the past for a few and the creation of a future for many more.

Both the living and the dead had to leave the dam site and the area to the south, which would become a vast lake. The TVA announced that it would purchase about three hundred thousand acres of this land, including farms, forests, roads, bridges, cemeteries, and a few small towns. To that end, federal officials had to negotiate purchases with some thirty-five hundred families and had to relocate more than two thousand graves to higher ground.[118] The TVA paid generally higher prices for doomed real estate than the current market value, thus easing some of the pain of resettlement and precluding all but a few complaints of inadequate compensation. Many of the displaced families chose to relocate nearby, frequently to new sites in the same counties, and so, no sizable migration outward took place. When requested, the TVA dug up graves or entire cemeteries and relocated them elsewhere. Such was the case in Birmingham, a town of about three hundred which ceased to exist when the reservoir waters rose. By 1940 fresh gravestones marked new resting places for old remains about a mile from where Birmingham used to be. The living residents had dispersed over a wider area.[119]

Other aspects of life could not be so easily transformed. Hundreds of mussel gatherers south of the dam were deprived of jobs as the rising waters buried their source of income. And the small Paducah factories that turned mussel shells into button blanks were forced to shut down. But the TVA employed a constant twenty-four hundred workers for a variety of jobs on and near the construction site.[120] The number of jobs periodically doubled and tripled when CCC camps and highway construction crews began the auxiliary tasks that brought prosperity to the region. The prospect of a better life could not compensate entirely for the personal sacrifices and lost heritage that accompanied the physical changes, however. Rena and John Jacob Niles captured some of these emotions in their article about the epic transformation. They reported that for many of the farmers the dam meant "saying goodbye to familiar surroundings and lifelong friends—separation from farms they probably inherited from their fathers and hoped to pass on to their children." And for those workers displaced by the project, "a dam's a damn good thing ef yuh kin get yohself a job on it . . . but a dam ain't worth a damn when you cain't."[121]

The Kentucky Dam, dedicated in October 1945, was the largest and one of the last monuments to the New Deal in the commonwealth. It stretched for a mile and a half across the Tennessee River, created a lake 184 miles long, and cost well over $100 million.[122] It also brought to an end more than a decade of acrimonious debate, which now disappeared in the roar of celebration. President Harry S. Truman joined Congressman Gregory and other dignitaries on a platform, with the dam looming behind them and fifteen thousand people cheering in front of them.[123] The Great Depression, New Deal, and World War II had passed into history. Franklin Roosevelt was dead, and all three Kentucky governors who had served during these tumultuous years—Laffoon, Chandler, and Johnson—had also left the scene. The dam, like the river it harnessed, rose above politics and transcended time.

The TVA attracted so much public attention in the state that it almost overshadowed another revolution taking place in rural Kentucky. The Rural Electrification Administration (REA) brought light and power to remote farms for the first time and, in the words of one historian, "stands out as one of the most significant contributions of the New Deal to the farmers and to the nation."[124] Because the cost of extending power lines into rural areas averaged two thousand dollars per mile—far more than in urban areas—and because revenues from rural consumers were 80 percent less than from urban customers, most private and municipal utility companies did not seek to expand into rural areas. Only 10 percent of American farms and only 4 percent of those in Kentucky had electricity in the early 1930s.[125] With the establishment of the TVA and the potential for transmitting additional power, President Roosevelt created the temporary Electric Home and Farm Authority in December

1933 to assist potential consumers in the TVA region to purchase electrical appliances. This agency would lend funds to
consumers in an effort to determine just how sizable a market
existed for TVA electricity. The results were immediate and
dramatic. Appliance sales in the test area, boosted by these
loans, rose by 300 percent.[126] Roosevelt and Congress responded to this experiment in 1935 with the REA to wage a full-scale,
but quiet, revolution in rural America.

The REA encouraged farmers to develop their own cooperatives by lending them money on generous terms to build either
electrical generators or transmission lines connected to an existing utility. To avoid conflict with private companies, the REA
would not extend loans to groups in an area already served by
power lines.[127] Despite the initial reluctance of a few private
utility firms to cooperate with the REA, most municipal, private, and even TVA officials by 1941 were working in tandem to
supply power to American farms through lines financed by the
REA. As America prepared to enter World War II, 35 percent of
its farms had electricity, up from 10 percent in less than one
decade. The REA had lent more than a billion dollars to co-ops
in forty-five states with 780,000 new consumers. In Kentucky
the change was even greater than elsewhere. In 1941 the number
of farms with electricity had risen to forty-four thousand, or 17
percent of the total (up from 4 percent); thirty-six thousand
farms were served by REA co-ops.[128]

Aggressive salesmanship and publicity encouraged farmers
to emerge from their dark age into inexpensive electrification.
REA officials arranged demonstrations and displays in rural
schools to acquaint families with modern conveniences of
which they could now take advantage with additional loans for
appliance purchases. Crowds of people in the Taylorsville
school gymnasium marveled at water pumps, milk coolers,
washing machines, irons, and radios. Newspapers in Louisville
and Lexington, whose populations had enjoyed electricity since
the nineteenth century, somewhat incredulously reported these
demonstrations and openings of new co-ops.[129] Retailers such
as Sears, Roebuck and Company ran full-page advertisements in
farm journals for home and barn wiring that would be compati-

ble with REA lines. One editor encouraged his rural readers to
join a co-op if for no other reason than to have colored lights on
their Christmas trees.[130]

Rural electrification brought immediate change to homes
and businesses. The elaborate ceremonies that surrounded the
founding of Henderson County's new co-op in 1937 revealed the
enthusiasm of Kentuckians for this change. A local 4-H group
buried a kerosene lamp beside the first utility pole to symbolize
the banishing of darkness, and their sponsor declared that electrification was "the greatest blessing of the century." Probably
remembering the darkness and poverty of his childhood there,
Governor Chandler predicted that the new co-op "will lift farm
women" out of a life of drudgery.[131] As farmers rushed to join
this and other Kentucky co-ops, the REA kept records of how
they utilized their new opportunities. The overwhelming majority purchased radios, obviously revealing a desire to have
greater access to news and entertainment. The next most popular purchase was refrigerators, followed by washing machines,
irons, and vacuum cleaners. One Boyle County farmer outfitted
his home and barn with twenty light fixtures and an assortment
of eleven time-saving appliances, ranging from a furnace to a
toaster, for which his monthly electric bill was only $10.33.[132]
The REA boasted, "The most widely quoted rural electrification story of the year" came from Pennyrile Co-op member
Albert Clark in 1939. Clark had recently electrified his hen-
house, and one of his pullets soon laid an egg that bore an
"astonishing likeness" to a light bulb. This egg captured the
attention of national radio and newspaper reporters and spent
some time on display at the New York World's Fair.[133]

Kentucky's rural population and high poverty level offered a
good measure of many of the New Deal's programs to revitalize
rural America. The New Deal accelerated two trends that were
already evident to a small degree in Kentucky. Its programs
helped narrow the gap between rural and urban populations and
increased the dependence of people on the federal government.
Electricity hastened the homogenization of a rural population
previously denied the devices usually reserved to urban families. Electric lights, radios, sweepers, and irons invaded remote

coves and hollows. This breakdown of geographical barriers and the consolidation of rural-urban interests came through the same wires that transmitted electrical current. The various agencies that pushed tenants and sharecroppers off their land to new locations assisted in this breakdown of provincialism and isolated poverty. Many of the resettled farmers improved their lives simply by leaving debilitating traditions; many raised their horizons by associating with government-sponsored communities; and many migrated to urban centers where greater opportunities existed. An obvious attitudinal change appeared as early as the first cotton plow-up of 1933. Farmers began to look to Washington for answers for their problems. Sometimes the answers were production control, price supports, soil conservation, or storage of surpluses, and most frequently, these answers came from the Department of Agriculture in Washington, not from the commissioner of agriculture in Frankfort. It is impossible to say whether the urban amenities, technological progress, and dependence on federal assistance caused a loss of state pride and identity as the agrarian authors feared in 1930 when they wrote *I'll Take My Stand*. Perhaps these changes were inevitable, and the New Deal merely accelerated them; and perhaps these changes were neither bad nor to be feared, anyway. What is clear, however, is that revolutionary changes did come—fast, deep, and enduring—and that Kentuckians took a willing stand in these newly plowed fields.

# 6. Getting Back to Business

When Congress amended the Volstead Act on March 22, 1933, legal beer and wine returned to America for the first time since 1920. President Roosevelt's signature on this bill also ushered in the gradual return of one of Kentcky's oldest industries, which had been dormant since the end of the Great War. The production and sale of alcoholic beverages—always controversial and always profitable—had been the leading manufacturing enterprise in the state, but national Prohibition virtually dried up this industry. Passage of the Beer Bill cheered millions of Americans who looked for signs of hope from the new administration, and it hastened the end of the Eighteenth Amendment. The end of Prohibition also brought prosperity back to the distillers and brewers and provided new tax revenues for the government. In Kentucky this return to legal liquor was the most dramatic of all the New Deal efforts to revive the nation's economy. Other administrative measures such as the National Recovery Administration (NRA) and the Wagner Act generated massive publicity or brought radical reforms to the working place, but neither produced such widespread enthusiasm as did the repeal of Prohibition. Repeal was a grand gesture that had mass appeal. It came early in the New Deal and started a momentum of restored confidence, which the other programs enhanced and solidified. World War II brought the sustained economic revival that New Deal planners were unable to produce, but that revival operated in an economic arena far different from the languishing situation of 1933.

Prior to the "noble experiment" of Prohibition, the liquor

industry in Kentucky was a major part of the state's economy. In 1910, approximately two hundred distilleries and breweries employed more than four thousand people in the commonwealth.[1] Bourbon whiskey, in particular, had become almost synonymous with the Bluegrass State. Named for the county of its origin, this distinctive blend of corn, rye, and limestone water, had become a popular product nationally by the time of the Civil War, and soon no mint julep or Kentucky Derby would have been complete without it. Meanwhile, another Kentucky native, Carrie Nation, was winning a nationwide reputation for her crusade against alcohol, but the efforts of Nation and other advocates of temperance did not have much success until the early twentieth century, when the Progressive reformers undertook a campaign for moral uplift and efficiency. State after state outlawed the production and sale of intoxicating drink, and by the time America entered the Great War in 1917, twenty-five states had become dry.[2] Kentucky's state legislature compromised on this issue in 1912. Its local option provision allowed counties and towns to make their own decisions, and soon a majority of the state's 120 counties exercised the dry option.[3] During the war Congress submitted and the states soon approved the Eighteenth Amendment to the Constitution. Kentucky ratified this measure in 1919 and at the same time added the Seventh Amendment to its state constitution. These amendments prohibited both the production and sale of alcoholic beverages. When they became effective in 1920 no intoxicating drink could be marketed, except for medicinal purposes.

The effect of Prohibition on Kentucky's liquor industry was swift and devastating. Distilleries and breweries either ceased production and shipping activities or curtailed operations to a minimum. More than three thousand employees lost their jobs, creating an industrywide depression nine years before the Great Crash. In 1933, just prior to the repeal of Prohibition, only five distilleries in Kentucky remained active, and they had only a few hundred employees on their payrolls.[4] These helped supply small quantities of liquor prescribed by physicians in twenty-six different states. Individual state laws determined the amounts of medicinal liquor allowable, and those states placed heavy taxes on each prescription. In Kentucky a person could buy one pint of liquor every ten days with a doctor's permit. The state treasury received fifty cents per pint sold, which a- mounted to approximately $175,000 per year from the 350,000 annual prescriptions.[5] This legal availability of liquor, tightly controlled as it was, kept a few distilleries dispensing whiskey from stored stocks and habitual drinkers visiting their doctors and pharmacies with metronomic regularity. The following dog- geral paid tribute to the transformations in business establish- ments during this dry decade:

> Never mind, little saloon,
> Don't you cry.
> You'll be a drugstore
> By and By.[6]

Repercussions of the Eighteenth Amendment on the general population were equally dramatic. Historian Thomas D. Clark has pointed out that the problems of enforcing Prohibition "proved impossible of solution. Instead of checking completely the manufacture of liquor, the amendment encouraged moon- shining and bootlegging."[7] Illicit production of intoxicating beverages flourished, and federal revenue agents could not hope to discover or destroy all the homemade stills and brewing vats operating in basements, bathrooms, and wooded areas. Golden Pond, a small, remote Kentucky community between the Ten- nessee and Cumberland rivers, became famous for its produc- tion of moonshine during the 1920s. Producers and runners from western Kentucky supplied secret contacts throughout the Midwest, and the Al Capone gang distributed some of the Gold- en Pond spirits to its Chicago clientele. An estimated five thou- sand gallons per day came from stills in this region alone, and small airplanes landed in nearby fields to carry freshly filled jugs to speakeasies as far away as New York.[8] Occasionally, licensed distilleries would report a truckload of their medicinal product lost or unaccounted for. Of more predictable quality than moon- shine, this missing legal liquor found ready customers at respectable clubs and restaurants. The lack of excitement that greeted the seizure of assorted liquors at Louisville's exclusive Pendennis Club in the summer of 1930 was only one example of the lax attitude toward Prohibition.[9]

As the nation made a mockery of the "noble experiment," former dry politicians began to turn wet and advocate repeal. Kentucky's Alben Barkley, who had enjoyed the support of the Anti-Saloon League, left the dry crusade at the end of the decade because he realized that prohibition was neither working nor popular. President Hoover's Wickersham Commission reported in 1931 what most people already knew, namely that prohibition had become an expensive failure.[10] In the spring of 1932 about four million Americans responded to a *Literary Digest* poll concerning Prohibition, and three-fourths of them favored its termination. The seventy-three thousand Kentuckians who participated in this poll conformed with the national results. In his keynote address at the Democratic National Convention later that year Barkley evoked a noisy demonstration when he urged repeal. Delegates thereupon voted a wet plank for the party platform.[11] Roosevelt's election in November virtually guaranteed the end of Prohibition, and in February, prior to his inauguration, Congress proceeded to initiate the repeal of the Eighteenth Amendment. It would take the requisite number of states until December of 1933 to ratify this repeal, but the New Deal administration accelerated the effort in March by liberalizing the Volstead Act and allowing the sale of beer and light wines.

Twenty states, including Kentucky, permitted the sale of beer on April 7, the first day it was permissible. Breweries worked overtime to prepare barrels for shipping their products. Employees at Louisville's Falls City and Oertel breweries labored during day and night shifts to meet the demand, and three hundred trucks from six states were lined up at the two plants to start hauling beer one minute past midnight on April 7. The supply of beer in Jefferson County taverns was adequate to the demand that day, but Frankfort's tap brew ran out early that evening. Customers from dry Tennessee had to travel across that state line to well-stocked Middlesboro and Bowling Green in order to celebrate the end of Prohibition.[12] While celebrations of beer continued in wet areas throughout 1933, the thirteen-year thirst

for hard liquor went unquenched. Not until three-quarters of
the states repealed the Eighteenth Amendment could whiskey
be legally produced, shipped, and sold. Kentucky did its part to
hasten this event. State officials called a special convention for
this purpose rather than wait until the following year for a
public referendum. Spectators packed the galleries of the House
of Representatives in Frankfort during this November convention and then cheered when delegates voted unanimously for
repeal.[13]

Although free from federal restraints on liquor traffic, Kentucky was still in a legal bind of its own making: the state
constitution continued to prohibit the production and sale of
liquors. The earliest possible date when the Seventh Amendment could be repealed would be November 1935, inasmuch as
the adoption of an amendment entailed considerations at a
regular session of the legislature and public approval during a
regular state election. Meanwhile a thirsty nation would be
denied Kentucky's famous product, and the state would be
denied tax revenues. These pressures prompted the state legislature in March 1934 to find a means of avoiding the legal
restrictions for the next twenty months until Kentucky could
amend its constitution. In a swift and clever move, the state
legislators declared that the repeal of the national Eighteenth
Amendment had "created an emergency which requires immediate control of intoxicating liquors" and revised the old state
enforcement provisions to allow temporary liquor traffic.[14]
Some observers doubted that this rushed measure was completely legal and thought that the legislated permission was
more expedient than constitutional.[15] Despite these doubts,
the Kentucky liquor industry revived rapidly and the formal
repeal of state prohibition took place as anticipated during the
November 1935 elections. Because the fact had already been
accomplished in 1934, little excitement accompanied this official 1935 blessing by the voters. Governor Laffoon issued a
quiet proclamation on December 4, 1935, declaring that the
people had rendered their verdict, and the production and sale of
liquor, which had been flourishing since 1934, was now entirely
legal.[16]

The end of Prohibition in Kentucky was as heartening economically as its birth had been depressing. The five distilleries operating in early 1933 had employed only a few hundred workers; five years later, fifty-seven distilleries and seven breweries were employing more than seventy-five hundred Kentuckians. The editors of the state public relations magazine, *In Kentucky,* estimated that an additional thirty-five thousand workers in the state also owed their jobs to the renewed industry.[17] Barrel makers, truck drivers, tavern employees, and many others found jobs thanks to the reopening of the liquor trade. These editors also reported that tax revenues generated from production and sale of alcoholic beverages were the state's second largest source of income, second only to the gasoline excise.[18] During that fiscal year, 1937-1938, the state collected revenues in excess of $7 million from production, sale, property, and licensing taxes levied on the liquor industry and its allied activities. This sum constituted 10 percent of the total state receipts for that year.[19] When the receipts were compared to the $175,000 per year that had come from Prohibition-era medicinal liquor taxes, state officials could not help but be pleased. And these taxes proved a steady and dependable source of income as the Depression waned but government services and responsibilities increased. Although the number of individual plants operating in 1940 was far below the number active prior to Prohibition, the number of employees was higher. Like many other business enterprises during this time, the liquor industry experienced the death of many small, family-owned operations, the consolidation of many others. If breweries in Lexington and Henderson did not reopen after repeal, and two older plants in Louisville did not survive Prohibition, Seagram's opened a new distillery in Louisville in 1937, which soon became the world's largest.[20] A Kentucky tradition was thus restored and dependable state revenues were guaranteed. Still, Carrie Nation would have been pleased that a majority of Kentucky counties opted to remain dry.

The spontaneous celebrations that greeted the end of Prohibition could not compete with the orchestrated ballyhoo of the NRA. When President Roosevelt, signing the National Industrial Recovery Act in June 1933, referred to it as "the most important and far-reaching legislation ever enacted by the American Congress," he set the stage for a program characterized by hyperbole and unrealistic goals.[21] Colorful NRA parades to enlist business and labor cooperation for reviving the economy were reminiscent of the idealistic homefront crusades during the Great War. Like America's activity in that war, the NRA's experience was brief and exciting, filled with temporary victories and considerable goodwill. Both relied heavily on volunteer efforts and massive publicity, and both ended with a legacy of botched triumphs, recriminations, and disenchantment. Because Kentucky's large rural population was not as directly involved with NRA programs as were urban dwellers, the agency did not affect the state as intensely as it did others. But most Kentuckians remembered the NRA's symbol, the Blue Eagle, which urged everyone to do his part in the battle against the Depression.

Business executives, labor leaders, politicians, and reformers all had a hand in the creation of the NRA, and the result was a compromise. The NRA attempted to revive and reform business by urging employers to accept codes of behavior "to eliminate unfair competitive practices, to promote the fullest possible utilization of the present productive capacity of industries."[22] Businesses would voluntarily abide by these codes and commit themselves to hire more employees, work them fewer hours, and pay them higher wages than had been the case. The use of child labor would also be restricted. Secretary of Labor Frances Perkins worked to make this ambitious program succeed. She knew that business attitudes, shaped by generations of free-enterprise competition, had to accept some severe "social adjustments" in order to abide by these new working conditions. Her experience as an industrial inspector and reformer in New York placed her more on the side of labor than of business, and her hopes for the NRA went beyond the mere revival of employment. Developing "a sound, socially just economic and industrial pattern" she later wrote, was equally important to her, and the crisis situation of the Depression could offer the necessary stimulant for such a transformation.[23] Senator Barkley, who helped draft the NRA legislation, was less visionary about its

goals than was Secretary Perkins. He later recalled the phrase
"fatal infirmity," which many critics used to describe this compromised NRA, the diversity of whose aims was partly responsible for some of its problems.[24]

To administer this multifaceted program Roosevelt chose
two men, Harold Ickes of the Interior Department and General
Hugh S. Johnson. Ickes took charge of the PWA in its attempts to
stimulate the construction industry, and Johnson assumed command of code development. Johnson was a West Point graduate
and a businessman who had helped organize the draft and the
War Industries Board in 1917-1918. He now relied on the same
moral and patriotic rhetoric to enlist business cooperation in
another crusade. Although angry that Roosevelt had not given
him control over both the PWA and the NRA, Johnson nevertheless threw his legendary energies and flamboyant personality into persuading employers to draw up the codes of fair
practice. He wanted to "eliminate eye-gouging and knee-groin-
ing and ear-chewing in business" so that both business and labor
would be more productive and less destructive. The results, he
said, would be "more chance for progress, more latitude for
ability, more chance for profit and stability than ever before."[25]
These were blithe predictions in the face of a business depression that had been around since 1930, but Johnson reflected the
early New Deal optimism. The martial spirit surrounding the
early days of this organization surfaced particularly in the NRA
emblem, the Blue Eagle. Johnson wanted an inspirational logo to
symbolize the crusading spirit of his organization, and he
sketched the original design. Clutching an industrial cogwheel
and bolts of electrical energy, this Blue Eagle—whether on a flag
or a poster—was issued to all participants in the NRA and
announced, "We do our part." Businesses that signed the codes
to resume production under reformed conditions would become
partners with the government.

Until such time as the NRA could negotiate and devise the
complex codes for the nation's industries, Johnson had to rally
business cooperation with temporary pacts known as the President's Re-employment Agreements (PRA). Federal officials
urged all employers to sign voluntary contracts that would bind

them to individual codes covering wages, hours, prices, and child labor restrictions. Small businesses and large, manufacturing and retail, would adhere to these new practices and march together under the Blue Eagle. At the same time NRA officials encouraged consumers to patronize only those businesses that displayed the Blue Eagle. Moral suasion and patriotic impulse would suffice to compel any right-thinking American business establishment to fall in line. In mid-July, General Johnson sent telegrams to thousands of civic organizations, asking for assistance in organizing and publicizing the campaign. He needed legions of local helpers to persuade businesses to sign the codes and to urge customers to reward them for their cooperation.[26]

Kentucky's initial response to Johnson's request was everything he could have hoped for. The Ashland Businessmen's Association replied that it was "heartily in sympathy"; the president of the Bowling Green Kiwanis Club promised that "we will all fall in line"; Owensboro's Chamber of Commerce indicated that "we will gladly cooperate"; and the Louisville Board of Trade offered to lead in whatever direction the NRA suggested to "speed the return of prosperity."[27] Louisville and Lexington also impressed Johnson with the kind of patriotic razzle-dazzle he enjoyed. Louisville's American Business Club organized a massive "Roosevelt Recovery Parade," which lasted three hours on August 10, one of the first of hundreds of such demonstrations in American cities during the coming weeks. With bands blaring "Happy Days Are Here Again" and the Blue Eagle emblazoned on uniforms and flags, Kentuckians sent up a cheery keynote for the NRA crusade. Floats, 175 of them, depicted full dinner pails and Uncle Sam slaying the Depression dragon.[28] The Man O'War Post of the American Legion sponsored a similar parade in Lexington, which thirty thousand people viewed on Labor Day. At Cheapside Park, following the parade, the chairman of the NRA Women's Division, Mary Hughes, a Lexington native, urged everyone to comply with the new codes.[29] Governor Laffoon and various local politicians had been working for several weeks to get Kentuckians to do just that. The governor had appointed Frederick A. Wallis chairman of the state NRA coordinating committee, and Wallis declared, "We want to see the Blue Eagle in every business house in the state." By Labor Day approximately eighteen thousand Kentucky firms had signed the agreements, and many of them ran newspaper advertisements announcing their compliance. The *Lexington Herald* estimated that payrolls in Fayette County alone had increased by twenty-four thousand dollars per month as a result of the additional hiring.[30]

In the midst of this rush to sign temporary agreements, leaders of major industries sat down in Washington to negotiate codes. More than seven hundred different agreements emerged from these talks; most shared features such as a forty-hour week and a minimum age of sixteen for full-time industrial laborers. These codes and agreements covered 96 percent of the nation's commercial and manufacturing establishments, a tribute to the NRA recruiting efforts.[31] Several Kentucky businessmen were involved in code formulation talks for their particular industries. Paul Blazer, president of Ashland Oil, for example, went to Washington to assist in hammering out the petroleum code, and Keen Johnson, publisher of the Richmond *Daily Register*, served on the national code committee for editors and publishers.[32] The codes ranged widely and affected Kentuckians in many ways. Blue Eagle banners fluttered over coal mines that signed Code 24, tobacco warehouses that endorsed Code LP 19, and barber shops that agreed to Code 398.[33] Hotels and hardware stores, plumbers and photographers all did their part to revive employment, wages, and the economy. Even the Gayety Burlesque in Louisville exposed its NRA emblem and adhered to the code that prohibited more than four strips per production.[34]

All of the carnivallike publicity that boosted the NRA could not mask the inherent difficulties of the agency. The original legislation had not provided for effective administration of the codes once the businesses had agreed to comply, and General Johnson was mistaken in his view that moral suasion would be sufficient enforcement. Each industry had a committee for self-regulation, but these were unwieldy and increasingly ineffective as the months wore on. After the initial burst of enthusiasm, some businesses still had not signed codes, some of the original signers were not complying, and consumers were not providing the pressure Johnson had hoped for. Examples of the disarray within NRA began to surface within a few weeks of its inception. One woman from Hopkinsville complained to General Johnson that the manager of the variety store in which she worked forced employees to work forty-eight hours a week rather than the forty promised in the code; furthermore he had threatened to fire anyone who reported the infraction.[35] The president of the Louisville Coal Exchange also complained to the NRA. Because he was complying with the appropriate code, his operating expenses were higher than those of competitors who had not signed. Thus he was losing business to these noncompliance rivals who could undersell his product. Especially galling was the fact that many federal employees in Jefferson County were purchasing cheaper coal from his rivals.[36] By early 1935 noncompliance was widespread. Of the 265 printers and publishers in Kentucky subject to NRA codes, only 155 were cooperating, and Keen Johnson scolded the guilty parties who he felt had "muffed a magnificent opportunity" to correct long-standing problems by refusing to participate.[37]

Administrative haste and bureaucratic complexity were partly responsible for the NRA's decline. Johnson's staff attempted too much too soon and produced confusion for state and local officials. The volatile director admitted to putting in eighteen-hour days, and referred to his routine as a "maelstrom." Local observers labeled the NRA organization a "sprawling administrative colossus," which had created an impossible system of codes that only an army could enforce.[38] It was little wonder that state headquarters had difficulty coping with the situation. Kentucky ran through four state compliance directors in the NRA's brief two-year existence and at one point endured the embarrassment of having two administrators appointed to do the same job at the same time. Prentiss Terry and Lorenzo Wood overlapped each others' activities until Washington administrators cleared up the chaos.[39] This confusion was also evident at the local level. Reports from regional compliance boards revealed that misunderstandings were rampant and that especially in Covington and Lexington, the lack of clear direction was critical.[40] By early 1935 there were more than four hundred lawsuits pending that involved broken NRA contracts and infractions. One of these had originated in Kentucky, where Federal District Judge Charles Dawson had questioned the legality of the bituminous coal code.[41]

The NRA's favoritism toward large businesses and its preoccupation with interstate commerce also caused problems, particularly in Kentucky. Representatives of large businesses—manufacturers and retailers alike—generally wrote the major codes, and many smaller businesses had difficulty complying with them. Rural and family-owned enterprises often found it impossible to add new employees or to rearrange working shifts. One compliance officer from Harrodsburg reported not only that neighborhood retailers found it burdensome to meet code requirements but that the small-town customers did not care about the NRA anyway.[42] Another inherent problem with the NRA was that many of the codes applied only to businesses involved in interstate traffic or trade. Many smaller businesses were purely intrastate in nature and therefore exempt from most NRA regulations and reforms. General Johnson tried to correct this problem by asking state legislatures to pass companion laws that would make intrastate and interstate standards uniform. He sent Governor Laffoon a model law that he hoped the Kentucky General Assembly would pass in its regular session in 1934.[43] This request set off a heated debate among several Kentucky businesses and politicians and resulted in a defeat for the New Deal. The Kentucky Retail Lumber Dealers Association lobbied for the state NRA law, and the Lousiville Board of Trade fought it, although this latter group favored most national NRA measures.[44] Governor Laffoon did little to promote the measure's passage, and one NRA official speculated that the governor assisted in its defeat in order to get Republican support for some of his own proposals.[45] Most other states joined Kentucky in rejecting the state NRA laws in 1934, perpetuating the enforcement problem and revealing a growing disenchantment among state politicians with the federal NRA program.

Despite the NRA's administrative and political difficulties,

Roosevelt believed it had provided enough benefits to be continued. In February 1935 he asked Congress to extend the life of the agency and to keep in mind that "the age-long curse of child labor has been lifted, the sweatshop outlawed, and millions of wage earners released from starvation wages and excessive hours of labor."[46] Before Congress had a chance to act, the Supreme Court invalidated part of the National Industrial Recovery Act with a unanimous decision saying, in part, that the codes were an unconstitutional means of regulating commerce. Little mourning accompanied the demise of the NRA; General Johnson had left the directorship the previous year; the PWA had pursued a separate life; and many of the codes had collapsed even before the Supreme Court dealt its death blow. The once proud Blue Eagle had begun to look like a "sick chicken" to most observers. Many businessmen were relieved to be rid of the federal regulations and to return to traditional free enterprise. Many of the Kentucky liquor distilleries, on the contrary, found that some of the NRA labor reforms worked to their advantage, and they maintained a semblance of the codes. For the moment the New Deal had to be content with the few firms that adopted this course of action.

As an experiment in government-industry partnership, the NRA was short-lived and relatively unsuccessful. Some aspects of the venture, however, produced more permanent repercussions, and Section 7a of the original NRA legislation is a case in point. Within that section the federal government made a commitment to the right of workers to organize and bargain collectively. For the first time in American history an administration had actively encouraged the growth of labor unions. Consequently, union organizing accelerated, membership grew, strikes and violence increased. Section 7a, a succession of arbitration boards, and favorable court decisions produced a major shift in government policy, making the New Deal the champion of the working people and resulting in new political alignments. Kentucky urban areas experienced a steady growth of union strength and activity, and the eastern coal communities saw old battles revived between operators and miners.

Organized labor in America needed Section 7a of the NRA as

a kind of Magna Carta. Labor had traditionally been on the defensive in a society that applauded the growth of business and regarded unions as impediments to economic progress and opponents of rugged individualism. The nation's largest labor organization, the American Federation of Labor, had tailored its wants to these societal attitudes. Its president in 1933, William Green, had devoloped a reputation for caution and respectability, avoiding political involvement and eschewing strikes whenever possible. Occasionally a member union, such as the United Mine Workers, departed from this norm and became aggressive. Its recent unsuccessful attempts to unionize miners in eastern Kentucky, for example, had damaged its reputation and virtually bankrupted its treasury. By the spring of 1933, AFL membership stood at only two million, down approximately one-third from its 1930 total. The massive unemployment of the Depression had drastically cut its strength.[47]

Like most southern and rural states, Kentucky had not experienced the widespread growth of unions. And the state had been spared the violence of labor unrest, with the exception of the Harlan County turmoil of 1930-1931. Unions in the state tended to be small, and their meetings relatively docile affairs. The Tobacco Workers International Union had organized in only one plant in Kentucky, Axton-Fisher in Louisville, and the United Mine Workers membership had fallen to a mere one hundred by 1932.[48] Individual unions enjoyed the assistance of central labor councils in only four areas of the state—Louisville, Lexington, Covington, and Paducah, revealing that union membership in the rest of Kentucky was not large enough to merit a coordinating body. Charles Gorman of Louisville was president of the Kentucky State Federation of Labor during the difficult years of the early 1930s, and he presided over the unenthusiastic annual conventions. Fewer than seventy delegates showed up at these meetings, mainly barbers, plumbers, carpenters, and unemployed distillery workers. They passed predictable resolutions that called for child-labor laws and better factory inspections and admitted in 1930 that it was useless to try to recruit more members or to strike because of the depression conditions.[49] Labor in Kentucky on the eve of the New Deal was barely organized and had little political power.

With the advent of NRA in 1933, all businesses that complied with a Blue Eagle code were bound by the provisions of Section 7a, which guaranteed to all employees that they could join a union of their own choosing and that they had the right to bargain collectively. The AFL thereupon undertook a campaign to recruit members for old organizations and to establish new unions where none had previously existed. Within six weeks of the NRA's establishment, unions across the United States claimed fifteen thousand new members, and by the spring of 1935 when the Supreme Court invalidated the NRA, about one million members had swelled union ranks, recouping what had been lost during the early Depression decline.[50] The AFL granted charters to 391 new chapters during 1933, up from the thirty-two new charters in 1932, and then continued its aggressive growth in 1934 by granting 1,262 new charters. The number of unions and delegates attending the annual conventions of 1933 and 1934 also increased dramatically, reflecting the new strength and optimism.[51] Most successful of all in its rebuilding efforts was the United Mine Workers. Throughout the Appalachian Mountains, President John L. Lewis had posters, billboards, and sound trucks blaring, "The president wants you to join the union," and within a few months the miners had pushed union membership to 500,000, or more than 92 percent of all coal miners in America.[52] These advances in the AFL and the UMW could be seen in the new vitality of the Kentucky State Federation of Labor. Its annual conventions in 1934 and 1935 were festive in contrast to the pre-New Deal days. More than 180 delegates crowded the ballroom in Lexington's Phoenix Hotel—triple the number of 1931—and praised Section 7a. Their numbers increased to 275 the following year, a total made possible by the attendance of many newly inducted miners.[53]

This rapid growth of unions encountered few obstacles in most of Kentucky, but in the eastern coal-mining communities union organizers met violent opposition similar to the bloody fights prior to the New Deal. Many mine owners and operators welcomed federal assistance to revive their industry but resisted the reforms mandated by Section 7a. Both Secretary of Labor Perkins and General Johnson later recalled the spectacle of coal operators making their pilgrimage to Washington in early 1933 to ask for government help and then balking at the NRA code provisions for union rights.[54] The result was an agreement that promised the Kentucky operators a fixed minimum sale price for their coal and guaranteed to the miners a forty-hour week, the right to join unions, and a minimum wage of $4.20 per day.[55] Once the compromise permitted union recruiting, the United Mine Workers started a new organizational campaign assisted by the Kentucky State Federation of Labor. Their efforts produced meager results, however. The entrenched business leaders and local newspapers, such as those in Harlan and Pineville, regarded the UMW as an alien and disruptive force. To prevent unionization, some of the mine operators offered their employees benefits superior to those in UMW contracts, and other owners hired deputy sheriffs as guards to stop union activity on mine premises. In Harlan County, in particular, Sheriff J.H. Blair and his deputies succeeded in keeping more than one-half of the mines union free.[56] A protest song of the era reflects the strained relations that existed in 1933.

> If you go to Harlan County,
> There is no neutral there.
> You'll either be a union man
> Or a thug for J.H. Blair.[57]

Similar resistance in Clay, Whitley, and Bell counties produced considerable violence and property destruction. Governor Laffoon responded by dispatching National Guard units into the area at least four times in 1934 and early 1935 to maintain order.[58]

Roosevelt had anticipated such difficulties and provided some remedies. He established the National Labor Board in August 1933 to mediate disputes, most of which involved unionization struggles. At first, the board set up several regional boards to hear complaints and help enforce the NRA regulations, but the National Labor Board had little power to solve the increasing number of disputes between labor and management. A stronger board replaced the original one in 1934, but it too lacked power of enforcement. It could investigate problems and recommend penalties for violators of Section 7a even though it had no means of insuring that anyone would follow its advice.[59] The board heard disputes involving the bituminous coal industry in Cincinnati, and received ninety-one complaints from Harlan County alone. After seven formal hearings and six recommendations, the rancorous situation there showed no improvement. One mine operator who openly violated his NRA code, informed the Board that "Roosevelt's not running this mine."[60]

Labor-management conflicts increased in 1935, and the new sheriff of Harlan County, Theodore Middleton, was even more aggressive than his predecessor in fighting unionization. Governor Laffoon described the situation as "very intense and very bitter" and explained that firearms abounded on both sides. He appointed a commission to investigate the problem and gave Adjutant General Henry Denhardt the post of chairman.[61] Throughout the spring of 1935, the Denhardt Commission held hearings in Frankfort and Harlan and visited Bell and Letcher counties, where union organization had proceeded more smoothly. Its final report in early June exonerated no one for the violence, but the weight of evidence showed workers to be less at fault than others. Denhardt spoke of the "monster-like reign of oppression" that sheriff's deputies used against union activity and condemned the collusion of political and legal forces that supported the mine operators. He called for Sheriff Middleton's removal from office and a reform of the deputy guard system. Only then, he predicted, would Kentucky see any improvement of the disgraceful conditions.[62] The sheaves of affidavits and testimony compiled by the commission testified to the deep differences between the UMW and operators and to the ineffectiveness of voluntary codes and toothless mediation boards.[63] New Deal efforts to encourage unions in eastern Kentucky had achieved no better results than the NRA had achieved with industrial firms when the Supreme Court killed the Blue Eagle in May 1935.

Two developments outside Kentucky in that same year clarified the government's support of labor and provided new impetus for union recruiting. In July Congress passed the National Labor Relations Act—popularly known as the Wagner Act—to rescue Section 7a from the moribund NRA. Also included in the Wagner Act was a reconstituted and more effective National Labor Relations Board. Union organizing efforts, which haad previously been stalled by business recalcitrance and unreliable legal protection, could safely resume, particularly in eastern Kentucky. A few weeks later in Atlantic City, discord within the AFL broke loose and set off a long internecine labor war. At the annual convention in October, the UMW's John L. Lewis physically assaulted Bill Hutcheson, president of the Brotherhood of Carpenters and Joiners. This scuffle represented in miniature the fight between militant industrial unions, which followed Lewis's lead, and the more conservative trade unions, led by Hutcheson.[64] Shortly after this fistfight, Lewis and friends formed an industrial coordinating committee within the AFL and by 1938 transformed it into the separate Congress of Industrial Organizations. Even before the divorce was official, the AFL and the CIO competed for members and spurred the growth of new unions. The New Deal was embarrassed by the civil war among labor leaders; at the same time it was pleased with the resurgence of union membership and activity.[65]

Internal competition and government support helped transform both the AFL and the CIO into healthy giants by the end of the decade. Unions unaffiliated with either of these two groups also experienced rapid growth. Estimates of memberships vary greatly, but the AFL was somewhat larger, with about four million members; the CIO followed with roughly two million, and nearly a million workers belonged to other unions.[66] In Kentucky, union membership grew and divided in a similar fashion, but in a different ratio. The CIO claimed the largest number of union members, forty-one thousand, followed by thirty-six thousand in AFL unions, and seven thousand workers belonged to other organizations, especially railroad brotherhoods.[67] These Kentuckians who had joined unions during the 1930s constituted more than 22 percent of the nonagricultural work force, hardly a substantial figure but certainly a much greater percentage than in the neighboring states of Tennessee and Virginia.[68] By all accounts, the largest single union in the state was the UMW, which by the end of the decade had overcome most of its opponents. Other sizable groups included carpenters and joiners, locomotive firemen and enginemen, and machinists. At the 1940 convention of the Kentucky State Federation of Labor, delegates celebrated recent efforts that had brought in thousands of new members among distillery and tobacco workers.[69]

The UMW did not emerge as the largest union in Kentucky without several struggles, some of which involved Kentucky electoral politics. To no one's surprise, as soon as the NRA expired in 1935, all but three of the forty-two mines in Harlan County reverted to nonunion status.[70] Even though the subsequent Wagner Act reasserted the rights of unions, both UMW leaders and coal operators maintained a kind of truce in their long war until the Supreme Court validated the act. In the meantime, both sides hoped to strengthen their relationship with the new state government and waged their battles in the 1935 gubernatorial campaigns instead. Governor Laffoon's Denhardt Commission had exposed the problems in Harlan County, and UMW leaders were optimistic about the removal of Sheriff Middleton and his deputies. For that reason alone they supported Laffoon's choice for the Democratic nomination, Thomas Rhea. Many Democrats crowded the primary ballot that spring, and Kentucky's election system required a runoff primary if no candidate won a clear majority of the votes. Rhea and his longtime adversary Lieutenant Governor Chandler, then, faced a second primary. Harlan County had become so politically polarized that the mine operators endorsed Chandler, if for no other reason than because the UMW supported Rhea. Chandler won both the runoff primary and the subsequent general election in November, with only a reluctant endorsement by labor leaders. The UMW could not help but suspect that more trouble was in store when Sheriff Middleton and some of his deputies served as Chandler's escorts at the December inauguration ceremonies in Frankfort.[71]

Governor Chandler did not wear the antiunion hat very comfortably, but he had difficulty discarding it as the UMW organizational campaign resumed during his new administration. Many delegates at the Kentucky State Federation of Labor convention of 1936 applauded the governor when he claimed that John L. Lewis was his "personal and close friend."[72] The following year, however, in another speech, Chandler equivocated on issues and managed to please business more than labor. The Supreme Court had just validated the Wagner Act, union recruiting had become more militant, and strikes and violence were becoming common again. The governor attempted in the midst of this turmoil to remain allied with the New Deal administration and, at the same time, to avoid alienating his conservative backers in Kentucky. He praised the Wagner Act and said that labor was now "adequately protected" by the federal government; he went on to deplore the sit-down strikes, work stoppages, and violence that characterized much CIO activity and especially UMW efforts in Kentucky.[73] Chandler, despite his protestations, appeared to be less than a friend of the coal miners.

A nationally publicized congressional hearing in 1937 embarrassed Kentucky and forced the governor to move closer to the UMW. The LaFollette Committee had been investigating abuses of civil liberties related to labor strife. In April and May the hearings focused on Harlan County, and for three weeks the nation received a condensed account of what eastern Kentucky had been experiencing for almost a decade. Representatives of the UMW and the mine owners paraded through the Washington committee chambers and recapitulated their stories. Day after day, the senators heard and America read about Sheriff Middleton's past imprisonment for bootlegging, his financial investments in the coal mines he protected, and the criminal records of his deputies, most of whose salaries were paid by the mine operators rather than the county. Testimony also revealed that the average miner in Harlan County earned only about seventy-five dollars per month, roughly one-half of what the deputies earned to keep the miners from joining the UMW. That several of the witnesses wore empty gun holsters at the hearing lent credence to the testimony of one union organizer, who told how snipers had killed his son.[74] At the end of the hearings, the committee recommended that "the Governor and the public conscience of Kentucky" restore citizens' rights, wipe out terrorism, and conduct a "top-to-bottom clean-up" in Harlan County.[75] The chronicler of the LaFollette Committee has stated that these hearings, with their widespread publicity, "performed yeoman service for John L. Lewis's miners."[76] Outraged Kentuckians demanded that Chandler get rid of "the law of the gun and thug," and by the end of 1937 the governor pledged "to restore peace and give justice to the people of Harlan County."[77]

Both Kentucky and the federal government responded with additional pressures in 1938 to break the chain of violence and to help the UMW to overcome the recalcitrance of Harlan County coal operators. Early that year, the Kentucky General Assembly replied to Chandler's request with new laws prohibiting the appointment of sheriffs' deputies with criminal records. The legislation also gave the state treasury some control over the deputies' salaries in an effort to improve the quality of law enforcement.[78] Later that year federal prosecutors brought to trial several mine operators, Harlan County law officers, and Theodore Middleton—recently retired as sheriff—for conspiring to deprive miners of their civil rights under the Wagner Act. Legions of witnesses, spectators, and Federal Bureau of Investigation and Justice Department personnel crowded into London for the midsummer trial, sorely taxing the hotel and restaurant facilities of this small Laurel County community. The local jurors listened to testimony far more complicated than that presented to the LaFollette Committee the previous year. They heard hundreds of witnesses whose stories filled thousands of transcript pages. Prohibited from all outside contacts, the jury spent most of June and July in confinement, reading and singing religious pieces, strolling through a local cemetery, and in the end, becoming "hopelessly deadlocked."[79] The judge declared a mistrial, and the mine owners followed their attorney's advice and signed contracts with the UMW to avoid a retrial. These coal operators had evaded Blue Eagle codes, defied National Labor Relations Board rulings, fought the UMW, violated the Wagner Act, and spent nearly a million dollars to insure a hung jury.[80] Despite these victories from 1933 to 1938, they lost the war. Unions came to Harlan County, and by the end of the decade fifteen thousand miners in the county belonged to the UMW and made up more than one-third of the largest union in the state.[81]

A coalition of officials in Frankfort and Washington had made it possible for the UMW to triumph in 1938, but John L. Lewis shattered that united front in 1939 and pitted state and federal governments against each other over his new plans. The UMW president demanded contacts including union shop agreements that would exclude from employment anyone who refused to join the UMW. President Roosevelt favored and Governor Chandler opposed this goal. Kentucky's governor had learned to accept unions, but forbidding jobs to nonunion members was another matter. The UMW began a nationwide strike in April 1939 to test the resistance of mine owners to their new contract demands. Nonunion miners had to cross picket lines to get to work, violence erupted, and owners everywhere shut down operations. Chandler demanded that both parties reach an agreement by May 14, or he would dispatch National Guardsmen to protect the property of those mines that reopened and the lives of those workers who crossed picket lines. Letters, petitions, and telegrams soon covered his desk, praising and condemning his stand.[82] Three nonunion miners from Kitts wrote about their poverty and desire to work. They requested "protection so that we might resume our work and support our families." Several UMW members warned against the use of troops and threatened that if the governor helped the owners dig coal with scab labor, "it will cause blood to run trickling down these little streams."[83] When the governor's deadline arrived, most Appalachian operators had signed the UMW contracts, and 86 percent of the miners in the region returned to work.[84] But not in Harlan County. Consequently, Governor Chandler ordered five hundred Kentucky guardsmen to maintain order as the mines reopened there. He announced, "No one can tell our people to work or not to work and no one can come into this state and cause trouble."[85]

In spite of and partly because of Chandler's rhetoric and

military intervention the conflict escalated to its highest level. For two months state and national leaders reinforced their allies in the coal camps and helped to produce unprecedented carnage and bitterness. The UMW sent in some of its top officials to bolster the picket lines, and the federal government supplied food to families of the strikers through the WPA. Chandler more than doubled the number of National Guardsmen, and defended his actions in a national radio debate. He insisted that the troops were there "to protect the right to work, *not* to prohibit the right to organize," an honest differentiation, but one that got lost on the battlefield.[86] In mid-July an armistice of sorts stopped the violence, although the issues remained unresolved. Harlan County residents once again buried their dead and bound the wounds of hundreds of their kin and neighbors. The National Guard withdrew, and the mines resumed operations.[87] Not all of the owners accepted the UMW demand for a union shop, however, and this refusal certainly pleased Chandler. He declared that "Kentucky won a victory for itself."[88] Shortly after the cessation of hostilities, one of the governor's supporters referred to John L. Lewis as "nothing but a red communist ungodley devel [sic]" indicating that the philosophical battlelines were still as firmly in place as before.[89] This war had raged on since the 1920s, and intervention by state and federal forces had merely intensified and prolonged the struggle. New Deal laws and agencies resuscitated the miners, and state military actions revived the owners. In the end, the UMW won. Quietly in 1941, after Chandler had departed the governor's mansion and the New Deal had become more concerned with conflicts in Japan and Germany than in Harlan County, the UMW negotiated new contracts containing the controversial closed-shop provision.[90]

New Deal efforts to revitalize and reform American industry produced extreme reactions in Kentucky. Kentuckians greeted federal programs with a combination of enthusiasm, resistance, and on rare occasions, apathy. When a New Deal measure was welcomed, as was the end of Prohibition, the state worked harmoniously with the federal government to implement necessary laws for restoring a profitable industry. But when Kentuckians disagreed with Washington officials, as many did on matters of labor relations, the results were sometimes bloody. And if a New Deal program simply did not work—consider the sickly Blue Eagle—the commonwealth ignored it until it expired. The effect of the New Deal on the state's economy nonetheless was dramatic and long lasting. Sometimes the result was immediate, as when the liquor industry was revived; at other times the result took years to materialize, as happened with the unionization of Harlan County. And even the short-lived NRA succeeded in creating a more receptive attitude about labor reforms that would come later. Federal child labor laws, minimum wages, and maximum hours—all soon became a normal part of the Kentucky workplace and built on the brief precedent set by the fair practices codes of 1933.

Inexorably the New Deal transformed business conditions from free enterprise to a more regimented economy a decade later. Many of these changes were administrative and affected Kentucky institutions more than individuals. Perhaps the most significant change in the economic system was that the federal government emerged from the 1930s with a new and permanent function in what had once been a free-market arena. The New Deal had established the right—even the duty—of Washington officials to intervene and alter the course of business practices for the common good. Most Kentucky businessmen by the onset of World War II knew that federal regulatory agencies and guidelines now played a larger role in their practices and profits than ever before. For example, the National Labor Relations Board continued to mediate labor disputes in Harlan County, and cigarette factories in Louisville had less control over how much they paid their workers. These federal responsibilities expanded throughout the New Deal and included new authority over previously unregulated activities. The Securities and Exchange Commission, the Federal Power Commission, and the Civil Aeronautics Authority all expanded the national government's role as a guarantor of standards and stabilizer of events. If nothing else, the New Deal had tried to restructure the economic machinery to prevent a recurrence of the boom-and-bust frenzy that had made the Depression so painful. Many of these new government agencies barely touched rural Kentucky in the 1930s, but as the state gradually became more urban and industrial, the New Deal legacy become more apparent to larger numbers. As more Kentuckians left the land to pursue their fortunes in manufacturing and finance, they found the rough edges of competitive capitalism less abrasive than previously.

# 7. Politics and Other Natural Phenomena

Politics—perhaps the most primal force in Kentucky—had to adapt to the unprecedented challenges of the New Deal, as did other institutions in the state. Businessmen, laborers, farmers, the young, and the elderly—all were compelled to alter their relationship with the national government during the 1930s. So too were state political leaders. Kentucky officials frequently found New Deal measures out of step with many of their southern, rural, and states-rights traditions. New Deal initiatives and federal regulations clashed with many time-honored customs. Loyalty for patronage jobs increasingly went to Washington rather than Frankfort. This dilemma was not exclusive to Kentucky, but the commonwealth's peculiar sensitivity to politics made it especially aware of the changes taking place in the balance of power during this decade. Neither denying the desperate situations that predicated the New Deal nor questioning the popularity of many of its programs, many Kentucky politicians nevertheless found themselves on unfamiliar ground with the new arrangements. Forces of nature intensified this uncertainty; natural disasters during the 1930s offered extraordinary challenges for politicians. The different state and federal responses to these natural crises revealed the widening gap between the two centers of political power, both in what was expected and what was delivered.

Kentuckians had taken their politics seriously for many years. Many believed literally James Milligan's famous poem describing the state's politics as "the damnedest." Debates over candidates and issues historically had produced feuds and violence. From the politically motivated duels of Henry Clay in the early nineteenth century to the assassination of Governor William Goebel in the early twentieth, state politicians and their followers reserved much of their passion for the electoral process and its potential rewards. The drafters of the state constitution scheduled state elections on uneven calendar years so that state and federal campaigns would not coincide. This measure guaranteed "separation of powers" between the two levels of government and kept voters going to the polls three out of every four years. Campaigning, therefore, was an almost nonstop occupation for office seekers and was an ongoing preoccupation for voters. The state's leading newspapers, the *Courier-Journal* and the *Lexington Herald*, gave inordinate coverage to political meetings and factional splits, and the smaller and weekly papers endorsed and attacked candidates with no pretense of objectivity. Vigorous debates within the letters-to-the-editor columns testified not only to the zeal of the writers but also to their awareness of political history and party platforms. The election of 1932, which produced the New Deal, was a good example of Kentucky's love affair with the ballot box. Of those Kentuckians eligible to vote, 67 percent did so, far exceeding the national percentage and more than doubling the voting rate elsewhere in the south.[1]

Democrats justifiably regarded themselves as Kentucky's majority party, and only three of the last ten governors had been Republicans. When Roosevelt's New Deal began in 1933, Democrats were thoroughly entrenched in most of the state's major political offices. Ruby Laffoon, occupant of the governor's mansion since late 1931, was as partisan a Democrat as the state had seen in many years. In Washington representing Kentucky in the newly elected Seventy-third Congress were nine congressmen and two senators—all Democrats.[2] The two sections of the state most likely to elect Republicans, Louisville and the southeast corner, both lost their Republican representatives in the 1932 sweep. Prior to that year, Kentucky had eleven congressional seats but, as a result of population shifts shown in the 1930 census, had lost two of them. Because of redistricting problems, Kentucky voters had to select their nine representatives in 1932 from "at-large" slates rather than from the usual geographical districts. Roosevelt's coattails and the unusual ballots that year combined to crush the few Republican enclaves in the state. Thus, the new president found his party completely in charge in Kentucky and, for the moment, willing to follow his lead. By the time of the 1934 elections, the nine new districts had been drawn, and the Republicans captured one of them; John Robsion from Barbourville became the only Kentucky Republican on Capitol Hill for the rest of the decade.[3] The New Deal produced no major shifts or realignments in this Democratic state with its deep regional political loyalties.

Roosevelt could count on the Kentucky delegation, Robsion excepted of course, to support the New Deal. Only on rare occasion would these congressmen and senators stray from the New Deal camp, and these infrequent departures came in response to local interests, not from loss of confidence in the national leadership. Unlike many southern Democrats, who abandoned the New Deal in the mid-1930s and became a part of an obstructionist conservative coalition, the Kentucky group remained loyal, and some became more fervent supporters of the New Deal as time passed.

Senator Alben W. Barkley dominated this Kentucky delegation by force of personality and longevity. He had survived many intraparty wars over the years, and by 1933 Kentuckians and Democrats everywhere regarded the Paducah politician as one of the finest statesmen around. He completely overshadowed his senatorial colleague, Marvel Mills Logan, and the other Kentucky representatives in the House. As a leading New Dealer, he helped draft several programs including the AAA, Social Security, NRA, and the banking reforms. His colleagues recognized his stature in 1937 by electing him Senate majority leader, and as such, he met weekly with Roosevelt in the Oval Office. There was a mutual fondness and respect between the president and the senator, and Barkley wore with pride the title "Dear Alben" that Roosevelt had given him.[4] Long after the New Deal declined as a political issue, Barkley still boasted of having helped create and nurture it. Congressman Fred M. Vinson of the Ashland area was probably the second most visible Kentuckian on Capitol Hill. He labored especially hard on legislation to benefit tobacco and coal-mining interests in his district, and in 1937, Roosevelt rewarded him with an appointment to the U.S. Court of Appeals. The New Deal could depend on Senator Logan for quiet, steady support and, except on a few minor issues, received the same loyalty from Paris's Virgil Chapman and Fort Thomas's Brent Spence in the House. The Gregory brothers were vocal in their advocacy of federal activities and were especially effective in getting the TVA expanded into their district. Despite Congressman Andrew May's notoriety for opposing the TVA's Kentucky Dam, he was a rather consistent supporter of New Deal programs.

As these Kentucky politicians and their other colleagues from the commonwealth sought reelection throughout the 1930s, their records on New Deal issues were common themes of their campaigns. Their opponents sometimes attacked the New Deal and sometimes promised to be even more zealous about it than the incumbents, but their tactics inevitably failed. By 1938 it was simply politically unwise to oppose such popular services as Social Security or even the controversial WPA. Voters who had benefited from or were currently employed by these programs were too numerous to alienate during an election year. Incumbents exploited the popularity of the New Deal in their bids for reelection. William Gregory's second election since the start of the New Deal gave him an opportunity to defend his and Roosevelt's record in 1936. He referred to the legislation of the past four years as "the most constructive record in the history of the nation," and he promised to "continue to advocate the program which Mr. Roosevelt has outlined."[5] As early as 1934 Vinson advertised himself as a loyal New Dealer. He pointed out that he had been "shoulder to shoulder, eye to eye with the President" on matters such as NRA and AAA, and praised the "magnitude" of these measures.[6] Audiences could depend on Barkley to make a glowing case for the New Deal at any occasion. The senator reminded the Democratic National Convention in 1948 that the New Deal had rescued a despairing country. "The new Roosevelt administration breathed into the nostrils of every worthy American enterprise a breath of new life, new hope and new determination. It put old agencies at the people's disposal and, where necessary, inaugurated new ones to make democracy live and work for the American people."[7]

Other Kentuckians in Washington assisted the congressional delegation in shaping the New Deal and implementing its policies, and they helped keep the bridges in good repair between federal and state government. Stanley Reed was a good example. Reed had worked his way up through the legal profession and the Kentucky state legislature to a distinguished career as an attorney in Washington. When the New Deal began he was general counsel for Hoover's RFC, where he remained during the hectic days of the Bank Holiday. In 1935, as Roosevelt's solicitor general, he defended several major New Deal cases before the Supreme Court. During his three years in that position, his calm manner, quaint pince-nez, and somber suits gave an appearance of stability and order that contrasted with the frequent disarray of the federal administration. As Roosevelt's adviser, the Harvard law professor Felix Frankfurter, commented to Reed, "The country and the President are fortunate to have your cool head here."[8] As solicitor general, Reed successfully defended cases involving the PWA, TVA, and the National Labor Relations Act, among others. He was not as successful on behalf of the AAA and NRA, however, and his dramatic collapse before the court in late 1935 revealed the Herculean efforts being made to salvage some of the early New Deal programs. In a speech delivered in 1936 at the University of Virginia, Reed applauded the New Deal philosophy of expanding federal responsibilities during national crises, and urged the Supreme Court to amend its conservative views regarding the limits of power. The Constitution should "guide and not curb necessary governmental processes," according to Reed, and he speculated that the Founding Fathers had not intended this document to become a straightjacket to make the federal government "helpless in the emergencies of today."[9] When Roosevelt appointed him to the Supreme Court in 1938, Reed took this philosophy with him to an increasingly liberal bench and joined two other Kentuckians already there, Justices Brandeis and Reynolds. Roosevelt appointed several Kentucky newspapermen to posts of varying importance in his administration. Robert Worth Bingham, publisher of the *Courier-Journal*, became ambassador to England in 1933 as a reward for his many contributions to the Democratic party; the president's chief political aide, Jim Farley, referred to Bingham as a "financial father" of the 1932 campaign. Though out of the country frequently during the decade, Bingham continued to influence politics. His personal touch could be seen especially in the 1935 primary elections and in his close working relationship with Secretary of Agriculture Henry A. Wallace regarding tobacco programs.[10] Urey Woodson, publisher of the *Owensboro Messenger* for many years, had attended every Democratic National Convention since 1880; he came to Washington in 1933 as alien property custodian. This sinecure afforded Woodson a strategic location in the capital from which to communicate news and gossip back to Governor Laffoon and other political allies. Such New Deal luminaries as Farley seldom refused Woodson's Derby Weekend invitations, which included lavish entertainments in Kentucky.[11] Probably the state journalist who occupied the most significant post in the New Deal administration was Marvin McIntyre. This native of La Grange had worked for a number of newspapers, including the *Louisville Times* and *Washington Times*, before joining Roosevelt's staff in 1920 during the vice-presidential campaign. By the time he became the president's appointments secretary in 1933, McIntyre—or Mac—had become a trusted friend and political adviser, and he remained in the inner circle of New Dealers. He had the ability to turn unwanted visitors away from the White House with tact, and he had the impresarial skills to arrange secret poker games for Roosevelt.[12]

Unlike the Kentucky native sons in Washington, many politicians in state offices had trouble adapting to the new federal administration. "Potomac fever" might turn Kentuckians into New Dealers when they arrived in Washington, but the political miasma around Frankfort immunized several state administrators against the new national phenomenon. Governor Laffoon was one of the immunized. Laffoon had endorsed Roosevelt's candidacy in 1932 and supported his early emergency measures, as did most Democrats in those desperate times. But an uneasy truce is about the best description of his relationship with the rest of the New Deal. The governor was a traditional politician of the old school, accustomed to a more leisurely pace of government than the crises of the 1930s demanded. Kentucky state government had always operated somewhat languidly once elections were concluded. The general assembly met only for a few weeks every second year unless the governor called it into special session. New Deal demands upset this relaxed routine, and the elderly Laffoon found the challenges too much for his precarious health. Frequent emergency trips to Washington drained his energy, and recurrent high blood pressure plagued his later years. Following the 1934 session of the state legislature, he entered the Waverly Hills Sanatorium near Louisville, suffering from mental and physical exhaustion.[13] Surgery for appendicitis hospitalized him the next year and curtailed his activities. Three-quarters of the way through his administration, the *Kentucky Post* openly discussed what many had whispered about Laffoon for some time: he was "heartily tired of the governorship" and was even "wishing his term were over."[14]

Philosophical differences with the New Deal also caused difficulties for Laffoon and his administration. Like many southern Democratic executives, he resisted relinquishing his power to federal officials. His basic conservatism and states'-rights orientation clashed with most New Deal programs. Bailey Wootton shared these attitudes and, as Laffoon's attorney general, reinforced the governor. His wife recalled that Wootton "did not approve of the trend of New Deal policies and was bitterly opposed to too much centralization of government."[15] Although Laffoon welcomed federal funds to combat human distress—his grandiose requests to Hoover's RFC had already proved that—he did not want Washington officials interfering with the state's use of those funds. The highly publicized flap with Harry Hopkins about matching grants for FERA was just an outward sign of his philosophical turmoil. These differences surfaced many times throughout his governorship. He helped to defeat the passage of state NRA legislation; he resisted coal miner unionization; and he postponed maintenance of CCC facilities in state parks. Laffoon was well aware that federal politicians held him in contempt. Urey Woodson reported that some of Roosevelt's cabinet members asked him early in the New Deal what kind of a "damn fool" Kentucky had for a governor.[16] Laffoon was also aware that a complete rupture in state-federal relations could seriously damage the state, however, and so he stopped short of that. The thousands of Kentuckians who received New Deal aid and the economic impact of that aid in the state were factors that kept him working, no matter how uneasily, with Washington.

Compounding Laffoon's problems were a series of political clashes with his lieutenant governor, an apparent New Deal ally. Unlike the governor, whose health was failing and whose long career had already peaked, Albert B. Chandler was young, full of vitality, and brimming with ambition. As Chandler's political star rose, it frequently collided with Laffoon's, and he became a leader of the anti-Laffoon faction in the Democratic party. As such, he helped kill Laffoon's sales tax proposal in 1933, partly to build his own power base and partly because he thought the tax would weigh heavily on the poor. Laffoon reciprocated the following year by getting the tax passed along with a "ripper bill" to remove many of the lieutenant governor's powers. Conflicts between the two men became so consuming and divisive that Roosevelt and other federal officials intervened to prevent further disruption of New Deal programs in the state.

Kentucky's state legislature had given political parties the option of picking gubernatorial candidates either by a convention or by primary election. The convention option was quicker, cheaper, and less divisive, and the minority Republicans usually nominated their candidates in that way. Democrats, on the other hand, generally chose the primary method, calling it the democratic method of allowing more people to participate in the selection process. In 1931 the state Democratic Executive

Committee had decided to revert to a convention.[17] Despite some protests, party delegates met in Lexington's Woodland Auditorium and selected Laffoon and Chandler to be the party's leaders. Bingham's *Courier-Journal* had opposed the convention method and later criticized most of Laffoon's major actions. In late 1934 the *Courier-Journal* began a campaign to force the Democratic Executive Committee to reinstate a primary for the 1935 elections. Most political observers thought that Laffoon delegates would dominate a convention, whereas a primary would be more likely to nominate a gubernatorial candidate who was in tune with New Deal principles. The newspaper mailed 250,000 ballots to Kentuckians in early January 1935 in a journalistic referendum to determine whether voters preferred a convention or a primary. One day before the meeting of the committee, on January 27, the *Courier-Journal* announced on its front page that Kentucky Democrats preferred a primary by an eleven-to-one margin.[18]

When the committee met the following day, it allowed proponents of each side to present their arguments. Although it would be erroneous to say the committee was "stacked" with Laffoon-convention supporters, as Chandler claimed, the governor did have tight control over party machinery and his anti-New Deal attorney general chaired the group.[19] Senator Barkley addressed the committee and pleaded for a return to primary elections. He then read a letter that Roosevelt had asked him to deliver, in which the president requested that the committee allow "the greatest freedom and the widest opportunity" for "all the people" to participate in "the selection of candidates." Laffoon responded with a denunciation of the *Courier-Journal* and charged that Bingham and his newspaper would exert inordinate influence on a primary. Following the arguments, the committee sided with Laffoon, by a vote of thirty to twenty and scheduled a convention for mid-May. As powerful and popular as the New Deal was, some aspects of Kentucky state politics were beyond its influence.[20]

What Roosevelt and Barkley had been unable to accomplish by themselves, Chandler managed to do with a hastily contrived coalition of friends. A succession of mistakes by Laffoon and a sequence of bold moves by his lieutenant governor gave Kentucky its primary elections and filled Frankfort with chaos greater than it had experienced since the assassination of Governor Goebel in 1900. Laffoon departed for Washington on February 5, accompanied by Thomas Rhea, his highway commissioner and his choice as successor. During Laffoon's absence from the state, Chandler used his temporary executive powers to call for an extraordinary session of the general assembly to pass legislation requiring a primary election. He stated, "The right of the people to have primaries is a fundamental one."[21] Laffoon rushed back from Washington to try to regain control of the situation. As soon as his train crossed the state line at Ashland he issued a proclamation to "revoke, rescind and annul" Chandler's call of the previous day and accused the lieutenant governor of serving "the interests of certain selfish politicians instead of the best interests of the Commonwealth."[22] Neither Chandler's nor Laffoon's forces were able to muster a quorum until the courts determined the legality of this controversial session. The Franklin County Circuit Court broke the impasse on February 11 by ruling that the original call by Chandler was valid; the Kentucky Court of Appeals immediately affirmed the decision and paved the way for the general assembly to convene.[23]

The legislators met in a highly charged atmosphere and produced not one but two primaries. Kentuckians subsequently trooped to the polls three times that year in one of the most memorable twelve months in Kentucky's political history. Laffoon's forces added to Chandler's proposal a second, or runoff, primary if no candidate received a clear majority of votes in the first. Following maneuvers and compromises by both sides, the double primary became law. Chandler wrote prophetically to a friend, "I gave them a damn good whipping and we are to have a Primary instead of a Convention. Of course the Primary will be considerable benefit to my friends and to me personally."[24] Energetic and ambitious, he faced four Democrats in the primary in August, the most formidable being Thomas Rhea, who had confided earlier to Urey Woodson, "Unless there is an earthquake or a revelation from Heaven . . . I am a sure winner."[25] Rhea did win a plurality of the votes but not a majority; so he faced Chandler again in September in the second primary he had helped to create. Chandler attracted many supporters with his pledge to repeal the recently enacted sales tax and many more with his vibrant, gregarious campaign style. Rhea lost votes because of his close involvement with unpopular decisions by Laffoon during the summer. The governor stirred up adverse publicity when he dispatched the National Guard twice to Harlan County and received much criticism for hardships caused during the awkward transition from the FERA to the WPA in 1935.[26] When Chandler defeated Rhea in September, the *New York Times* declared that the victory had "saved Kentucky for President Roosevelt," a somewhat premature judgment.[27] But the ensuing campaign against Republican King Swope did turn out to be an important referendum on New Deal policies.

Kentucky's general election that fall, as one of the few elections in 1935, drew much national attention. Although the Republican candidate did not openly attack the New Deal, Chandler's advisers welcomed the opportunity to portray the Lexington lawyer and judge as a conservative opponent of Roosevelt's programs.[28] The president and several of his Washington staff members discarded their neutral stance once the primaries were over and entered into the fray as though this were an important vote of confidence. Early in the campaign, Roosevelt made an effort to bestow his blessings on Chandler and, at the same time, to heal the wounds left over from the recent primaries. He had scheduled a trip through southern Ohio and Indiana and invited Laffoon, Rhea, Chandler, and the candidate for lieutenant governor, Keen Johnson, to visit with him aboard the train as it passed through Cincinnati. An unfortunate mixup in the delivery of the invitations offended Laffoon's sense of protocol, and both he and Rhea refused to join the president's party, despite Marvin McIntyre's attempts to repair the damage. Chandler and Johnson, however, basked in the publicity that surrounded their conference, and Johnson later wrote that Roosevelt "flashed that winsome smile" for the benefit of photographers and Democrats.[29] Jim Farley told young Democrats in Louisville the following week that all of America was watching their actions and that they "must elect Happy Chandler . . . if Kentucky wishes to uphold the hands of President Roosevelt."[30] In his familiar green ink, Farley wrote to many voters in the state, urging "a sweeping Democratic victory."[31] By the end of the campaign, Chandler had so thoroughly allied himself with the national administration that he speculated Abraham Lincoln would have endorsed the Roosevelt-Chandler team.[32]

The WPA and its influence on voters also played a role in the general election of 1935. Both Roosevelt and Harry Hopkins had reiterated that politics and relief were to remain separate, but it was difficult to keep them apart, especially during a heated campaign. State WPA director George Goodman confided to an associate that, although he wanted to keep politics out of relief activity, Democrats were "preferable" to Republicans as co-workers, and the outcome of this election would be important to the WPA in Kentucky.[33] State Republicans were quick to notice the rapid acceleration of WPA hiring during the autumn campaign. Fewer than five thousand Kentuckians had been employed on WPA projects in September; by mid-November that number had risen to more than thirty thousand. King Swope's staff charged the Democrats with using jobs to purchase votes, and the Republican candidate accused federal officials of allowing state Democrats the use of relief rosters for campaign mailings. Campaign rhetoric to the contrary, recent research has shown that the WPA was much less politically involved than Republicans claimed. The employment surge did coincide with the political campaign, but this same hiring increase occurred in most other states as well, none of which was holding an election that fall.[34] In any event, Chandler defeated Swope handily in November, and the WPA was only a minor factor in the victory. The lieutenant governor was simply a more appealing figure than Swope, and his campaign style offered great entertainment. There were more Democrats in the state than Republicans, and they voted in record numbers that year. Chandler's promise to repeal the sales tax was an important issue, and the New Deal was undeniably popular. Following his victory, Governor-elect Chandler made his way to Lexington's Union Station to see Senator Barkley off to Washington. As the senator left on an eastbound train, he said, "I'm going to tell President Roosevelt all is well."[35]

Chandler's administration worked far more compatibly with the New Deal than had Laffoon's. A few stylistic parallels between the new governor and the president even created an illusion of similar methodology. Chandler appointed several educators to his staff in a manner reminiscent of Roosevelt's Brain Trust. Notable among these were the University of Kentucky's Dr. James Martin, who became commissioner of revenue, and Frank Peterson, who had been with the Department of Education and NYA and now went to the Finance Department. The new governor also developed a closer rapport with Washington administrators than did his predecessor, and his trips to the nation's capital had less of an emergency air about them. Jim Farley asked Chandler to bring his vibrant campaigning style to Roosevelt's aid during the president's reelection campaign in 1936, and the governor responded with a flurry of oratorical rallies in Ohio, Missouri, Illinois, and North Dakota.[36] Even when many Democrats abandoned the president in 1937 during his unsuccessful attempt to add more justices to the Supreme Court, Chandler defended Roosevelt and referred to the "court-packing" proposal as a "reform."[37] Under the governor's leadership the Kentucky General Assembly endorsed several New Deal measures, passed state enabling laws to expedite federal programs, and provided matching funds without the public disputes of previous years. At the end of Chandler's first year in office, the state director of the National Emergency Council, the coordinating body for federal agencies, complimented the governor on the "pleasant relations" that existed between state and national governments.[38]

It would be wrong, however, to assume that Chandler was a Roosevelt puppet or that his many state reforms constituted a "Little New Deal" as some observers concluded. Chandler was at heart a fiscal conservative who valued state autonomy and regarded Harry F. Byrd, the conservative former governor of Virginia and now anti-New Deal senator, as his mentor and friend. Byrd had been Chandler's choice for president in 1932; he had attended Chandler's inauguration in 1935; and he had been the inspiration for Kentucky's reorganization plan in 1936.[39] When Chandler left office in late 1939, the state government was more efficiently consolidated and was operating less expensively than before; Governor Keen Johnson could report in early 1940 a surplus of more than two million dollars in the General Fund.[40] All of this was in direct contrast to the burgeoning federal bureaucracy and debt under Roosevelt's New Deal. Of course some of Chandler's success was due to massive federal spending in Kentucky during his administration, a general improvement in the national and state economy, and a new tax structure that included liquor revenues. Moreover, part of the state's new solvency had come at the expense of indigent citizens. Kentucky participants in Social Security and other relief programs fell below the national average in their benefits, and the state administration had allowed or determined this situation. One historian stated that Chandler was "among the most frugal in appropriations for relief and welfare" and that he "professed his sympathy with the national administration while doing relatively little in the state to prove it."[41]

Chandler's conservatism was philosophical as well as fiscal, and this also placed him at odds with the New Deal. His improvements in public education and penal institutions sprang more from necessity than from humanitarian instincts, and he frequently delivered lectures on individualism to constituents in search of government assistance. To one family seeking a NYA position for a son, he recalled "that without such assistance I largely made my own way through college, including law school, with absolutely no help."[42] When he handed out the first Social Security checks to elderly recipients, he reminded them, "It is not money that you are entitled to"; it was, instead, a gift that was not to be spent "riotously."[43] Late in his term, Chandler lectured the New Deal administration itself. In a Jackson Day address in North Carolina he urged the federal government to adhere to sound business practices and to return many powers and responsibilities to the states.[44] On some matters, Chandler openly clashed with federal officials. He chafed under Social Security personnel guidelines, quarreled with the CCC about park maintenance, and fought with Roosevelt over unions in Harlan County. In each of these conflicts Chandler appeared to be a states'-rights conservative at war with federal liberalism.

Chandler's personal ambitions and his increasing disaffection with the New Deal caused him to challenge Barkley in 1938 for a seat in the Senate. The ensuing primary campaign, which engaged two powerful and talented politicians and called much of the New Deal into question, garnered national press coverage. In early 1938 Chandler was entering the second half of his gubernatorial term, and the state constitution prevented him from running for a second term. Restless and possibly bored, he had already accomplished most of his agenda as governor, and by his own admission, Frankfort was just a stepping-stone to higher office.[45] The only higher office available in the foreseeable future was Barkley's Senate seat.

Rumors had been circulating for some time that Chandler would challenge Barkley, and the senator began his reelection plans early. Approximately thirteen hundred Barkley supporters gathered for a testimonial dinner at Louisville's Brown Hotel on January 22 and heard presidential aide Marvin McIntyre read a letter from Roosevelt. "I wish you would go down to Louisville and tell the homefolks how much we in Washington think of their senior Senator. . . . his integrity, his patriotic zeal, his courage and loyalty, and his eloquence . . . give him exceptional equipment as a legislator and a leader."[46] In a meeting with Chandler a few days later, Roosevelt discouraged the governor from entering the race. Chandler recalled later that Roosevelt said "I was a young fellow and had lots of time. . . . But I told the President that I wanted to do what he had done—run while the running was good."[47] Shortly after the president's attempt to forestall his candidacy, Chandler met with several conservative senators in Washington; some observers speculated that the governor intended to turn the Senate contest into part of a southern conservative attack on the New Deal.[48] There were to be thirty-two senatorial races in 1938, and Roosevelt decided to intervene in some of them—including the primaries—to defend his supporters and "purge" some of the troublesome critics. The Kentucky primary was one of those. Harold Ickes recalled a cabinet meeting in the spring of that year in which the president pledged his assistance to Barkley and called Chandler "a dangerous person," a politician "of the Huey Long type but with less ability."[49]

Chandler rose to this challenge and launched his campaign not just against Barkley but against the federal administration as well. Sounding increasingly conservative, he attacked the unbalanced budget in Washington and the ever-growing number of government employees. Comparing these excesses with the manner in which he had consolidated offices, improved efficiency, and reduced the state payroll and debt, the governor promised to use the same techniques as a senator. "We've got to undertake to pay the national debt. . . . We've got to cut governmental costs. We've done it in Kentucky and now we are prepared to lead the way in Washington." According to Chandler, Barkley was part of the problem in the nation's capital. He was only a Roosevelt pawn, the "number one coat-tail rider of the nation."[50]

Barkley's campaign started later than Chandler's because of the senator's inability to leave Washington during the final weeks of the Seventy-fifth Congress. But in June he launched a concerted effort to show Kentuckians just how much they had benefited from federal programs. He distributed mimeographed forms to audiences around the state, which listed, county by county, the thousands of workers employed on New Deal projects and the millions of dollars expended for such programs as AAA, FERA, Social Security, and WPA. "Those are the policies I helped to write," he told a large crowd at the Lexington Trotting Track; "those are the policies for which I will continue to stand for the next six years."[51] Letters from Barkley campaign headquarters reminded voters that Chandler's success in balancing budgets and reducing debts had been achieved by keeping Social Security benefits low. Despite the senator's desire for elderly Kentuckians to receive thirty dollars per month as did recipients in some states, the governor had been more interested in cutting costs than in serving human needs. Consequently, Barkley said, Kentucky benefits averaged less than ten dollars per month.[52]

On July 8, Roosevelt visited Kentucky for several appearances on behalf of Barkley. In a speech at Latonia Racetrack, he reiterated the senator's argument about federal benefits to the state. Since its inception in 1933, the New Deal had disbursed more than $300 million to Kentuckians in direct relief and jobs and additional millions through loans and underwritten mortgages. He asked voters to consider how much they had needed this assistance the next time someone asked "why the national government hasn't balanced its budget." Firmly but diplomatically, Roosevelt then cast his personal ballot. "I have no doubt that Governor Chandler would make a good Senator—but I think he would be the first to acknowledge that . . . it would take him many, many years to match the national knowledge, the experience . . . of that son of Kentucky of whom the whole nation is proud, Alben Barkley."[53] Chandler anticipated the effect of the president's visit and attended the Latonia event either to observe the blessing or to salvage as much as possible from the occasion. And he managed to accomplish the latter with style. Those who only glanced at the newspaper photographs the following day and did not read about Roosevelt's endorsement of Barkley would have formed the opposite opinion. There in the back seat of the president's open car sat Chandler in the middle, smiling broadly, with Roosevelt on his right and Barkley, looking none too pleased, on his left. Barkley later remembered that Chandler, in an attempt to get whatever advantage he could and "much to the horror of the Secret Service men, literally leaped over the President and ensconced himself beside him before I could get into the car." Many years later, Chandler hotly denied any rudeness or presumption on his part in this affair; he maintained that the president arranged the seating positions himself.[54] Whatever the case, Chandler had managed to capture at least some publicity while Barkley held on to the president's coattails.

Welfare and politics, which had played a minor part in the 1935 gubernatorial election, became a major part of this senatorial primary and damaged both candidates. The use of WPA funds to assist Barkley and the use of Social Security benefits and other relief programs to aid Chandler both became prime issues of the campaign. Although the candidates themselves were not guilty of misuse of government funds, their staffs and overzealous supporters did abuse the welfare machinery to influence the votes of needy Kentuckians. Publication of the details of these activities in the state won a Pulitzer Prize for an enterprising journalist and helped produce a new federal law to prevent such abuses in the future.

The potential for political use of WPA jobs appeared early in the spring of 1938. Thomas Rhea joined the Barkley campaign against his old enemy Chandler and hoped to use the federal relief network to guarantee a large majority for the senator in August, but to his dismay, he complained to Urey Woodson in Washington, "We are having one hell of a time getting any action out of the W.P.A."[55] The Kentucky WPA director, George Goodman, seemed reluctant to involve his agency in politics; his friendship with Barkley spanned many years, but his working relationship with Chandler was forthright and professional. If WPA jobs were to become political bait, it would have to happen without his knowledge. Political primaries were occurring in more than half the states in 1938, so the problem was common to other state administrators as well. Harry Hopkins tried to prevent political abuse before it became widespread. He directed a communiqué on May 5 to all WPA officials and employees, which declared that "anyone who used his position with the W.P.A. in any way to influence the votes of others . . . will be dismissed. . . . What's more, I want you to let me know if anyone tries to tell you anything different."[56]

Hopkins's invitation to protest brought responses within the month. Governor Chandler's campaign manager, Brady Stewart, accused the WPA "of frankly and brazenly operating upon a political basis" that favored Barkley. His accusations appeared in most major newspapers. With affidavits to substantiate his case, Stewart charged Goodman's staff of discriminatory hiring, assessment of salaries, use of WPA vehicles for campaign transportation, and distribution of commodity foods in containers that endorsed Barkley.[57] Goodman and state WPA officials denied the charges, point by point, and refuted them with other affidavits. For example, they quashed the matter of Barkley endorsements by the Laurel County commodity center. Local WPA administrators in Laurel County had refused to provide bags for relief recipients to carry commodities home, and the district director pointed out that "there is a merchant across the street from the commodity distribution area. He is a friend of Barkley and had many bags printed up, 'Paper Bags donated by Friend of Alben Barkley.' Very frequently people go over to his store to get bags in which to carry their commodities. Neither the Commodity Project nor any W.P.A. employee have had anything to do with this."[58]

Thomas L. Stokes, a staff writer for the Scripps-Howard newspaper chain, was intrigued with this debate and not entirely convinced by the WPA's refutations. He visited Kentucky to conduct his own investigation, traveled some fourteen hundred miles throughout the state, and then published eight articles in June. No Kentucky newspaper carried the series, but it did appear in the *Cincinnati Post,* and perhaps most damaging, the *Washington Daily News.* He repeated some of the original accusations and added more to the list. Some WPA offices, he charged, had assumed the atmosphere of a Barkley campaign headquarters. "It is open and flagrant."[59] Goodman proceeded to deny each of the new charges, and Hopkins rushed his field agent Howard Hunter to Kentucky to assist in discrediting the Stokes series. In a telephone conversation shortly after his arrival, Hunter assured his chief that the WPA had "an answer to every charge" and was completely innocent.[60] After further study, however, Hunter, Goodman, and Hopkins admitted that a few of Stokes's accusations were valid and reprimanded one WPA foreman, who had threatened to fire an employee if he did not support Barkley. Other evidence implicated Goodman in partisan activities.[61]

Several factors contributed to the credibility of Stokes's articles and ultimately gained him a Pulitzer Prize. One was the fact that he was philosophically a supporter of Barkley, and another was that he also uncovered evidence that Chandler's staff was playing the same political games with state relief money. Stokes quoted Chandler's finance commissioner, J. Dan Talbott, as saying, "If I find a man on a state job who's not for Happy, I'll fire him."[62] Other observers publicized similar activities in the governor's campaign. A column by Joseph Alsop in the *Washington Star* accused Chandler of having Social Security checks delivered in person by state welfare workers rather than by mail as usual.[63] The *Courier-Journal* and *Time* magazine both investigated state relief procedures and reported that these thirty-three thousand hand-delivered Social Security checks were accompanied by a few good words for the governor's candidacy. They also reported that Chandler's administration was assessing campaign contributions from state welfare workers, whose salaries came from federal revenues.[64] Some of this was secondhand evidence, but the *Kentucky Welfare News*, edited by Chandler's associate Orval Baylor, admitted that relief checks had been personally delivered that summer, mainly to cut expenses.[65]

This highly publicized debate over politics and relief became the subject of a special Senate investigation that autumn. The Sheppard Committee reviewed charges of political misconduct from several elections, and regarding the Kentucky situation, two questions were outstanding. To what extent were federal and state funds misused in the campaign, and in what measure could the two candidates be held responsible? When the senators completed their review of testimony, affidavits, tally sheets, and other material, they listed fifteen episodes in which WPA officials had been politically active. The committee also determined that government employees—those paid from national appropriations—had contributed twenty-four thousand dollars to Barkley and seventy thousand dollars to Chandler.[66] None of these revelations came as a great surprise to close observers of the primary campaign, but the committee's complete exoneration of Barkley and Chandler was a bit unexpected. The report concluded that none of the evidence showed that either candidate "had any knowledge of this activity."[67]

Chandler could derive some satisfaction from the committee report that Barkley's campaign had committed more acts of questionable ethics than his. This was cold comfort, however, and it came too late; he had lost the election anyway by a sizable seventy-one thousand votes. Barkley continued to deny that the WPA had contributed to his victory, and Chandler maintained that the senator "would not have been elected" without it.[68] It is likely, however, that other factors were involved; the margin of victory was too great to have been brought about by manipulation of a few thousand relief workers and recipients. Barkley was successful in all the state's urban counties, where organized labor strongly supported his candidacy. The same was true in most of the coal-mining counties in the southeast corner of the state where the UMW was angry with Chandler. The senator also swept the western agricultural counties, which were happy with AAA programs. In short, the Roosevelt coalition defeated Chandler. Laborers, farmers, and relief recipients owed too much to the New Deal to abandon it for a singing, smiling governor who promised them less of what they were enjoying.[69]

Chandler joined Barkley in the Senate the following year in spite of his resounding defeat in 1938. Senator Logan died in late 1939, creating a vacancy that Chandler quickly filled by resigning as governor in the final weeks of his term and having his successor, Keen Johnson, appoint him to the unexpired term. New Deal budgets, debts, and bureaucracy—which had comprised much of Chandler's campaign the previous year—did not occupy much of the new senator's attention. By the time he moved from the governor's mansion to Capitol Hill, the New Deal was phasing out many of its relief and public works programs and concentrating on defense appropriations and preparation for war. Both Chandler and Barkley may have learned something from the 1938 primary, and their votes in favor of the Hatch Act of 1940 gave an indication of that lesson. The legislation they helped to pass, as the junior and senior senators from Kentucky, placed tight restrictions on the political activities of government employees.

Keen Johnson, as the third governor of Kentucky during the New Deal, proved more friendly to the federal administration than either Laffoon or Chandler. He faced neither the economic crises nor the political challenges that had troubled his predecessors, so his tenure as chief executive was comparatively

easier than theirs. His zeal for continuing, improving, and en-
larging the New Deal, however, far exceeded that of his colleagues and surprised many Kentuckians who knew him only as
a conservative newspaper publisher and Chandler's loyal lieutenant governor. As the national New Deal wound down,
Johnson goaded the Kentucky General Assembly to take up the
slack by increasing state Social Security benefits and improving
workmen's compensation laws.[70] His battle to permit municipalities the use of TVA electricity became almost a religious
crusade and endeared him to New Dealers even though most of
them were now on other missions. Whereas Laffoon and
Chandler had clashed with the New Deal over its youthful and
experimental programs, Johnson benefited from its maturity
and momentum.

Meanwhile, two natural catastrophes within two years devastated Kentucky and tested the resources of the state and
federal governments. The drought of 1936 and the flood of 1937
brought unprecedented suffering to large numbers of Americans, who demanded that political leaders provide both immediate aid and corrective measures. State and federal governments responded to these challenges, as did individuals in the
private sector. Government leaders in both Frankfort and Washington were justifiably proud of their actions during these episodes. In the end, New Deal aid was greater, thus highlighting
what other events of the decade had revealed with increasing
regularity: individuals as well as state governments looked to
Washington for answers to their problems. Whether the problems were political, economic, or in this case, natural, Kentuckians received better answers from the federal government
than from their traditional self-reliance and state leaders.

Kentucky's drought of 1936 did not equal the spectacle of the
Dust Bowl, which had carried away tons of topsoil from the
Midwest and forced the evacuation of hundreds of farms. Farm
Security Administration photographers and John Steinbeck's
*The Grapes of Wrath* documented this ravaging of America's
landscape. But the months of heat and sparse rainfall brought
similar suffering to Kentucky and called for emergency mea-
sures. The shortage of rain became noticeable in April, and

tobacco farmers found it difficult to prepare their fields because of the unusual dryness. Corn and pasture crops soon began to wither from the heat and lack of moisture, and as streams and ponds ran dry in the summer, many farmers had to sell their livestock, including family milk cows.[71] Day after day the temperature rose above a hundred degrees in central and western Kentucky, and by late August state and federal officials agreed that this was "the most serious drought—the most serious emergency that ever affected our state."[72] The Governor's Committee on Drought Relief estimated in September that as many as fifty-one thousand farmers in the state would not be able to purchase feed for their livestock, and thousands would "be reduced to poverty." Yields of gardens and truck farms would probably be down about 85 percent, and approximately sixteen million dollars in aid would be necessary for human subsistence, livestock feed, and production assistance for 1937.[73]

As a new governor of a rural state pledged to budget balancing, Chandler faced a serious problem with this drought. The needs were extraordinary and either state resources for emergency aid were not available or Chandler could not reconcile their use with his frugal philosophy. The governor solved a major part of his dilemma by appealing to the federal government. President Roosevelt made a special "drought tour" of the Midwest and held a conference with several governors in Indianapolis, which Chandler attended. At the meeting, the governor requested aid for sixty-five thousand Kentucky families.[74] His Drought Committee subsequently documented the specific needs to appropriate New Deal agencies, such as the WPA and the Resettlement Administration. Their wells running dry, commonwealth officials carried their buckets to Washington to be filled with emergency loans, jobs, commodities, and reduced freight rates.

The New Deal responded with generous benefits for Kentuckians. Eighty-six counties qualified for the "emergency drought area" designation that opened the door for fast assistance from a variety of agencies. The WPA quickly certified 13,500 farm families for temporary jobs, and the Department of Agriculture purchased livestock and distributed meat through its Surplus Commodities program. Resettlement Administration and FCA offices increased their loans; the AAA shipped carloads of livestock feed to stricken areas; and the Soil Conservation and Domestic Allotment service made extra payments to farmers as "a measure of crop income insurance."[75] New Deal agencies—already established to handle economic crises—easily readjusted their personnel and schedules and coped with this natural disaster. Earlier droughts had brought havoc and administrative confusion; the drought of 1936 turned state politicians into tillers of very bountiful federal fields.

Most of the rain that nature withheld from Kentucky in 1936 fell early in 1937 and created one of the greatest floods in the history of the Ohio Valley. From Pittsburgh to the Mississippi River, too much rain fell too fast. Louisville normally received about two inches of precipitation in January, but in January 1937 the city got nearly twenty.[76] Floods from the Kentucky River in the southeast and the Wabash in the north dumped into the already swollen Ohio, forcing that river to spill over its banks into cities and farms. When the water receded in February, the devastation left behind was staggering. Two-thirds of Maysville had been under water; Frankfort's state prison, which had been above flood level since its construction in 1802, was a total wreck; brown water crested four feet deep at Louisville's Fourth and Broadway intersection; refugees trapped in the upper floors of Paducah's Irvin Cobb Hotel reportedly burned furniture in tile bathrooms to keep warm. Those who had prayed for rain the year before now blamed it for approximately two hundred deaths and nearly $200 million in damages.[77] In light of all this, Governor Chandler could be forgiven his overstatement, which was as out of control as the rivers, when he declared the flood "the most destructive catastrophe that has ever occurred on this continent."[78]

Chandler was not in Kentucky when he first heard about the flooding. He was visiting with his wife's family in Virginia, and Lieutenant Governor Johnson contacted him from Frankfort. Immediately Chandler telephoned Harry Hopkins and discovered that the WPA chief in Washington knew far more about Kentucky's crisis than did the governor. They agreed that the

WPA should proceed with emergency evacuation work in the river towns while Chandler was returning to the state.[79] From this point on, heroic efforts to combat Kentucky's greatest natural disaster came from a combination of volunteer efforts, state government resources, and federal agencies. Of the three, federal assistance was the first requested, the best coordinated, and the most important in handling the emergency.

Volunteer workers and generous private contributions eased the rescue efforts. A group of Florida grocery store managers shipped a railroad carload of fruit and vegetables to Kentucky flood victims; the Carnation Milk Company sent 750 cases of evaporated milk; Harlan County's coal mine operators got some rare good publicity by donating $5,500 and offering fifty carloads of coal.[80] Following a request in the *New York Times* for Kentucky Colonel donations, more than nine thousand dollars came to the governor's office by February 1.[81] The American Red Cross provided aid and comfort to more than eighty thousand dislocated families throughout the state. For several weeks it supplied rescue equipment, nurses, food, and other services—all of which cost approximately nine million dollars.[82]

Lieutenant Governor Johnson and Governor Chandler coordinated these volunteer activities and directed state emergency efforts with little rest and inadequate resources. Prior to Chandler's return from Virginia, Johnson alerted private, state, and national agencies of the emergency needs. He placed all State Highway Department equipment at the disposal of rescue workers, and he directed the presidents of all state colleges to use campus facilities to house and care for flood refugees.[83] Within an hour of his return to Frankfort, Chandler was in a pair of hip boots, touring the flooded prison, with its twenty-nine hundred stranded convicts. He yelled to them from his small open boat, "This is a hell of a mess, but I'm going to get you out. Just sit tight and keep your chins up. . . . God made this flood, I didn't."[84] Because of power outages and disruption of communications and transportation, he dispatched the National Guard to help maintain order in several areas, including Maysville, Paducah, and Louisville. Leaving State Health Officer A.T. McCormack in charge of relief activity in Frankfort, the governor then inspected flood damage along the entire Kentucky border of the Ohio River, from West Virginia to Missouri. During this tour, he kept a personal list of the devastation he witnessed. At a site near his boyhood home in Henderson County, he noted that thirty horses had drowned and fourteen floating buildings had come to rest.[85] Soggy and exhausted, Kentucky's two top government executives sent telegrams, gave orders, and made lists, but their efforts were not enough.

State officials soon recognized that the crisis was beyond their ability to remedy. Lieutenant Governor Johnson warned Chandler even while the governor was still in Virginia that "all resources of the State are being utilized. But, it is apparent that they will be inadequate."[86] Chandler agreed and sent at least three telegrams to President Roosevelt within twenty-four hours in which he described the Kentucky situation as "frightful" and requested Coast Guard cutters, army engineers, and a "generous supply of money." Federal response to these requests, he explained, would be the "only way to prevent cruel and extensive suffering" in the state.[87] Washington officials moved quickly and generously. Army personnel from Fort Knox and other military installations helped maintain order, evacuate victims, and supply blankets, cots, and assorted emergency equipment. George Goodman rushed more than twelve thousand WPA employees to flooded areas in forty counties to construct levees, build latrines, distribute food, repair buildings, and organize refugee camps. He was particularly pleased with the stockade and tent city that his workers built to house the twenty-nine hundred convicts from the evacuated state prison.[88] Many CCC enrollees left camp sites and did emergency rescue and construction work along the river banks. NYA youth also assisted, especially with Red Cross and hospital work. In Louisville several NYA students operated a flood relief canteen that, on one brief occasion, became one of Jefferson County's finest dining spots. The driver of a stranded delivery truck—rather than abandon his wares—donated to the NYA his cargo of crabmeat, lobster, and caviar.[89]

Other New Deal agencies contributed to the process of reconstruction once the flood waters receded and to the documentation of the episode. Congressman Brent Spence, whose district included badly damaged Covington, conferred with Harry Hopkins about flood relief. One result of this meeting was the creation of the Disaster Loan Corporation, which extended credit to individuals, municipalities, and institutions for rebuilding and repair. The HOLC, FHA, RFC, FCA, and the Resettlement Administration all pledged low-interest loans for affected families and property owners.[90] And for those who wanted to reminisce about aquatic horrors in a civilized setting, the Farm Security Administration captured dramatic portions of the flood in its documentary film *The River*. Pare Lorentz had been shooting this film on the Mississippi when the January flood intervened. He quickly revised his script and guided his boat up the raging Ohio, "shooting pictures of the ruined cities" as he plied upstream.[91] The completed film, which opened in commercial theaters several months later, included several references to Hickman, Paducah, and Henderson.

Both the nature of politics and the politics of nature made Kentuckians aware of the shifting balance of power in the 1930s. This shift could be seen in the return of primary campaigns, the rise of new voting blocs such as organized labor, and the influence of federal relief and presidential coattails during elections. The New Deal had become a primal force. A damaging drought and an equally devastating flood confirmed that the federal government commanded greater resources for combating natural emergencies than did individuals and the commonwealth. The crises accelerated a shift from self-reliance and state autonomy to greater dependence on national ministrations. Kentuckians transplanted to Washington seemed to adapt with greater ease to these shifts than did their political counterparts who remained at home in the commonwealth. Some—such as Barkley, Vinson, and Reed—welcomed the transfer of power, helped to advance it, and reaped political rewards for their efforts. Others—such as Laffoon and Chandler—fought rearguard battles against the New Deal and generally lost. Chandler's request for a "generous supply" of flood relief in 1937, juxtaposed to his attacks on federal deficit spending in 1938, reveals the dilemma of a man unable to adapt to the new political realities. By 1940, however, Keen Johnson and most Kentuckians had accepted the shifting balance of power and learned to live in harmony with the New Deal. Even the Republican party in the state adapted to the new ground rules, as John Sherman Cooper—one of the GOP's most successful vote-getters in the 1940s and 1950s—demonstrated many times in the Senate. His earlier praise for the WPA was prophetic of his later defenses of TVA and other New Deal legacies.

# 8. New Deal Legacy in Kentucky

Beyond the political shift of power to Washington, the temporary strengthening of the Democratic party, and the liberalizing of the Republican party in Kentucky, the New Deal had a lasting impact on the state. Early and incomplete statistics revealed that federal programs during the 1930s spent more than $650 million in the state, or roughly $250 for every resident.[1] The immediate effect of this financial infusion was obvious in the revival of Kentucky's economy, and its Keynesian aftereffects remained usable and visible in new roads, bridges, and public facilities. But when the emergency programs such as WPA, CCC, and NYA expired during World War II, was life really that much different than before? Was the New Deal only a brief and dramatic attack on the Great Depression, which passed into history once its mission was complete? Or did it sink roots in Kentucky soil and continue to thrive for years thereafter? The answer has to be the latter. These roots were probably not as pervasive as those that flourished in Tennessee's river valleys or in the industrial centers of Indiana and Ohio, but they were stronger than those that struggled to penetrate the hostile soil of Virginia.[2] Life was different from what it had been, because the New Deal introduced new ideas and accelerated other trends that had already begun to transform the commonwealth.

The most obvious legacy of the New Deal in Kentucky was the enrichment and improvement of the land. Memories of Henry A. Wallace notwithstanding, Kentucky farms were more productive and profitable and the land was better managed because of New Deal innovations. The CCC transformed thousands of acres of scrubby, barren, or eroded hillsides into renewed farms and forests. By planting millions of seedlings, improving fire control, and slowing erosion, the corps not only reversed the decline of some land but also created new natural resources on previously desolate sites. The enlargement and improvement of the state parks system by Roosevelt's "forest army" helped turn it into one of the nation's finest. TVA's Kentucky Dam and its reservoir, perhaps the most visible legacy of New Deal land management, helped control floods, provided inexpensive fertilizers for soil enrichment, and developed new recreational potential. The area between the Tennessee and Cumberland rivers once produced poor crops and moonshine; it now enjoys bountiful agricultural and tourist profits. The AAA collaborated with both the CCC and the TVA to assist Kentucky farmers in better soil conservation. Seminars, test farms, greenhouse experiments, and model projects helped bring more scientific and productive planning to Kentucky crop- and pastureland. The Resettlement and Farm Security Administrations convinced some farmers that the best way to use their land was to abandon it and have it turned into forests. By purchasing hundreds of exhausted plots, moving families to other areas, and ceding the land to the forestry service, Rexford Tugwell's staff redeemed both soil and people. That private or state initiatives might later have accomplished all these things is a moot point; the New Deal plowed quickly and thoroughly through these new fields.

Stabilizing the economy and guaranteeing its continued stability was another legacy of the New Deal. The FDIC restored confidence in banks, protected depositors, and guaranteed that there would be no recurrence of the panic and hysteria that earlier had devastated the state. The SEC brought greater order to securities markets. Kentuckians who invested and traded at America's stock exchanges would no longer be gambling in unregulated bull and bear markets as they had in 1929. The New Deal attacked and partially corrected the historical problem of agricultural surpluses and penniless farmers. Although the specific AAA programs of the 1930s have given way to other measures, the concept of federal production controls and price supports prevails. Kentuckians still participate in surplus commodity purchase-and-distribution activity, and tobacco farmers are heavily dependent on the Department of Agriculture. Federal measures to liberalize credit and provide new mortgage options saved thousands of Kentucky properties from sheriffs' auctions during the Depression. Like the changing agricultural programs, many lending activities of that era have evolved into new ones, but the principle of government-underwritten loans continues. These and other examples of "managed capitalism" have replaced much of the boom-and-bust economics that preceded the Great Crash.

From the ill-fated NRA Blue Eagle in 1933 to the Fair Labor Standards Act of 1938, the New Deal brought about major changes in conditions for labor. Through a combination of federal and state laws, favorable court decisions, and sometimes violent recruiting, labor unions became a force to be reckoned with in corporate planning and political campaigns. Eastern Kentucky coal mine operators were among the most reluctant to accept this new reality, but they gradually fell into line. During this decade, child labor restrictions, unemployment compensation, retirement pensions, minimum wages, maximum working hours, and tighter federal regulations on various corporate activities emerged as government policies. Subsequent legislation, most notably the Taft-Hartley Act of 1947, altered many of these labor policies; the basic direction of the government, however, has remained. Today, when a grocery clerk in Pikeville earns minimum wage and a factory worker in Paducah exercises union privileges it is because the New Deal took up the cause of the country's workers.

Without coercive legislation the New Deal also wrought lasting social changes in Kentucky. Through a variety of programs it introduced twentieth-century technology to rural areas of the state. REA and TVA electricity made available modern conveniences that had been standard for more than a generation among urban Kentuckians. Incandescent bulbs brightened life; vacuum sweepers and milking machines reduced burdens and brought additional leisure time; and radios hastened the cultural homogenization of the commonwealth. The New Deal sent thousands of CCC youth to distant parts of America, where they lived and worked with enrollees from Idaho, New York, and Florida, broadening their horizons and weakening provincial barriers and stereotypes. These changes in the 1930s brought about an increasing sophistication concerning worldly things. The rest of the state did not become more like Louisville because of the New Deal; rural Kentucky did, however, narrow the cultural gap and learn to better understand and appreciate the urban benefits the Falls City had enjoyed for years.

Among the most important legacies the New Deal left the state was the rescue and resuscitation of education. Many Kentuckians were ashamed of the state's high illiteracy rate and its low level of financial support for public schools. Both threatened to become even worse as the Depression kept children out of the classroom and reduced school funding. The NYA programs allowed thousands of Kentucky youths to stay in high school and college. Thousands more learned from the NYA vocational workshops. This federal program helped prevent the intellectual atrophy of one academic generation and the potential scarcity of trained leaders in the next. The WPA and PWA performed the same rescue operation for educational facilities. They built hundreds of classrooms, gymnasiums, libraries, and laboratories that otherwise would not have existed until after World War II. Many unemployed teachers stayed in their profession during this decade only because of WPA projects. CCC camps enhanced these efforts by offering classes for illiterates and by arranging, in conjunction with nearby schools, for several young men to complete high school degrees while on the job. In the process of these human salvage operations, many institutions—both public and private—benefited from stabilized enrollments and the improvement of physical facilities. At the very least, the New Deal educational activities kept Kentucky from falling further behind, no mean achievement in the 1930s.

A particularly enduring—albeit comparatively minor—contribution the New Deal made to the future was to preserve part of Kentucky's past. Several programs during the 1930s collected and conserved fragments of the state's history that could well have been lost. The often-maligned WPA undertook most of these projects, and it frequently used professional historians to assist in the recapture of Kentucky's heritage. Both the American Guide series and the interviews with former slaves were flawed but valuable. Likewise, the Folk Song Project provided a rich source of oral traditions. The Historical Records Survey and the Historic American Buildings Survey compiled inventories of documents and architectural monuments around the state, which are still useful to researchers. Other WPA employees microfilmed newspaper collections, refurbished historic shrines, cataloged museum holdings, and duplicated indigenous art forms for the Index of American Design. All these federally sponsored activities prevented the loss of irreplaceable artifacts. For this specialized legacy alone the New Deal should command the gratitude of historians.

Perhaps the most controversial legacy of the Roosevelt years was the never-ending debate over the relationship of the individual to the state. The Depression and the New Deal tested traditional concepts of individualism and government authority. Did the private sector and charitable institutions have sole responsibility for jobs, relief, housing, and pensions? Or was a "welfare state" permissible? Would government assumption of these responsibilities destroy individual initiative? A western Kentucky physician complained in 1939 that seeing the "reliefers" on government work projects made him "mad thru and thru"; they should be "hustling for themselves" instead of having easy welfare sap their initiative away.[3] A few months later a journalist from the eastern part of the state doubted that government relief had much to do with the level of self-reliance. He argued that desperate "conditions already had destroyed initiative before the WPA came along."[4] An incident in late 1932 indicated that the latter viewpoint was the more reasonable. Governor Laffoon requested huge amounts of relief funding from President Hoover's RFC, and Kentucky local governments and individuals exhausted those revenues before the New Deal ever inaugurated its welfare programs. The federal government did not have to force bankrupt governments to apply for these funds; nor did it have to persuade the citizens to clamor for them.

Some conservatives feared that state autonomy might join individualism in the ranks of the endangered and obsolete. Would continued reliance on federal aid weaken local and state governments as their constituents looked increasingly to Washington for help? With measures including the WPA, Social Security, and the Federal Housing Administration, national responsibilities increased and those of the states diminished. Frankfort officials generated fewer initiatives while Washington planners assumed more. Even when the New Deal attempted to decentralize some of its activities by establishing regional offices, these were located, more often than not, outside of Frankfort; the WPA was in Louisville, the AAA in Lexington, Social Security in several cities. As temporary programs of the 1930s evolved into lasting services of the welfare state, the pattern remained the same. National headquarters continued to be the primary source of funding, whether the conduit was the Job Corps in the 1960s or Revenue Sharing in the 1970s. Recent attempts by the Nixon and Reagan administrations to reverse this trend and return some responsibilities to states and individuals are an indication that the half century of debate has not ended. Perhaps their more conservative "New Federalism" will prompt a renewed growth of state powers and private duties. But after five decades without these financial burdens, private citizens and Kentucky politicians may not want them back.

# Notes

## Introduction

1. Bank Holiday Proclamation, Feb. 28, 1933, box 17, Governor's Papers, 1931-35, Kentucky Department of Libraries and Archives, Frankfort. See also, *Frankfort State Journal*, March 1, 1933.
2. Commonwealth of Kentucky, Division of Banking, *Annual Reports, 1928-32*, n.p.
3. Susan E. Kennedy, *The Banking Crisis of 1933* (Lexington: Univ. Press of Kentucky, 1973), 151.

## 1. Hard Times in the Commonwealth

1. Bureau of the Census, *Statistical Abstracts of the U.S., 1930* (Washington: GPO, 1931), 387.
2. *Fifteenth Census of the United States, 1930*, 6:10.
3. *Statistical Abstracts, 1930*, 387.
4. *Census, 1930*, 6:52.
5. William A. White, *A Puritan in Babylon: The Story of Calvin Coolidge*, (New York: Macmillan, 1930), 395.
6. *Kentucky Progress Magazine* 1, no. 1 (Sept. 1928).
7. Speech manuscript, Jan. 15, 1929, box 53, Keen Johnson Collection, Eastern Kentucky Univ. Archives, Richmond.
8. *Census, 1930*, 1:15.
9. Ibid., 24, 31.
10. Ibid., 6:588.
11. *Thirteenth Census of the United States, 1910*, 9:392, 394.
12. *Census, 1930*, 6:590.
13. Commonwealth of Kentucky, Department of Mines and Minerals, *Annual Report, 1938*, 15-16.
14. "Kentucky Leads," *Kentucky Progress Magazine*, 1, no. 1 (Sept. 1928): 9, 68.

15. Kentucky Progress Commission, *First Report* (Dec. 6, 1929), 21.

16. *Statistical Abstracts of the United States, 1932* (Washington: GPO, 1933), 344, 351.

17. Commonwealth of Kentucky, Department of Agriculture, *Kentucky Agricultural Statistics, 1950*, 22-24.

18. *Statistical Abstracts, 1932*, 592.

19. "First Report" *Kentucky Progress Magazine* (Jan. 1930), 79.

20. John Kenneth Galbraith, *The Great Crash, 1929* (Boston: Houghton Mifflin Co. 1954), 117.

21. John Slaughter, *Income Received in the Various States, 1929-1935* (New York: National Industrial Conference Board, 1937), 33.

22. *Lexington Herald*, Oct. 26, 1929.

23. Kennedy, *Banking Crisis* 147.

24. Kentucky Division of Banking, *Annual Reports, 1928-30*, n.p.

25. *Courier-Journal*, (Louisville), Nov. 17, 1930.

26. Ibid., Dec. 19, 1937.

27. Emma G. Cromwell, *Woman in Politics* (Louisville: Standard Printing, 1939), 192.

28. Ibid., 196.

29. Kentucky Division of Banking, *Annual Report, 1931-32*, n.p.

30. Commonwealth of Kentucky, Agricultural and Industrial Development Board, *Deskbook of Kentucky Economic Statistics, 1952*, table I, p. 2.

31. Ibid., table I, p. 14.

32. U.S. Department of Labor, *Industrial Employment Information Bulletin* (May 1932), 13.

33. W.F. Axton, *Tobacco and Kentucky* (Lexington: Univ. Press of Kentucky, 1975), 111-12.

34. Kentucky Department of Mines, *Annual Report, 1938*, 15-16.

35. For an exhaustive treatment of the Harlan County situation, see John W. Hevener, *Which Side Are You On? The Harlan County Coal Miners, 1931-1939* (Urbana: Univ. of Illinois Press, 1978). See also Tony Bubka, "The Harlan County Coal Strike of 1931," *Labor History* 11 (Winter 1970): 41-57; John F. Day, *Bloody Ground* (1941; reprint, Lexington: Univ. Press of Kentucky, 1981), chap. 19.

36. Flem D. Sampson to Adjutant General W.H. Jones, May 6, 1931, box 2, Governors' Papers.

37. *New York Times*, Oct. 10, 1931; Kentucky Department of Mines, *Annual Report, 1931*, 10.

38. *Census, 1930* 1:391.

39. L.A. Halbert, Report, Oct. 6, 1931, box 245, ser. 10, President's

Organization on Unemployment Relief, RG 73, National Archives. See also James T. Patterson, *The New Deal and the States: Federalism in Transition* (Princeton: Princeton Univ. Press, 1969), 26.

40. Commonwealth of Kentucky, Department of Labor, *Biennial Report, 1931-33,* 6.

41. *Congressional Record,* 72d Cong., 1st sess., 3075.

42. Commonwealth of Kentucky, Department of Health, *Bulletin of the State Board of Health* (1930-33).

43. Kentucky Department of Agriculture, *Agricultural Statistics, 1950,* 22-24.

44. Frankfort *State Journal,* Aug. 6, 9, 1930.

45. *New York Times,* Feb. 5, 1933.

46. John L. Johnson, *Income in Kentucky* (Lexington: Univ. Press of Kentucky, 1955), 13.

47. *Lexington Herald,* Feb. 3, 1933.

48. *Statistical Abstracts of the United States, 1930,* 387, *1931,* 405, *1932,* 360, *1933,* 336.

49. Harris G. Warren, *Herbert Hoover and the Great Depression* (New York: Norton, 1967), 22, 29.

50. Herbert C. Hoover, *The State Papers and Other Public Writings of Herbert Hoover,* ed. William Starr Myers (New York: Doubleday, 1934), 1:12.

51. Herbert C. Hoover, *The Memoirs of Herbert Hoover: The Great Depression, 1929-1941* (London: Hollis and Carter, 1953), 33-37.

52. Gilbert C. Fite, *George N. Peek and the Fight for Farm Parity* (Norman: Univ. of Oklahoma Press, 1954), 226.

53. Warren, *Hoover,* 94.

54. Patterson, *New Deal and the States,* 27-29.

55. Warren, *Hoover,* 197.

56. Frankfort *State Journal,* Oct. 3, 1929.

57. See George W. Robinson, "Conservation in Kentucky: The Fight to Save Cumberland Falls, 1926-1931," *Register of the Kentucky Historical Society* 81 (Winter 1983); 25-58.

58. Frankfort *State Journal,* March 21, 1930.

59. Flem Sampson, Proclamation, Oct. 15, 1930, box 2, Governors' Papers.

60. Ibid., Dec. 3, 1930.

61. L.A. Halbert, Report, Oct. 16, 1931, box 245, ser. 10, POUR Records.

62. Halbert, report, Oct. 30-Nov. 7, 1931, ibid.

63. Harry Bullock to Walter Gifford, Dec. 4, 1931, ibid.

64. *Congressional Record,* 72d Cong. 1st sess. 3070.

65. Ibid., appendix, 3144-45.

66. Edgar E. Robinson and Vaughn D. Bornet, *Herbert Hoover, President of the U.S.* (Stanford: Hoover Institution Press, 1975), 220.

67. Vernon Gipson, *Ruby Laffoon, Governor of Kentucky, 1931-1935* (Hartford, Ky.: McDowell, 1978), 4.

68. Griffenhagen and Associates to Ruby Laffoon, Feb. 15, 1932, copy in box 102, Albert Benjamin Chandler Papers, Special Collections, University of Kentucky Library, Lexington.

69. Kentucky Bankers Association, "Official Proceedings" (40th Annual Convention, June 1932), 2; "RFC-First Quarterly Report," April 1, 1932, *Senate Documents* no. 75, 72d Cong., 1st sess., 4; "Activities and Expenditures of the RFC," Dec. 19, 1932, *House Documents* no. 515, 72d Cong. 2d sess., 6; "Report of Activity of the RFC," March 31, 1933, *House Documents* no. 13, 73d Cong., 1st sess., 7; "Report of the RFC," May 9, 1933, *House Documents* no. 34, ibid., 14.

70. *Frankfort State Journal,* March 4, 1932.

71. *New York Times,* March 27, 1932.

72. Laffoon to RFC, July 21, 1932, box 35, ser. 86 RFC Records, RG 234, National Archives.

73. Bullock to Fred Croxton, July 22, 1932, ibid.

74. *Courier-Journal,* July 31, 1932.

75. Ibid., July 23, 1932.

76. Rowland Haynes to Croxton, Sept. 1, 1932, box 35, ser. 86, RFC Records.

77. Petition to RFC, Sept. 1932, ibid.

78. *Courier-Journal,* Sept. 25, 1932.

79. Croxton to Laffoon, Dec. 30, 1932, box 35, ser. 86, RFC Records.

80. *Courier-Journal,* Oct. 6, 1932.

81. Harper Gatton to Croxton, Jan. 18, 1933, box 35, ser. 86, RFC Records.

82. John B. Rodes, "Bowling Green Benefits Thru Constructive Efforts of RFC Labor," *Kentucky City* 4 (Aug. 1933): 5-6.

83. Gatton to Laffoon, Financial Report, Feb. 28, 1933 box 35, ser. 86, RFC Records.

84. *Louisville Times,* March 14, 1933.

85. Gatton to Laffoon, May 31, 1933, box 35, ser. 86, RFC Records.

86. *Louisville Times,* Feb. 14, 1933.

87. "Report of the RFC," 2, 14.

88. Robert F. Sexton, "Kentucky Politics and Society, 1919-1932" (Ph.D. diss. Univ. of Washington, 1970), 231.

89. Alben W. Barkley, *That Reminds Me* (New York: Doubleday, 1954), 139.

## 2. Banks, Homes, and the Indigent

1. Frankfort *State Journal*, March 2, 1933; Frank Freidel, *Franklin D. Roosevelt: Launching the New Deal* (Boston: Little, Brown, 1973), 202.

2. Kennedy, *Banking Crisis*, 161.

3. Franklin D. Roosevelt, *The Public Papers and Addresses of Franklin D. Roosevelt*, ed. Samuel I. Rosenman 13 vols. (New York: Random House, 1938-50), 2:11-15.

4. Proclamation, March 9, 1933, box 17, Governor's Papers.

5. *Lexington Herald*, March 1-8, 1933; Frankfort *State Journal*, March 8, 1933.

6. *Congressional Record*, 73d Cong., 1st sess., 209.

7. Kennedy, *Banking Crisis*, 177-79.

8. Roosevelt, *Public Papers*, 2:61-65.

9. Frankfort *State Journal*, March 16, 1933.

10. Ibid., March 17, 1933.

11. David Maynard to Harry Hopkins, Dec. 10, 1934, container 66, Harry L. Hopkins Papers, Franklin D. Roosevelt Library, Hyde Park, N.Y.

12. *American Bankers Association Journal* (June 1933), 28.

13. *Ibid.*, (May 1934), 37.

14. James F.T. O'Conner, *The Banking Crisis and Recovery under the Roosevelt Administration* (1938; reprint New York: Da Capo; 1971), 24.

15. Federal Deposit Insurance Corporation, *Annual Report, 1941* (Washington: GPO, 1942), 102.

16. Kentucky Division of Banking, *Annual Reports, 1933-35*, n.p.; *Courier-Journal*, Sept. 13, 1935.

17. Roosevelt, *Public Papers* 2:136.

18. A.J.B. to Fred Vinson, May 31, 1933, box 25, Frederick M. Vinson Papers, Special Collections, University of Kentucky Library, Lexington.

19. Federal Home Loan Bank Board, *Annual Report, 1933* (Washington: GPO, 1934), 4, 9.

20. Roosevelt, *Public Papers* 2:13.

21. HOLC, *Report, 1936* (Washington: GPO, 1937), 41.

22. *Courier-Journal*, July 25, 1933.

23. HOLC, *Report, 1933*, 53, *1934*, Exhibit "A"; *Louisville Times*, Aug. 17, 1934.

24. *Louisville Times*, Aug. 17, 1934.

25. HOLC, *Report, 1937*, 180.

26. *Louisville Times*, April 20, 1936.

27. *Courier-Journal*, Feb. 2, 1940.

28. Roosevelt, *Public Papers* 2:85-89.

29. Ibid., 180.

30. Arthur M. Schlesinger, Jr., *The Coming of the New Deal* (Boston: Houghton Mifflin, 1959), 45.

31. William Gregory to Henry Morgenthau, Oct. 25, 1933, William Voris Gregory Papers, Pogue Library, Murray State Univ., Murray, Ky.

32. *Courier-Journal*, March 1, 1936.

33. Marvel Logan, Speech Manuscript, April 8, 1936, copy in box 100, Chandler Papers.

34. National Emergency Council Report, "Kentucky, February 23, 1938," box 1938, Brent Spence Papers, Special Collections, Univ. of Kentucky Library, Lexington.

35. Federal Housing Administration, *7th Annual Report for the Year Ending, December 31, 1940* (Washington: GPO, 1941), 8.

36. Ibid.

37. *Courier-Journal*, Sept. 21. 1935.

38. Proclamation, Sept. 27, 1935, box 20, Governors' Papers.

39. *Courier-Journal*, Sept. 8, 1935.

40. FHA, *7th Annual Report*, 59; *Courier-Journal*, Oct. 21, 1940.

41. Paul K. Conkin, *The New Deal* (New York: Thomas Y. Crowell, 1967), 63.

42. Federal Works Agency, *Annual Report, 1941* (Washington: GPO, 1942), 399-400; *Courier-Journal*, Oct. 25, 1939.

43. *Lexington Herald*, Jan. 2, 1938.

44. Roosevelt, *Public Papers*, 4:472.

45. For a brief, general overview of the Social Security provisions, see Social Security Board, *1st Annual Report of the Social Security Board, Fiscal Year Ending June 30, 1936* (Washington: GPO, 1937), 1-9.

46. Ibid., 9; Patterson, *The New Deal and the States*, 85-86.

47. Constantine W. Curris, "State Public Welfare Developments in Kentucky," *Register of the Kentucky Historical Society* 64 (Oct. 1966): 303, 312-13.

48. Robert S. McElvaine, ed., *Down and Out in the Great Depression: Letters from the "Forgotten Man"* (Chapel Hill: Univ. of North Carolina Press, 1983), 103, 106.

49. E.J.H. to A.B. Chandler Nov. 15, 1935, and D.J. to Chandler, Nov. 14, 1935, box 4, Chandler Papers.

50. J.L.G. to Chandler, May 26, 1935, box 8, ibid.

51. Urey Woodson to Arthur Krock, Nov. 26, 1935, Urey Woodson Papers, Special Collections, Univ. of Kentucky Library, Lexington.
52. *Louisville Times*, July 6, 1935.
53. Ibid., Aug. 15, 1935.
54. Campaign material, 1935, boxes 7, 10, Chandler Papers.
55. Jasper B. Shannon, "Happy Chandler: A Kentucky Epic," in *The American Politician*, ed. J.T. Salter (Chapel Hill: University of North Carolina Press, 1938), 175.
56. Inaugural Address, 1935, box 586, Chandler Papers.
57. Commonwealth of Kentucky, *House Journal*, 1936, 1:22.
58. Frankfort *State Journal*, Feb. 6, 1936; *Courier-Journal*, Feb. 15, 1936.
59. Social Security Board, *1st Annual Report*, 102, 105.
60. Terry L. Birdwhistell, "A.B. 'Happy' Chandler," in *Kentucky: Its History and Heritage*, ed. Fred J. Hood (St. Louis: Forum Press, 1978), 212-15.
61. Commonwealth of Kentucky, *Acts of the General Assembly*, special sess. 1936, 25.
62. Keen Johnson, Speech Manuscript, 1936, "New Deal in Kentucky," box 53, Johnson Papers.
63. *Lexington Herald*, May 2, 1936.
64. Kathleen Lowrie, Social Security Board district representative, to Chandler, June 15, 1936, box 84, Chandler Papers.
65. Donald Slone, Public Administration Service director, to Chandler, July 13, 1936, ibid.
66. Speech Manuscript, 1936, box 586, ibid. For a detailed account of the early administrative problems, see Charles McKinley and Robert W. Frase, *Launching Social Security: A Capture-and-Record Account, 1935-1937* (Madison: Univ. of Wisconsin Press, 1970), 177-80.
67. *Louisville Times*, Aug. 24, 1936; *Courier-Journal*, Aug. 25, 1936; Carrollton *News-Democrat*, Aug. 27, 1936.
68. W.R.M. to Chandler, Aug. 25, 1936, box 84, Chandler Papers.
69. Kentucky Old Age Assistance Grants, Report, Aug. 1936, ibid.
70. Report from Division of Public Assistance, Oct. 1937, box 83, ibid.
71. Frederick Wallis to Chandler, Oct. 19, 1937, ibid.
72. Frank Peterson to Chandler, Oct. 19, 1937, and A.Y. Lloyd to W.C., May 6, 1938, ibid.
73. Report from Division of Public Assistance, May and June 1938, ibid.
74. Social Security Board, *6th Annual Report of the Social Security*

*Board for the Fiscal Year Ended June 30, 1941* (Washington: GPO, 1941), 196, 199.

75. Chandler to Arthur Altmeyer, May 10, 1938, box 81, Chandler Papers.

76. Patterson, *New Deal and the States*, 91.

77. Schlesinger, *Coming of the New Deal*, 314-15.

## 3. Relief and Public Works

1. Roosevelt, *Public Papers* 2:183-85.

2. Theodore E. Whiting, *Final Statistical Report of the Federal Emergency Relief Administration* (Washington: GPO, 1942), iii.

3. Work Projects Administration, *Final Report on the W.P.A. Program, 1935-1943* (Washington: GPO, 1946), 2-3.

4. Neville Miller, "Relief—the American Way," *Kentucky City* 7(June 1936): 6.

5. *Courier Journal*, Nov. 2, 1933.

6. Searle F. Charles, *Minister of Relief: Harry Hopkins and the Depression* (Syracuse: Syracuse Univ. Press, 1963), 36.

7. In container 57, Hopkins Papers, are several folders of field agent reports from Kentucky.

8. *New York Times*, July 12, 1933; Russel Kurtz, "Two Months of the New Deal in Federal Relief," *Survey* 69(April 1933): 286.

9. Orval W. Baylor, *J. Dan Talbott: Champion of Good Government* (Louisville: Kentucky Printing Corp. 1942), 231.

10. *Courier-Journal*, Aug. 3, 1933.

11. Proclamation, Aug. 10, 1933, box 17, Governors' Papers.

12. Frankfort *State Journal*, Aug. 23, 1933.

13. Ibid., Sept. 5, 1933.

14. Baylor, *J. Dan Talbott*, 247-49; *Woodford Sun* (Versailles), Sept. 28, 1933.

15. Thomas H. Coode and John F. Bauman, "Dear Mr. Hopkins: A New Dealer Reports from Eastern Kentucky," *Register of the Kentucky Historical Society* 78 (Winter 1980): 56.

16. Lorena Hickok to Hopkins, Sept. 6, 1933, container 67, Hopkins Papers.

17. Maynard to Hopkins, Dec. 10, 1934, and Mary Atkinson to Aubrey Williams, June 8, 1935, containers 66, 57, ibid.

18. National Emergency Council, Conference of State Directors, Report, Jan. 31-Feb. 3, 1934, copy in case 19, box 438, Frank Walker Papers, University of Notre Dame Archives, Notre Dame, Ind.

19. Robert F. Hunter, "Virginia and the New Deal," in *The New Deal: The State and Local Levels*, ed. John Braeman et al. (Columbus: Ohio State Univ. Press, 1975), 111.

20. Frankfort *State Journal*, Oct. 3, 4, 5, 1933.

21. *Courier-Journal*, Nov. 6, 1933.

22. Howard Hunter to Hopkins, Nov. 6, 1933, container 57, Hopkins Papers.

23. *Courier-Journal*, Nov. 8, 1933.

24. Hunter to Hopkins, Dec. 7, 1933, Jan. 19, 1934, container 57, Hopkins Papers.

25. Laffoon to J. Dan Talbott, May 18, 1934, box 18, Governors' Papers.

26. Hunter to Hopkins, Sept. 18, 1934, Hopkins Papers. container 57.

27. Frankfort *State Journal*, Sept. 12, 1934.

28. *Herald-Post* (Louisville), Sept. 27, 1934; *Courier-Journal*, Oct. 1, 1934.

29. Whiting, *FERA*, 265.

30. Ibid., 129, 169-70.

31. KERA Bulletins, Nov., Dec. 1934, box 301, Records of the WPA in Kentucky, Kentucky Department of Libraries and Archives, Frankfort.

32. KERA, Bulletin no. 182, ibid.; (hereinafter cited as WPA-KY Records) L.F. Brashear, "A Relief Officer Looks at Relief," *Mountain Life and Work* (Oct. 1934), 8.

33. KERA Account Statement, box 115, Chandler Papers.

34. Brashear, "Relief Officer," 8-9; Rosemary Kutak, *Unemployment Relief in Kentucky* (Louisville: KERA, 1934), 6.

35. *Herald-Post*, March 5, 1935; *Louisville Times*, Nov. 27, 1935.

36. WPA, *Final Report*, 6.

37. Patterson, *New Deal and the States*, 71.

38. Whiting, *FERA*, 7.

39. WPA, *Final Report*, 3.

40. Charles, *Minister of Relief*, 47.

41. WPA, *Final Report*, 3-4.

42. Paul A. Kurzman, *Harry Hopkins and the New Deal* (Fairlawn, N.J.: R.E. Burdick, 1974), 96.

43. WPA,*Final Report*, 4.

44. Edward R. Ellis, *A Nation in Torment: The Great American Depression, 1929-39* (New York: Coward-McCann, 1970), 499.

45. Roland R. Pyne, "The Civil Works Program in Kentucky," *Kentucky City* 4(May 1934): 5, 7.

46. "Federal Aid in Kentucky," *Kentucky City* 4 (March 1934): 7.

47. William F. McDonald, *Federal Relief Administration and the Arts* (Columbus: Ohio State Univ. Press, 1969), 371; CWA, Final Report, reel 37, WPA-KY Records.

48. CWA, Final Report.

49. *Courier-Journal*, March 11, 1934.

50. *Lexington Herald*, March 17, 1934.

51. Charles, *Minister of Relief*, 61.

52. Roosevelt, *Public Papers* 4:19-20, 163.

53. WPA, *Final Report*, 111, 120.

54. George Goodman to Chandler, Dec. 10, 1935, box 114, Chandler Papers.

55. Chandler to Talbott, "Revenue Transfer Authorizations," Dec. 20, 1935, Feb. 6, March 13, 1936, boxes 114, 115, Chandler Papers.

56. WPA Scrapbook, no. 3, George H. Goodman Papers, Special Collections, Univ. of Kentucky Library, Lexington; *Lexington Herald*, June 6, 1936.

57. WPA Scrapbook, no. 2, Goodman Papers.

58. Monthly Narrative Reports, July 20-Aug. 20, 1936, box 5, Goodman Papers. See successive narrative reports for hiring fluctuations.

59. WPA, *Final Report*, 111, 124.

60. Ibid., 135.

61. WPA Scrapbooks, nos. 1, 4, Goodman Papers.

62. WPA, *Final Report*, 136.

63. *Lexington Herald*, May 25, 1937.

64. "Directory and Description of Professional and Service Projects in Kentucky" (1940), 6, in box 309, WPA-KY Records.

65. Sewing Project, "WPA in Kentucky, Final Report," box 21, WPA-KY Records.

66. WPA, *Final Report*, 134.

67. Sewing Project, "WPA in Kentucky, Final Report."

68. Mattress Project, ibid.

69. "Directory and Description," 13.

70. Goodman to Chandler, Feb. 24, Aug. 26, 1937, box 115, Chandler Papers.

71. School Lunch Program, "WPA in Kentucky, Final Report," box 21, WPA-KY Records.

72. Garden and Canning Program, ibid.

73. "Directory and Description," 26; Austin Welch, "W.P.A. Recreation Programs in Kentucky Cities," *Kentucky City*, 9 (Dec. 1938-Jan. 1939): 5.

74. Recreation Project, "WPA in Kentucky, Final Report," box 23, WPA-KY Records.

75. "Directory and Description," 27.

76. Welch, "W.P.A. Recreation," 6-7; "Directory and Description," 27; Recreation Project "WPA in Kentucky, Final Report."

77. *Leisure Leader* (Feb.-Mar. 1941), 10, copy in box 23, WPA-KY.

78. WPA, *Final Report*, 62; "Directory and Description," 22.

79. Robert Beach, "Book Extension Services in Eastern Kentucky," *Mountain Life and Work* (Summer 1941), 7; Michael S. Blayney, "Libraries for the Millions: Adult Public Library Services and the New Deal," *Journal of Library History* 12 (Summer 1977): 245.

80. "Kentucky Packhorse Libraries, 1938", box 309, WPA-KY Records; *Courier-Journal*, Dec. 11, 1938.

81. *Lexington Herald,* July 24, 1938; *Courier-Journal*, Aug. 23, 1936, April 15, 1938.

82. *New York Times*, Nov. 12, 1939; Ellen Woodward, "WPA Library Projects," *Wilson Bulletin for Librarians*, 12 (April 1938): 518-20.

83. McDonald, *Federal Relief*, 172.

84. Jerre Mangione, *The Dream and the Deal: The Federal Writers' Project, 1935-1943* (New York: Avon Books, 1972), 4.

85. Ibid.; WPA, *Final Report*, 63.

86. *Ashland Daily Independent,* June 13-14, 1936; Monthly Narrative Report May 20-June 20, 1936, 18, box 5, Goodman Papers.

87. Jean Thomas, *Ballad Makin' in the Mountains of Kentucky* (New York: Henry Holt and Co. 1939), 244.

88. McDonald, *Federal Relief*, 624.

89. Music Project, "W.P.A. in Kentucky, Final Report," box 22, WPA-KY Records.

90. WPA, *Final Report*, 64-65.

91. FAP, "WPA in Kentucky, Final Report," box 22, WPA-KY Records; "Directory and Description," 28. The U.S. Treasury Department also provided art works for federal buildings, twenty-four of which were in Kentucky. Since its commissions were open to all competitors, not just the unemployed, this project was not considered a relief measure. See Marlene Park and Gerald E. Markowitz, *Democratic Vistas: Post Offices and Public Art in the New Deal* (Philadelphia: Temple Univ. Press, 1984).

92. Ibid.; *Courier-Journal*, Feb. 15, 1939; "The Index of American Design, *Design* 40 (Sept. 1938): n.p.; Gordon Smith, "The Shaker Arts and Crafts," in *Art for the Millions*, ed. Francis V. O'Connor (Boston: New York Graphic Society, 1975), 173-75.

93. Richard D. McKinzie, *The New Deal for Artists* (Princeton: Princeton University Press, 1973), 139-41.

94. Irvin S. Cobb to L.C. Turner, Dec. 22, 1935, box 114, Chandler Papers.

95. *Courier-Journal*, Nov. 27, 1938.

96. Harlan Hatcher to Henry Alsberg, Oct. 28, 1938; Thomas D. Clark to Alsberg, March 30, 1939, ser. 13, WPA Records, RG 69, National Archives. See also box 43, WPA-KY Records.

97. Review in *Journal of Southern History* (Nov. 1941), 580-81.

98. Mangione, *Dream and the Deal*, 338-39.

99. Review in *Filson Club History Quarterly* (Oct. 1940), 230.

100. "America Eats" file, box 43, WPA-KY Records.

101. "These Are Our Lives" files, boxes 107-9, WPA-KY Records.

102. See Tom Terrill and Jerrold Hirsch, eds., *Such as Us: Southern Voices of the Thirties* (New York: Norton, 1978); John L. Robinson, *Living Hard: Southern Americans in the Great Depression* (Washington: Univ. Press of America, 1981)

103. B.A. Botkin, ed., *Lay My Burden Down: A Folk History of Slavery* (Chicago: Univ. of Chicago Press, 1945), x-xi.

104. Federal Writers' Project, Introduction, Slave Narratives, vol. 1, Manuscript Division, Library of Congress.

105. Alsberg to Urban Bell, Aug. 2, 1937, in Slave Narratives, box 192, ser. 21, WPA Records.

106. FWP, Slave Narratives, 7: 29, 66.

107. "Directory and Description," 37.

108. George Gallup, *The Gallup Poll: Public Opinion, 1935-1971* (New York: Random House, 1972), 157.

109. "Federal Work Relief in Kentucky," *Kentucky City*, 9 (April 1938):5.

110. Charles, *Minister of Relief*, 229.

111. Goodman to Chandler, Jan. 23, 1936, box 115, Chandler Papers.

112. Bill Cooper interview with John Sherman Cooper, Oral History Project, Special Collections, Univ. of Kentucky Library, Lexington.

113. *Louisville Times*, July 8, 1940.

114. H.L. Donovan to Goodman, Jan. 20, 1943, copy in box 44, Thomas Poe Cooper Papers, Special Collections, Univ. of Kentucky Library, Lexington.

115. *Courier-Journal*, Feb. 16, 1942.

116. FWA, *Annual Report, 1940* (Washington: GPO, 1941), 318.

117. Harold L. Ickes, *The Secret Diary of Harold L. Ickes* (New York: Simon and Schuster, 1954), 2: 139-40.

118. Ibid., passim.
119. FWA, *Annual Report, 1940*, 318.
120. Jack F. Isakoff, *The Public Works Administration* (Urbana: Univ. of Illinois Press, 1938), 90, 94.
121. *Courier-Journal*, July 25, 1937.
122. Public Works Administration, *America Builds: The Record of the PWA* (Washington: GPO, 1939), 107.
123. Ibid., 56, 267-71; "PWA in Kentucky," *Kentucky City* 6 (March 1935): 24-25.
124. PWA Investigations, reel 323, ser. 94, Public Works Administration Records, RG 135, National Archives.
125. *Herald-Post*, July 29, 1935; *Courier-Journal*, July 25, 1937.
126. Chandler to Harold Ickes, Jan. 8, 1937, and Chandler to Alben Barkley, Feb. 15, 1937, boxes 100, 85, Chandler Papers.
127. *Lexington Herald*, June 15, 1937.
128. W.H. Richeson to Barkley, May 18, 1936, Chandler to Ickes, May 25, 1936, and Horatio Hackett to Chandler, July 9, 1936, ser. 44, PWA records.
129. *Times-Journal* (Bowling Green), July 11, 1936.
130. *Louisville Times*, April 10, 1940.

## 4. Kentucky Youth and the New Deal

1. Cromwell, *Woman in Politics*, 237.
2. "NYA for Kentucky" (Nov. 1, 1936), 47, in box 302, WPA-KY Records.
3. Freidel, *Launching the New Deal*, 257.
4. Roosevelt, *Public Papers* 2:80-81.
5. John Salmond, *The Civilian Conservation Corps, 1933-1942: A New Deal Case Study* (Durham: Duke Univ. Press, 1967), 30.
6. Ibid., 27-28.
7. Civilian Conservation Corps, *Handbook for Agencies Selecting Men for Emergency Conservation Work* (Washington: GPO, 1933), 4-5.
8. Perry H. Merrill, *Roosevelt's Forest Army: A History of the Civilian Conservation Corps* (Montpelier, Vt.: privately printed, 1981), 196.
9. Ibid., 130-31; Civilian Conservation Corps, *Annual Report, 1940-41*, 61.
10. CCC, *Annual Report, 1936-37*, 15; Goodman to Chandler, Sept. 30, 1938, box 123, Chandler Papers.
11. CCC, *Annual Report, 1940-41*, 4.

12. CCC, *Handbook*, 6.

13. Salmond, *The CCC*, 100-101.

14. Dean Snyder, Report on Field Trip to Kentucky, April 18, 1935, ser. 59, Civilian Conservation Corps Records, RG 35 National Archives.

15. *Courier-Journal*, Aug. 8, 1941.

16. John D. Minton, *The New Deal in Tennessee, 1932-1938* (New York: Garland, 1979), 59.

17. *Courier-Journal*, Aug. 7, 1939.

18. "Doughboys of 1933 off to the Wood," *Literary Digest*, April 29, 1933, 22; CCC, *Annual Report, 1938-1939*, 4.

19. Frank Linkenberg to Frank Persons, Survey of Social Value of CCC, Aug. 16, 1934, ser. 32, CCC Records.

20. CCC, *Report, April-September 1933*, 4; Kenneth Holland and Frank Hill, *Youth in the CCC* (Washington: American Council on Education, 1942), 77.

21. Mcrrill, *Roosevelt's Forest Army*, 84, 89; author's interviews with Kentucky CCC alumni Oscar Huffman, Willie Himes, Russell Stanford, Oct. 1984.

22. CCC, *Annual Report, 1933-1934*, 7; Salmond, *The CCC*, 34.

23. *Courier-Journal*, Nov. 15, 1936.

24. V.J.F. to Brent Spence, Nov. 26, 1937, box 1937, Spence Papers; Harlan Kiwanis Club to Chandler, April 6, 1939, box 97, Chandler Papers.

25. CCC Camp Directories, 5th period, 1935, ser. 13, CCC Records.

26. Camp Inspection Report, London, 1937, Danville, 1941, and Paducah, 1940, box 115, ibid.

27. Agricultural Extension Service, Annual Report of J.E. Bradfute, 1938-39, box 8, Cooper Papers.

28. CCC, *Annual Report, 1933-34*, 33, and *1935-36*, 38.

29. *Louisville Times*, Oct. 5, 1934; *In Kentucky* (Spring 1937), 18 (Spring 1938), 19.

30. "Cumberland Falls State Park," 14-15; Spindletop Research Project, 311A, Documents Department, Univ. of Kentucky Library, Lexington. See also *Lexington Herald*, April 6, 1940.

31. "CCC Activity in Kentucky, 1935-1942," Photo Albums, ser. 75, CCC Records.

32. Cromwell, *Woman in Politics*, 262-63.

33. Commonwealth of Kentucky, Division of State Parks, *Annual Report, 1940*, 5, 9.

34. CCC, *Annual Report, 1933-34*, 3; Salmond, *The CCC*, 135.

35. CCC, *Annual Report, 1935-36,* 5; *Courier-Journal,* Nov. 15, 1936.

36. Camp Inspection Report, Pine Ridge, 1935, box 115, CCC Records; author's interview with Willie Himes.

37. Holland and Hill, *Youth in the CCC,* 98.

38. CCC, *Report, 1935-36,* 19, and *1939-1940,* 36.

39. Salmond, *The CCC,* 140; Camp Inspection Report, London, March 1937, box 115, CCC Records.

40. P.E. Williams, "The School in the Camps," *Kentucky School Journal* 14 (Jan. 1936): 20.

41. "Columbus-Belmont State Park," 10-12, Spindletop Research Project; Nat Frame, "Kentucky Mountain Boys in the CCC," *Mountain Life and Work* (Oct. 1935), 21.

42. *Courier-Journal,* June 26, Oct. 20, 1940; Salmond, *The CCC,* 195; author's interviews with Kentucky CCC alumni Leroy Brown, Tom Mayne, and Russell Stanford, Oct. 1984.

43. CCC, *Report, 1935-36,* 3.

44. Linkenberg to Dean Snyder, Jan. 26, 1939, ser. 56, CCC Records.

45. Robert Fechner to Laffoon, Feb. 26, 1935, and Laffoon to Fechner, March 19, 1935, ser. 9, CCC Records.

46. Fechner to Chandler, March 15, 1937, ser. 9, CCC Records.

47. Conrad Wirth to Fechner, Dec. 19, 1938, ser. 9, CCC Records.

48. *Louisville Times,* Jan. 27, 1939.

49. Ibid., March 8, 1939.

50. *Henderson Gleaner* and *Pineville Sun,* reprinted in *Louisville Times,* June 14, 1939.

51. *Courier-Journal,* June 23, 1939.

52. Betty Lindley and Ernest K. Lindley, *A New Deal for Youth: The Story of the NYA* (1938; reprint New York; Da Capo Press, 1972), 7; John Salmond, *A Southern Rebel: The Life and Times of Aubrey Willis Williams.* (Chapel Hill: Univ. of North Carolina Press, 1983), 73.

53. Lindley and Lindley, *New Deal for Youth,* 12, 158.

54. Roosevelt, *Public Papers,* 4:281.

55. Ibid., 285-86.

56. Salmond, *A Southern Rebel,* 67.

57. Ibid., 23, 96.

58. Ibid., 138.

59. *Herald-Post,* Jan. 18, 1936.

60. Peterson Interview, July 1977, in the A.B. Chandler Oral History Project, Special Collections, Univ. of Kentucky Library, Lexington.

61. Transcript of "Radio Discussion of Youth Problems and NYA

Activities in Kentucky and Indiana," broadcast over WAVE (Dec. 15, 1937), 3, copy in box 304, WPA—KY Records.
62. NYA for Kentucky, "General Information Bulletin," 1935, box 302, ibid.
63. NYA for Kentucky, "Program Review of Activities," 1935-36, Ibid.
64. "Radio Discussion," 10; "Review of Activities in Kentucky, 1935-1943," 156, box 2, NYA Records, RG 119, National Archives.
65. NYA for KY, "General Information Bulletin."
66. *Herald-Post,* Jan. 18, 1936; Lindley and Lindley, *New Deal for Youth,* 160; "Review of Activities," 126.
67. T.T. Jones and S.B. Holmes, "Administration of Student Aid under NYA," 2, box 110, Chandler Papers.
68. *Herald-Post,* Jan. 18, 1936; "NYA Student Aid Program, Berea College 1936-37," ser. 51, NYA Records; W.G. Marigold and E.S. Bradley, *Union College, 1879-1979* (Barbourville: Union College, 1979), 112; Robert Snyder, *A History of Georgetown College* (Georgetown, Ky.: Georgetown College, 1979), 111-12.
69. NYA for KY, "Program Review," 40-41; "Negro Activities in Kentucky," unpaged, undated pamphlet, NYA Records.
70. "Review of Activities in Kentucky," 85-86. For an analysis of NYA's critics, see Susan Wladaver-Morgan, "Young Women and the New Deal: Camps and Resident Centers, 1933-1943" (Ph.D. diss., Indiana Univ., 1982), chap. 6.
71. W.E. Baxter, "National Youth Administration," *Kentucky School Journal* 15 (Nov. 1936): 26.
72. *Courier-Journal,* April 10, 1938; box 303, WPA-KY Records.
73. "Radio Discussion," 11.
74. "Radio Discussion," 7; "NYA Work Projects in Kentucky, 1936-37," box 302, WPA-KY Records.
75. "Review of Activities," 32.
76. Lindley and Lindley, *New Deal for Youth,* 31; "Outstanding Projects," no. 8231, box 644, ser. 250, NYA Records.
77. W.E. Baxter, "NYA Diversified Program Aids Kentucky Cities," *Kentucky City* 8 (July 1937): 9-11.
78. "Radio Discussion," 6, 8.
79. *Courier-Journal,* April 24, 1941.
80. Palmer O. Johnson and O.L. Harvey, *The National Youth Administration* (1938; reprint New York: Arno Press, 1974), 67.
81. Robert Salyers to Richard Brown, May 1, 1937, and Brown to Salyers, May 4, 1937, ser. 51, NYA Records.

82. Lindley and Lindley, *New Deal for Youth*, 53-54.

83. Salyers to Orren Lull, Aug. 24, 1938, ser. 52, NYA Records.

84. "Basic Information on NYA Workers in Kentucky," 1, box 302, WPA-KY Records.

85. Ibid., 26-47; "NYA Work Projects in Kentucky," 59-76.

86. Mark Bridges to NYA Supervisors, April 12, 1937, ser. 52. NYA Records.

87. Baxter, "NYA Diversified Program," 9.

88. *Courier-Journal*, April 22, 1941.

89. "Review of Activities," 28.

90. Salmond, *A Southern Rebel*, 133; Lindley and Lindley, *New Deal for Youth*, 87, 106.

91. "Review of Activities," 51.

92. *Courier-Journal*, April 23, 1941; Francis Shouse, "The Mountain Youth in NYA," *Mountain Life and Work* (Summer 1940), 26-27.

93. *Courier-Journal*, Dec. 4, 1938.

94. Shouse, "Mountain Youth," 27; *Courier-Journal*, April 23, 1941.

95. *National Youth Advocate* (publication of Murray Resident Center) (July 1940), in State Publications, NYA Records.

96. "Resident Projects for Negro Youth" (unpaged, undated brochure), NYA Records.

97. "Review of Activities," 74; William H. Wooten, "National Youth Administration," *Mountain Life and Work* (Winter 1942) 16; *Courier-Journal*, Jan. 3, 1941.

98. Wooten, "NYA," 18.

99. Lindley and Lindley, *New Deal for Youth*, 10, 211.

100. Author's interview with Tom Mayne, October 1984.

101. Johnson and Harvey, *The National Youth Administration*, 21.

102. Author's interview with Russell Stanford, October, 1984.

## 5. Newly Plowed Fields

1. *Historical Statistics of the U.S.* (Washington: GPO, 1975), pt. 1:483.

2. Henry A. Wallace, *Democracy Reborn* (New York: Reynal and Hitchock, 1944), 40.

3. Roosevelt, *Public Papers* 1:695.

4. Theodore Saloutos, *The American Farmer and the New Deal* (Ames: Iowa State Univ. Press, 1982), 50.

5. Roosevelt, *Public Papers*, 2:74.

6. Saloutos, *The American Farmer*, 48-49.

7. Roosevelt, *Public Papers*, 2:178.

8. Saloutos, *The American Farmer*, 67.
9. Wallace, *Democracy Reborn*, 53.
10. Roosevelt, *Public Papers* 1:709.
11. *Hickman Courier*, July 20, 1933.
12. *Yearbook of Agriculture, 1934*, (Washington: GPO, 1935), 29-32.
13. E.J. Kilpatrick, Extension Service Agent Report (Dec. 1, 1932-Nov. 30, 1933), 12, in College of Agriculture Papers, Special Collections, Univ. of Kentucky Library, Lexington. See also *Hickman Courier*, Aug. 24, 1933.
14. Wallace, *Democracy Reborn*, 53.
15. *Agricultural Statistics, 1942*, (Washington: GPO, 1943), 100.
16. Dennis A. Fitzgerald, *Corn and Hogs under the Agricultural Adjustment Act* (Washington: Brookings Institution, 1934), 2, 7.
17. Dennis A. Fitzgerald, *Livestock Under the Agricultural Adjustment Administration* (Washington: Brookings Institution, 1935), 62.
18. Howard R. Tolly, Reminiscences, 264-65, in Oral History Research Office, Columbia Univ.
19. AAA, Division of Information, "Changes in the Agricultural Situation in Kentucky, 1932-1936," 3, copy in box 1938, Spence Papers.
20. Dean Albertson, *Roosevelt's Farmer: Claude R. Wickard in the New Deal* (New York: Columbia Univ. Press, 1961), 68. Wickard later joined the AAA Corn-Hog Division and then succeeded Wallace as secretary of agriculture.
21. *Chicago Daily Tribune*, Aug. 19, 1933.
22. "Emergency Hog Marketing Program: A Letter from the Secretary of Agriculture," *Senate Documents*, no. 140, 73d Cong., 2d sess., 21-23; Fitzgerald, *Corn and Hogs* 19-20.
23. Henry A. Wallace, *New Frontiers* (New York: Reynal and Hitchcock, 1934), 180.
24. AAA, *Agricultural Adjustment: A Report of Administration of the AAA, May 1933 to February 1934* (Washington: GPO, 1934), 321.
25. Ibid., 113, 322.
26. *Courier-Journal*, Aug. 30, 1933; *Henderson Gleaner*, Aug. 28, 1933.
27. James Benton to Paul Porter, Sept. 8, 1933, box 58, ser. 2, Agricultural Adjustment Administration Records, RG 145, National Archives.
28. Clyde Johnson to Henry Wallace, Sept. 6, 1933, and A.G. Black to Clyde Johnson, Sept. 13, 1933, ibid.
29. Larkin Bell to Vinson, Nov. 12, 1933, and A.H. Calvert to AAA, n.d. [1933], box 59. ibid.
30. Fitzgerald, *Livestock*, 66.

31. AAA, *Report, 1933*, 118.
32. *St. Louis Post-Dispatch*, Sept. 21, 1933.
33. *Courier-Journal*, Aug. 27, 1933.
34. Barkley, *That Reminds Me*, 148.
35. See George T. Blakey, "Ham That Never Was: The 1933 Emergency Hog Slaughter," *Historian* (Nov. 1967), 56.
36. See annual extension service agent reports, arranged by name and county, College of Agriculture Records.
37. AAA, "Changes in the Agricultural Situation," 3; *Lexington Herald*, Feb. 20, 1933.
38. *Congressional Record*, 73d Cong., 2d sess., June 15, 1934, 12331.
39. AAA, *Report, 1933*, 85.
40. *Lexington Herald*, Dec. 12-16, 1933.
41. Ibid., Dec. 17, 1933; Anthony J. Badger, *Prosperity Road: The New Deal, Tobacco, and North Carolina* (Chapel Hill: Univ. of North Carolina Press, 1980), 52.
42. Tobacco Proclamation, Dec. 16, 1933, box 18, Governors' Papers.
43. *Lexington Herald*, Dec. 21, 1933.
44. Ibid., Jan. 1, 1934.
45. *Congressional Record*, 73d Cong., 2d sess., June 15, 1934, 12331.
46. Extension Service, *Annual Report, 1935*, 3; Edwin G. Nourse, et al., *Three Years of the AAA* (Washington: Brookings Institution, 1937), 585.
47. AAA, "Changes in the Agricultural Situation," 2-3, 5.
48. AAA, *Report 1934*, 382-84; Henry I. Richards, *Cotton and the AAA* (Washington: Brookings Institution, 1936), 6, 92.
49. Extension Service, *Annual Report, 1935*, 6.
50. Leroy Northington to Thomas P. Cooper, July 14, 1934, box 14, Cooper Papers.
51. AAA, *Report, 1933-35*, 149, 174, 296; AAA "Changes in the Agricultural Situation," 3, 5.
52. *Farmers Home Journal* (May 1935), 375.
53. *Washington Post*, Dec. 11-12, 1935.
54. Wallace, *Democracy Reborn*, 109.
55. *Farmers Home Journal* (Feb. 1936), n.p.
56. *Frankfort State Journal*, Jan. 7, 17, 1936.
57. William E. Leuchtenburg, *The New Deal: A Documentary History* (Columbia: Univ. of South Carolina Press, 1968), 122.
58. AAA, "Changes in the Agricultural Situation," 6; Albertson, *Rooevelt's Farmer*, 102-3.
59. AAA, "Changes in the Agricultural Situation," 1937 revision, 6.
60. Murray R. Benedict and Oscar C. Stine, *The Agricultural Com-*

*modity Programs: Two Decades of Experience* (New York: Twentieth Century Fund, 1956), xxii, xxv, xxx.

61. *Courier-Journal,* Oct. 16. 1937.

62. AAA, *Report, 1937-38,* 103-4; Albertson, *Roosevelt's Farmer,* 114-15; Edward L. Schapsmeier and Frederick H. Schapsmeier, *Henry A. Wallace of Iowa: The Agrarian Years, 1910-1940* (Ames: Iowa State Univ. Press, 1968), 242-43.

63. *Courier-Journal,* Sept. 22, 1941; David MacFarlane and Max M. Tharp, "Trends in Kentucky Agriculture, 1929-1940," Univ. of Kentucky, Agricultural Experiment Station *Bulletin* 429 (June 1942): 4-5, 16, 48; *Louisville Times,* March 25, 1940.

64. AAA, *Report, 1938-39,* 65; Benedict and Stine, *Commodity Programs,* 66-67.

65. Saloutos, *The American Farmer,* 242-43.

66. Ibid., 98, 106, 262.

67. *Sixteenth Census of the United States, 1940,* vol. 1, pt. 4:4.

68. Earl Mayhew to Goodman, July 15, 1935, copy in box 44, Cooper Papers.

69. Cooper to Goodman, July 18, 1935, ibid.

70. Saloutos, *The American Farmer,* 157-58; Charles, *Minister of Relief,* 87-88.

71. "Project Description Book," LA-KY-1, ser. 13, Farm Security Administration Records, RG 96, National Archives.

72. Roosevelt, *Public Papers,* 4:143-44.

73. Paul K. Conkin, *Tomorrow a New World: The New Deal Community Program* (Ithaca: Cornell Univ. Press, 1959), 147.

74. "What the Resettlement Administration Has Done," Nov. 1936, box 100, Chandler Papers.

75. Rexford Tugwell, "A Fresh Start," *Courier-Journal,* June 14, 1936.

76. "Summary of Farm Security Administration," 1939, box 19, Cooper Papers.

77. Saloutos, *The American Farmer,* 264.

78. FSA, *Report, 1941,* 31; FSA, "Report of Loan Activities," 1942, box 19, Cooper Papers.

79. *Louisville Times,* April 25, 1938.

80. Paul V. Maris, *The Land Is Mine: From Tenancy to Family Farm Ownership* (Washington: GPO, 1950), 211-27.

81. Tugwell, "A Fresh Start."

82. Ibid.; *Herald-Post,* Nov. 8, 1935; "Project Description Book," LD-KY-1, LD-KY-4.

83. *Herald-Post*, Oct. 7, 1935; *Courier-Journal*, Dec. 21, 1935, May 22, 1936.

84. *Louisville Times*, July 25, 1938.

85. Sidney Baldwin, *Poverty and Politics: The Rise and Decline of the Farm Security Administration* (Chapel Hill: Univ. of North Carolina Press, 1968), 111.

86. London *Sentinel-Echo*, Nov. 28, 1935; *Herald-Post*, Nov. 15, 1935.

87. "Project Description Book," FS-KY-10; *Courier-Journal*, Nov. 19, 1936.

88. FSA *Report, 1941,* 33; *Lexington Herald*, May 7, 23, 1937.

89. London *Sentinel-Echo*, Sept. 10, 1936, Dec. 2, 1937.

90. *Courier-Journal*, Sept. 3, 1939.

91. Conkin, *Tomorrow a New World*, 330-31.

92. Ibid., 230; FSA, *Report, 1945-46,* 17.

93. "Project Description Book," RR-KY-14; *Report, 1941,* 36.

94. *Courier-Journal*, Oct. 24. 1937.

95. "Project Descriptions," 1943, ser. 13, FSA Records.

96. Resettlement Administration, *Annual Report, 1937,* 3.

97. Marion Post Wolcott, "Autobiographical Statement," 2, ser. 2G, Roy Stryker Papers, Univ. of Louisville Photographic Archives.

98. Marion Post Wolcott to Roy Stryker, July 28, Aug. 16, Sept. 9, 1940, box 37, ser. 8, ibid.

99. Marion Post Wolcott, Photograph Prints, box 29, ser. 4, ibid.; Beverly Brannan, "Things as They Were: FSA Photographers in Kentucky, 1935-1943," Univ. of Louisville Photographic Archives, 1984, p. 3.

100. L.S. Dodson, "Living Conditions and Population Migration in Four Appalachian Counties," mimeo., (Washington: GPO, 1937), 88, 111-12.

101. Tennessee Valley Authority, *Annual Report 1933-34,* 1-4.

102. *Congressional Record*, 73d Cong. 2d sess., 11822-23.

103. Gregory campaign materials, July 29, 1936, William Gregory Papers.

104. *Louisville Times*, March 28, 1935.

105. TVA, *Annual Report, 1936-37,* 9-12; Noble Gregory to L.J. Hortin, April 19, 1937, box 17, Noble J. Gregory Papers, Pogue Library, Murray State Univ., Murray, Ky.

106. Univ. of Kentucky, Agricultural Experiment Station, *Annual Report, 1937,* 32; TVA, *Annual Report, 1936-37,* 37.

107. *Congressional Record*, 73d Cong., 2 sess., 11822.

108. "TVA Possibilities for Kentucky Cities," *Kentucky City* 7 (Nov. 1936), 21; *Courier-Journal*, July 30, 1937.

109. Paducah *Sun-Democrat*, April 25, 1938. For activities of the Lower Tennessee Valley Association, see box 17, 1937-38, Noble Gregory Papers.

110. Kentucky Department of Mines, *Annual Report, 1941*, 14.

111. Noble Gregory to Clyde Washam, April 29, 1938, box 17, Noble Gregory Papers.

112. Paducah *Sun-Democrat*, Feb. 12, 17, 1939.

113. *Middlesboro Daily News*, Dec. 20, 21, 1940.

114. TVA, *Annual Report, 1939-40*, 89.

115. Keen Johnson, *The Public Papers of Governor Keen Johnson, 1939-1943*, ed. Frederick D. Ogden (Lexington: Univ. Press of Kentucky, 1982), 60-67.

116. Frankfort *State Journal*, Feb. 17, 1942.

117. TVA, *Annual Report, 1941-42*, 10.

118. Ibid., *1938-39*, 15.

119. *Courier-Journal*, April 14, 1940.

120. TVA, *Annual Report, 1939-40*, 39-40; *Courier-Journal*, July 23, 1939.

121. *Courier-Journal*, July 23, 1939.

122. TVA, *Annual Report, 1943-44*, 31, *1944-45*, 39.

123. Paducah *Sun-Democrat*, Oct. 10, 11, 1945.

124. Saloutos, *The American Farmer*, 221.

125. Ibid., 209; *Census, 1940*, vol. 1, pt. 4, pp. 4, 11.

126. Saloutos, *The American Farmer*, 214.

127. Roosevelt, *Public Papers*, 4: 173-74.

128. Rural Electrification Administration, *Annual Report, 1940-41*, 25; Saloutos, *The American Farmer*, 219.

129. *Lexington Herald*, June 11, 1938; *Courier-Journal*, June 12, 1938.

130. *Farmers Home Journal* (Feb. 1937), 614, and (Sept. 1937), 771.

131. *Louisville Times* and *Courier-Journal*, May 20, 1937.

132. REA, *Annual Report, 1938-39*, 222-23.

133. Ibid., 223.

## 6. Getting Back to Business

1. *Census, 1910*, 9:392-94.

2. Anti-Saloon League of America, *Yearbook* (Westerville, Ohio, 1917) 65.

3. Thomas D. Clark, *A History of Kentucky* (Lexington: John Bradford Press, 1960), 399.

4. *In Kentucky* (Summer 1938), 46.

5. *New York Times*, Aug. 11, 1929.

6. *Lexington Herald*, Feb. 26, 1933.

7. Clark, *History of Kentucky*, 399.

8. J. Winston Coleman, Jr., *Kentucky: A Pictorial History* (Lexington: Univ. Press of Kentucky, 1971), 198; Esther Kellner, *Moonshine: Its History and Folklore* (Indianapolis: Bobbs-Merrill, 1971), 146-47.

9. *Frankfort State Journal*, Aug. 10, 1930.

10. Barkley, *That Reminds Me*, 141-42; Andrew Sinclair, *Era of Excess: A Social History of the Prohibition Movement* (New York: Harper and Row, 1962), 364-65.

11. *Louisville Times*, April 29, 1932; Barkley, *That Reminds Me*, 143-44.

12. Frankfort *State Journal* and *Courier-Journal*, April 6-8, 1933.

13. *Herald Post*, Nov. 27, 1933.

14. *Acts of the General Assembly*, March 17, 1934, 664.

15. George L. Willis, *Kentucky Democracy* (Louisville: Democratic Historical Society, 1935), 1: 482.

16. Laffoon proclamation, Dec. 4, 1935, box 20, Governors' Papers.

17. *In Kentucky* (Summer 1938), 46; Warren M. Persons, *Beer and Brewing in America: An Economic Study* (New York: United Brewers Industrial Foundation, 1938), 15.

18. *In Kentucky* (Summer, 1938), 46.

19. Commonwealth of Kentucky, Department of Revenue, *Report, 1938-39*, 6; idem, Department of the Treasury, *Report, 1939*, 8.

20. Manfred Friedrich and Donald Bull, *The Register of United States Breweries, 1876-1976* (Trumbull, Conn.: privately printed, 1976), 116; George Yater, *Two Hundred Years at the Falls of the Ohio* (Louisvile: Heritage Corp. 1979), 199.

21. Roosevelt, *Public Papers*, 2:246.

22. Leverette S. Lyon et al. *The National Recovery Administration: An Analysis and Appraisal* (Washington: Brookings Institution, 1935), 889.

23. Frances Perkins, *The Roosevelt I Knew* (New York: Viking Press, 1946), 208-9, 212.

24. Barkley, *That Reminds Me*, 28.

25. Hugh S. Johnson, *The Blue Eagle from Egg to Earth* (New York: Doubleday, Doran and Co. 1935), 282.

26. Ibid., 258; NRA, *What the Blue Eagle Means to You and How You Can Get It* (Washington: GPO, 1933), 2.

27. *Courier-Journal*, July 25, 1933.

28. *Louisville Times* and *Herald-Post, Aug. 11, 1933.*

29. *Lexington Herald*, Sept. 5, 1933.

30. *Herald-Post,* Aug. 21, 1933; *Courier-Journal,* Aug. 23, Sept. 1, 1933; *Lexington Herald,* Sept. 3, 1933.

31. Hugh S. Johnson, *The Blue Eagle,* 267-68; Lyon et al. *The NRA,* 29, 900.

32. Otto J. Scott, *The Exception: The Story of Ashland Oil and Refining Company* (New York: McGraw-Hill, 1968), 107; *Kentucky Press* (Sept. 1933), 4.

33. Lyon et al. *The NRA,* appendix D, Approved Codes.

34. *Courier-Journal,* Sept. 13, 1933; William E. Leuchtenburg, *Franklin D. Roosevelt and the New Deal* (New York: Harper and Row, 1963), 68.

35. L.M. to Hugh Johnson, Feb. 7, 1934, ser. 120, National Recovery Administration (RG 9), National Archives.

36. M.G.S. to Hugh Johnson, Sept. 21, 1934, ser. 101, ibid.

37. Keen Johnson, Speech to Kentucky Press Association, Jan. 18, 1935, box 53, Johnson Papers.

38. Hugh S. Johnson, *The Blue Eagle,* 211, 288; Lyon et al. *The NRA,* 29, 288.

39. *Louisville Times,* Sept. 20, 1934.

40. NRA Compliance Board, Progress Reports, Oct.-Dec. 1933, ser. 120, NRA Records.

41. Roosevelt, *Public Papers,* 4:222; NRA Press Release, May 22, 1934, ser. 78, NRA Records.

42. NRA Compliance Questionnaire, July 3, 1934, ser. 219, NRA Records.

43. Hugh Johnson to Laffoon, Sept. 2, 1933, ser. 80, ibid.

44. W. Morrow to L. Klarer, April 4, 1934, ser. 78, ibid.

45. Memo of telephone conversation between Howard Wahrenbrock and J.R. Layman, May 15, 1934, ibid.

46. Roosevelt, *Public Papers,* 4:80.

47. AFL *Report of the Proceedings,* 61st Annual Convention, 1941, 44.

48. F. Ray Marshall, *Labor in the South* (Cambridge: Harvard Univ. Press, 1967), 139, 215.

49. Kentucky State Federation of Labor, *Book of Laws and Proceedings,* Annual Conventions (1929), 17-18, 30 (1930), 15 (1931), 14-15.

50. Lyon et al., *The NRA,* 492; Milton Derber, "Growth and Expansion," in *Labor and the New Deal,* ed. Milton Derber and Edwin Young (Madison: Univ. of Wisconsin Press, 1961), 23.

51. AFL, *Proceedings, 1932-34.*
52. Hevener, *Which Side Are You On?* 95.
53. Kentucky Federation of Labor, *Proceedings, 1934-35.*
54. Perkins, *The Roosevelt I Knew,* 229-30; Hugh S. Johnson, *The Blue Eagle,* 243.
55. Hugh S. Johnson, *The Blue Eagle,* 178; Hevener, *Which Side Are You On?* 97.
56. Hevener, *Which Side Are You On?* 27, 100, 104.
57. Ibid., x.
58. Laffoon proclamations, box 19, Governors' Papers.
59. R.W. Fleming, "The Significance of the Wagner Act," in *Labor and the New Deal,* ed. Derber and Young, 127.
60. Hevener, *Which Side Are You On?* 120.
61. Executive Order, Feb. 12, 1935, box 18, Governors' Papers.
62. *Congressional Record,* 74th Cong., 1st sess. (June 10, 1935), 8987-88.
63. Denhardt Commission Materials, 1935, box 19, Governors' Papers.
64. Melvyn Dubofsky and Warren Van Tyne, *John L. Lewis: A Biography* (New York: Quadrangle, 1977), 220-21.
65. Edwin Young, "The Split in the Labor Movement," in *Labor and the New Deal,* ed. Derber and Young, 72; Fleming, "Significance of the Wagner Act," 146.
66. Leo Troy, *Distribution of Union Membership among the States, 1939-1953* (New York: National Bureau of Economic Research, 1957), 4-5; Irving Bernstein, *Turbulent Years: A History of the American Worker, 1933-1941* (Boston: Houghton Mifflin, 1969), 774.
67. Troy, *Distribution of Union Membership,* 4-5.
68. Marshall, *Labor in the South,* 299.
69. Frank DeVyver, "The Present Status of Labor Unions in the South," *Southern Economic Journal* 5 (April 1939): 491-92; Kentucky Federation of Labor, *Proceedings, 1940,* 36, 39.
70. Hevener, *Which Side Are You On?* 103.
71. See Olivia Frederick, "Kentucky's 1935 Gubernatorial Election" (M.A. thesis, Univ. of Louisville, 1967); *Courier-Journal,* Dec. 11, 1935.
72. Kentucky Federation of Labor, *Proceedings, 1936,* 15.
73. Speech File, 1937, box 586, Chandler Papers.
74. *New York Times,* April 16, 1937; *Time Magazine,* May 3, 1937, 13-14.
75. *New York Times,* May 7, 1937.
76. Jerold Auerbach, *Labor and Liberty: The LaFollette Committee and the New Deal* (Indianapolis: Bobbs-Merrill, 1966), 115.

77. W.K.T. to Chandler, Nov. 20, 1937, and Chandler to W.K.T., Dec. 1, 1937, box 103, Chandler Papers.

78. *Acts of the General Assembly*, Jan. 24, 1938, 141-47.

79. London *Sentinel-Echo*, May 12, July 28, Aug. 4, 1938; Hevener, *Which Side Are You On?* 151; Day, *Bloody Ground*, chap. 20.

80. Auerbach, *Labor and Liberty*, 120; Hevener, *Which Side Are You On?* 151.

81. Marshall, *Labor in the South*, 147.

82. See box 54, Chandler Papers.

83. Three Miners to Chandler, May 8, 1939, and Union Coal Miners of Eastern Kentucky to Chandler, May 10, 1939, ibid.

84. Hevener, *Which Side Are You On?* 161.

85. *Lexington Herald*, May 14, 1939.

86. Transcript of Radio Address, May 21, 1939, Chandler File, Thomas R. Underwood Papers, Special Collections, Univ. of Kentucky Library, Lexington.

87. Report, Brig. Gen. Ellerbe Carter to Chandler, July 22, 1939, box 68, Chandler Papers; *Courier-Journal*, July 14, 1939.

88. Frankfort *State Journal*, July 22, 1939.

89. A.R.W. to Chandler, Aug. 7, 1939, box 103, Chandler Papers.

90. Hevener, *Which Side Are You On?* 171.

## 7. Politics and Other Natural Phenomena

1. Malcolm E. Jewell and Everette W. Cunningham, *Kentucky Politics* (Lexington: Univ. Press of Kentucky, 1968), 8.

2. *Biographical Directory of the American Congress, 1774-1971* (Washington: GOP, 1971), 370.

3. Ibid., 376, 382, 388.

4. Barkley, *That Reminds Me*, 156; James K. Libbey, *Dear Alben: Mr. Barkley of Kentucky* (Lexington: Univ. Press of Kentucky, 1979), 76. See also Polly Ann Davis, *Alben W. Barkley: Senate Majority Leader and Vice President* (New York: Garland, 1979), 27-29, 39.

5. Campaign Speech Manuscript, 1936, William Gregory Papers.

6. *Congressional Record*, 73d Cong., 2d sess., 12330-32.

7. Barkley, *That Reminds Me*, 201.

8. Felix Frankfurter to Stanley Reed, June [2], 1935, Scrapbook, no. 1, Stanley Reed Papers, Special Collections, Univ. of Kentucky Library, Lexington.

9. Speech manuscript, July 13, 1936, ibid. This speech later appeared in the *American Bar Association Journal* (Sept. 1936).

10. *Courier-Journal*, Dec. 19, 1937; James A. Farley, *Behind the*

*Ballots: The Personal History of a Politician* (New York: Harcourt, Brace, 1938), 72.

11. Biographical Data Sheet and assorted invitations, clippings, and correspondence, Woodson Papers.

12. *Who's Who in Kentucky, (1936); New York Times*, Sept. 1, 1940; Ickes, *Secret Diary* 2:32, 288.

13. Gipson, *Ruby Laffoon*, 118-19.

14. *Kentucky Post*, Sept. 12, 1934.

15. Clara Wootton, *They Have Topped the Mountain* (Frankfort: Blue Grass Press, 1960), 138.

16. Urey Woodson to J.M., Dec. 12, 1933, Woodson Papers.

17. Fredrick, "Kentucky's 1935 Gubernatorial Election," 26-27.

18. *Courier-Journal*, Jan. 16, 27, 1935.

19. Chandler to Joe Schneider, Jan. 21, 1935, box 9, Chandler Papers.

20. *Courier-Journal*, Jan. 29, 1935.

21. Chandler proclamation, Feb. 6, 1935, box 19, Governors' Papers.

22. Laffoon proclamation, Feb. 7, 1935, ibid.; *Courier-Journal*, Feb. 8, 1935.

23. Frankfort *State Journal*, Feb. 12, 13, 1935.

24. Chandler to William Kennedy, March 15, 1935, box 8, Chandler Papers.

25. Thomas Rhea to Woodson, Jan. 21, 1935, Woodson Papers.

26. Robert J. Leupold, "The Kentucky WPA: Relief and Politics, May-November 1935," *Filson Club History Quarterly* 49 (April 1975): 160-61.

27. *New York Times*, Sept. 15, 1935.

28. Republican Platform, 1935, Speech Folder, King Swope Papers, Special Collections, Univ. of Kentucky Library, Lexington.

29. *Lexington Herald* and *Kentucky Post*, Sept. 27, 1935; *Cincinnati Times Star*, Sept. 28, 1935; *Richmond Daily Register*, Sept. 30, 1935.

30. *Courier-Journal*, Oct. 6, 1935.

31. Jim Farley to Fellow Democrat, Oct. 30, 1935, Scrapbook, Swope Papers.

32. Frankfort *State Journal*, Oct. 29, 1935.

33. Goodman to Cecil Williams, Oct. 4, 1935, box 3, Goodman Papers.

34. Frankfort *State Journal*, Nov. 2, 1935; Leupold, "The Kentucky WPA," 161, 165-67.

35. *Lexington Herald*, Nov. 7, 1935.

36. Farley to Chandler, July 30, 1936, box 99, Chandler Papers; *Woodford Sun*, Oct. 15, 1936.

37. Speech Manuscript (Tennessee), 1937, box 586, Chandler Papers.

38. E.S. Leggett to Chandler, Jan. 13, 1937, box 100, ibid.

39. Chandler to Harry F. Byrd, July 11, 1932, box 7, ibid; *Lexington Herald*, Jan. 5, 1936.

40. Keen Johnson, "State of the Commonwealth Address," Jan. 2, 1940, in idem, *Public Papers*, 23.

41. Patterson, *New Deal and the States*, 160.

42. Chandler to M.R., June 4, 1938, box 110, Chandler Papers.

43. *Louisville Times*, Aug. 24, 1936.

44. *Woodford Sun*, Jan. 12, 1939.

45. *Time Magazine*, Aug. 1, 1938, 11.

46. Roosevelt to Marvin McIntyre, Jan. 21, 1938, General File XII, Miscellaneous and Personal Folder, Alben W. Barkley Papers, Special Collections, Univ. of Kentucky Library, Lexington.

47. Walter Davenport, "Happy Couldn't Wait," *Colliers*, July 16, 1938, 13.

48. *Lexington Herald*, Feb. 2, 1938; Shannon, "Happy Chandler," 188.

49. Ickes, *Secret Diary* 2:342.

50. Frankfort *State Journal*, Feb. 20, 1938; *Lexington Herald*, May 6, 1938.

51. Mimeographed fliers, 1938, Political File IX, Barkley Papers; *Lexington Herald*, June 19, 1938.

52. Barkley-for-Senator letter, July 26, 1938, box 45, Chandler Papers.

53. Roosevelt Speech Manuscript, July 8, 1938, box 3, Goodman Papers; *Lexington Herald*, July 9, 1938.

54. Barkley, *That Reminds Me*, 166; Chandler, "Open Letter, Aug. 1, 1966," *Filson Club History Quarterly* (Oct. 1966) 336.

55. Rhea to Woodson, March 31, 1938, Woodson Papers.

56. Hopkins Memo, May 5, 1938, box 2, Goodman Papers.

57. *Courier-Journal* and *New York Times*, May 26, 1938.

58. Ernest Rowe to Goodman, May 28, 1938, box 3, Goodman Papers.

59. *Washington Daily News*, June 8, 1938.

60. Telephone conversation of Hunter and Hopkins, June 20, 1938, transcript, container 74, Hopkins Papers.

61. *Courier-Journal* and *New York Times*, July 1, 1938.

62. Thomas L. Stokes, *Chip off My Shoulder* (Princeton: Princeton Univ. Press, 1940), 535; *Washington Daily News*, June 6, 1938.

63. *Washington Star*, July 13, 1938.

64. *Courier-Journal*, Sunday Magazine, July 24, 1938; *Time Magazine*, Aug. 1, 1938, 11.

65. *Kentucky Welfare News*,n.d., Chandler File, Underwood Papers.

66. Special Committee to Investigate Senatorial Campaign Expenditures and Use of Governmental Funds in 1938, *Senate Report*, 76th Cong., 1st sess., no. 1, pt. 1: 12-13.

67. Ibid., 18.

68. Barkely, *That Reminds Me*, 166; Chandler to author, Oct. 17, 1964.

69. Malcolm E. Jewell, *Kentucky Votes* (Lexington: Univ. Press of Kentucky, 1963), 1:30-31; Walter Hixon, "The 1938 Kentucky Senate Election: Alben W. Barkley, 'Happy' Chandler, and the New Deal," *Register of the Kentucky Historical Society* 80 (Summer 1982): 326-27.

70. Keen Johnson, *Public Papers*, 18-20.

71. Governor's Committee on Drought Relief, "The Drought Situation in Kentucky," Sept. 17, 1936, 1-2, box 99, Chandler Papers.

72. Goodman to Chandler, Aug. 25, 1936, ibid.

73. Governor's Committee, "Drought Situation," 2, 5.

74. *Courier-Journal*, Sept. 6, 1936.

75. AAA, "Changes in the Agricultural Situation," 1937 revision, 5-7; Goodman to Chandler, Aug. 25, 1936, box 99, Chandler Papers.

76. Willard R. Jillson, *The Great Flood of 1937 in Louisville, Kentucky* (Louisville: Standard Printing, 1937), 96.

77. Frankfort *State Journal*, Jan. 29, Feb. 18, 1937; Jillson, *The Great Flood*, 27; A.P.P. to Chandler, Jan. 28, 1937, box 101, Chandler Papers; Woodson to H.A. Sommers, March 10, 1937, Woodson Papers.

78. Chandler to *Yale Daily News*, Jan. 28, 1937, box 101, Chandler Papers.

79. Telephone conversation of Chandler and Hopkins Jan. 22, 1937, transcript, container 74, Hopkins Papers; *Woodford Sun*, Jan. 28, 1937.

80. F.P.C. to Chandler, E.H.S. to Chandler, G.S.W. to Chandler, all Jan. 27, 1937, box 101, Chandler Papers.

81. Kentucky Colonel Contribution List, Feb. 1, 1937, ibid.

82. R.F.A. to Chandler, July 8, 1937, box 102, ibid.

83. Keen Johnson telegrams, Jan. 22, 1937, box 100, ibid.

84. *Lexington Leader*, Jan. 24, 1937.

85. Chandler Flood List, Feb. 4, 1937, box 101, ibid.

86. Keen Johnson to Chandler, Jan. 22, 1937, box 100, ibid.

87. Chandler to Roosevelt, Jan. 24, 25, 1937, box 101, ibid.

88. *Courier-Journal*, Feb. 21, 1937, Ky. WPA, Monthly Narrative Report, Jan. 20-Feb. 20, 1937, box 5, Goodman Papers.

89. Frank Peterson to Richard Brown, Feb. 15, 1937, box 19, ser. 62, NYA Records.

90. "Federal Flood Aid Agencies Listed," *Kentucky City* (Feb. 1937), 9; Mayhew to Chandler, Jan. 28, 1937, box 101, Chandler Papers.

91. Robert L. Snyder, *Pare Lorentz and the Documentary Film* (Norman: Univ. of Oklahoma Press, 1968), 58.

## 8. New Deal Legacy in Kentucky

1. Don C. Reading, "New Deal Activity and the States, 1933 to 1939," *Journal of Economic History* 33 (Dec. 1973): 794.

2. See Minton, *New Deal in Tennessee*, 275; Ronald L. Heinemann, *Depression and New Deal in Virginia: The Enduring Dominion* (Charlottesville: Univ. Press of Virginia, 1983), 172; James H. Madison, *Indiana Through Tradition and Change: A History of the Hoosier State and Its People, 1920-1945* (Indianapolis: Indiana Historical Society, 1982), 130, 243-44; David J. Maurer, "Relief Problems and Politics in Ohio," in *The New Deal*, ed. Braeman et al., 94-99.

3. F.A.J. to James Farley, Jan. 20, 1939, Roosevelt Papers. Democratic National Committee Section, box 38, Franklin D. Roosevelt Papers, Franklin D. Roosevelt Library, Hyde Park, N.Y.

4. Day, *Bloody Ground*, 173.

# Bibliography

## Manuscript Collections—Individuals

Barkley, Alben W. Special Collections, University of Kentucky Library, Lexington.

Chandler, Albert Benjamin. Special Collections, University of Kentucky Library, Lexington.

Cooper, Thomas Poe. Special Collections, University of Kentucky Library, Lexington.

Governors' Papers. Flem Sampson, Ruby Laffoon, A.B. Chandler. Kentucky Department of Libraries and Archives, Frankfort.

Goodman, George H. Special Collections, University of Kentucky Library, Lexington.

Gregory, Noble J. Pogue Library, Murray State University, Murray, Ky.

Gregory, William Voris. Pogue Library, Murray State University, Murray, Ky.

Hopkins, Harry L. Franklin D. Roosevelt Library, Hyde Park, New York.

Johnson, Keen. Eastern Kentucky University Archives, Richmond, Ky.

Reed, Stanley. Special Collections, University of Kentucky Library, Lexington.

Roosevelt, Franklin D. President's Official Files. Franklin D. Roosevelt Library, Hyde Park, New York.

Spence, Brent. Special Collections, University of Kentucky Library, Lexington.

Stryker, Roy. Photographic Archives, University of Louisville.

Swope, King. Special Collections, University of Kentucky Library, Lexington.

Underwood, Thomas R. Special Collections, University of Kentucky Library, Lexington.

Vinson, Frederick M. Special Collections, University of Kentucky Library, Lexington.

Walker, Frank. University of Notre Dame Archives, Notre Dame, Indiana.
Woodson, Urey. Special Collections, University of Kentucky Library, Lexington.

## Manuscript Collections—Agencies

Agricultural Adjustment Administration (AAA). RG 145, National Archives.
Civilian Conservation Corps (CCC). RG 35, National Archives.
Farm Security Administration (FSA). RG 96, National Archives.
Federal Writers' Project, Slave Narratives. Manuscript Division, Library of Congress.
National Recovery Administration (NRA). RG 9, National Archives.
National Youth Administration (NYA). RG 119, National Archives.
President's Organization on Unemployment Relief (POUR). RG 73, National Archives.
Public Works Administration (PWA). RG 135, National Archives.
Reconstruction Finance Corporation (RFC). RG 234, National Archives.
Resettlement Administration (RA). RG 96, National Archives.
University of Kentucky, College of Agriculture Records. Special Collections, University of Kentucky Library, Lexington.
Work Projects Administration (WPA) (including records of Federal Emergency Relief Administration). RG 69, National Archives.
Work Projects Administration in Kentucky Records (including records of Civil Works Administration). Kentucky Department of Libraries and Archives, Frankfort.

## Oral History Interview Collections

Columbia University, Oral History Research Office (Howard Tolly, John B. Hutson).
University of Kentucky, Oral History Project (John Sherman Cooper, Frank Peterson).
Kentucky CCC Alumni (Leroy Brown, Willie Himes, Oscar Huffman, Robert Kellen, George Mayne, Tom Mayne, Russell Stanford). Interviews with author.

## Federal Publications

Agricultural Adjustment Administration. Periodic reports.

Biographical Directory of the American Congress, 1774–1971. 1971.
Bureau of the Census. *Statistical Abstracts of the United States.* 1929, 1930, 1931, 1932, 1933.
*Census of the United States* (1910, 1920, 1930, 1940).
Civilian Conservation Corps. Periodic and annual reports.
Committee of Industrial Analysis. *The National Recovery Administration.* 1937.
*Congressional Record*
Department of Labor. *Industrial Employment Information Bulletin* (May 1932).
Farm Security Administration. Annual reports.
Federal Deposit Insurance Corporation. Annual reports.
Federal Home Loan Bank Board. Annual reports.
Federal Home Loan Bank Board. *Summary of the Operations of the Agencies under the Federal Home Loan Bank Board as of June 30, 1941, for the State of Kentucky.* 1941.
Federal Housing Administration. Annual reports.
Federal Works Agency. Annual reports.
*Historical Statistics of the U.S.* 1975.
Kutak, Rosemary. *Unemployment Relief in Kentucky.* Louisville: KERA, 1934.
Maris, Paul V. *The Land Is Mine: From Tenancy to Family Farm Ownership.* 1950.
NRA. *What the Blue Eagle Means to You and How You Can Get It.* 1933.
Public Works Administration. *America Builds: The Record of the PWA.* 1939.
Resettlement Administration. Annual reports.
Rural Electrification Administration. Annual reports.
Schwartz, Charles F., and Robert E. Graham, Jr. "Personal Income by State, 1929-1954." *Survey of Current Business*, Sept. 1955.
Social Security Board. Annual reports.
Tennessee Valley Authority. Annual reports.
Whiting, Theodore E. *Final Statistical Report of the Federal Emergency Relief Administration.* 1942.
Work Projects Administration. *Final Report on the W.P.A. Program, 1935-1943.* 1946.

## State Publications

*Acts of the General Assembly.*

Agricultural and Industrial Development Board. *Deskbook of Kentucky Economic Statistics.* 1952.
Agricultural Experiment Stations. University of Kentucky. Annual reports.
Department of Agriculture. *Kentucky Agricultural Statistics.* 1950.
Department of Health. *Bulletin of the State Board of Health.* Monthly.
Department of Labor. Biennial reports.
Department of Mines and Minerals. Annual reports.
Department of the Treasury. Biennial reports.
Division of Banking. Annual reports.
Division of State Parks. Annual reports.
*House Journal.*
Kentucky Commission on Human Rights. *Kentucky's Black Heritage.* 1971.
Kentucky Progress Commission. *First Report,* December 6, 1929.
*Kentucky Progress Magazine (In Kentucky* from 1937).
*Senate Journal.*
State Tax Commission (Department of Revenue after 1936). Annual reports.

## Newspapers

*Ashland Daily Independent*
Bowling Green *Times-Journal*
Carrollton *News-Democrat*
*Chicago Daily Tribune*
*Cincinnati Times-Star*
*Courier-Journal* (Louisville)
Frankfort *State Journal*
*Henderson Gleaner*
*Herald-Post* (Louisville)
*Hickman Courier*
*Kentucky Post* (Cincinnati)
*Lexington Herald*
*Lexington Leader*
London *Sentinel-Echo*
*Louisville Times*
*Middlesboro Daily News*
*New York Times*
Paducah *Sun-Democrat*
*Richmond Daily Register*

*St. Louis Post-Dispatch*
*Washington Daily News*
*Washington Post*
*Washington Star*
*Woodford Sun*(Versailles)

## Unpublished Materials

Birdwhistell, Terry L., "Fayette County, Kentucky and the New Deal Farm Program, 1933-36" Graduate Research Paper, Univ. of Kentucky, 1973.

Boddy, Julie M., "The Farm Security Photographs of Marion Post Wolcott: A Cultural History." Ph.D. diss., State Univ. of New York at Buffalo, 1982.

Conrad, James E. "History and Development of Banking in Kentucky." Kentucky Bankers Association Headquarters, Louisville, 1964.

Frederick, Olivia M. "Kentucky's 1935 Gubernatorial Election." M.A. thesis, Univ. of Louisville, 1967.

Pettit, Noble Gregory. "The New Deal in Kentucky—Limited Partnership: Political and Governmental Developments in Kentucky, 1931-1939." Senior thesis, Princeton Univ., 1981.

Rawick, George P., "The New Deal and Youth: The Civilian Conservation Corps, the National Youth Administration, and the American Youth Commission." Ph.D. diss., Univ. of Wisconsin, 1957.

Sexton, Robert F. "Kentucky Politics and Society, 1919-1932." Ph.D. diss., Univ. of Washington, 1970.

Skaggs, James. "The Rise and Fall of Flem D. Sampson, 1927-1931." M.A. thesis, Eastern Kentucky Univ. 1976.

Spindletop Research Project. "Kentucky State Parks." Univ. of Kentucky, Documents Library, 1975.

Taylor, Paul F. "Coal and Conflict: The United Mine Workers Association in Harlan County." Ph.D. diss., Univ. of Kentucky, 1969.

Watkins, Charles A. "The Blurred Image: Documentary Photography and the Depression South." Ph.D. diss., Univ. of Delaware, 1982.

Wladaver-Morgan, Susan. "Young Women and the New Deal: Camps and Resident Centers, 1933-1943." Ph.D. diss., Indiana Univ. 1982.

## Books

Albertson, Dean. *Roosevelt's Farmer: Claude R. Wickard in the New Deal.* New York: Columbia Univ. Press, 1961.

Allied Liquor Industries. *Beverage Distilling Industry Facts and Figures, 1934-1944.* New York: Allied Liquor Industries, 1945.

Auerbach, Jerold. *Labor and Liberty: The LaFollette Committee and the New Deal.* Indianapolis: Bobbs-Merrill, 1966.

Axton, W.F. *Tobacco and Kentucky.* Lexington: Univ. Press of Kentucky, 1975.

Badger, Anthony J. *Prosperity Road: The New Deal, Tobacco, and North Carolina.* Chapel Hill: Univ. of North Carolina Press, 1980.

Baldwin, Sidney, *Poverty and Politics: The Rise and Decline of the Farm Security Administration.* Chapel Hill: Univ. of North Carolina Press, 1968.

Barkley, Alben W. *That Reminds Me.* New York: Doubleday, 1954.

Baylor, Orval W. *J. Dan Talbott: Champion of Good Government.* Louisville: Kentucky Printing Corp., 1942.

Benedict, Murray R., and Oscar C. Stine. *The Agricultural Commodity Programs: Two Decades of Experience.* New York: Twentieth Century Fund, 1956.

Bernstein, Irving. *Turbulent Years: A History of the American Worker, 1933-41.* Boston: Houghton Mifflin, 1969.

Botkin, B.A., ed. *Lay My Burden Down: A Folk History of Slavery.* Chicago: Univ. of Chicago Press, 1945.

Braeman, John, et al., eds. *The New Deal: The State and Local Levels.* Columbus: Ohio State Univ. Press, 1975.

Brown, D. Clayton. *Electricity for Rural America: The Fight For REA.* Westport, Conn.: Greenwood Press, 1980.

Brown, Josephine C. *Public Relief, 1929-1939.* 1940. Reprint. New York: Octagon Books, 1971.

Charles, Searle F. *Minister of Relief: Harry Hopkins and the Depression.* Syracuse: Syracuse Univ. Press, 1963.

Clark, Thomas D. *Greening of the South* Lexington: Univ. Press of Kentucky, 1984.

Clark, Thomas D. *A History of Kentucky.* Lexington: John Bradford Press, 1960.

Cobb, James C., and Michael V. Namorato, eds. *The New Deal and the South.* Jackson: Univ. Press of Mississippi, 1984.

Coleman, J. Winston, Jr., ed. *Kentucky: A Pictorial History.* Lexington: Univ. Press of Kentucky, 1971.

Conkin, Paul K. *The New Deal.* New York: Thomas Y. Crowell, 1967.

―――. *Tomorrow a New World: The New Deal Community Program.* Ithaca: Cornell Univ. Press, 1959.

Couch, W.T., ed. *These Are Our Lives.* Chapel Hill: Univ. of North Carolina Press, 1939.

Cromwell, Emma G. *Woman in Politics.* Louisville: Standard Printing, 1939.

Davis, Joseph S. *Wheat and the A.A.A.* Washington: Brookings Institution, 1935.

Davis, Polly Ann. *Alben W. Barkley: Senate Majority Leader and Vice President.* New York: Garland, 1979.

Day, John F. *Bloody Ground.* 1941. Reprint. Lexington: Univ. Press of Kentucky, 1981.

Derber, Milton, and Edwin Young, eds. *Labor and the New Deal.* Madison: Univ. of Wisconsin Press, 1961.

Dubofsky, Melvyn, and Warren Van Tyne. *John L. Lewis: A Biography.* New York: Quadrangle, 1977.

Ellis, Edward R. *A Nation in Torment: The Great American Depression, 1929-1939.* New York: Coward-McCann, 1970.

Farley, James A. *Behind the Ballots: The Personal History of a Politician.* New York: Harcourt, Brace, 1938.

Fite, Gilbert C. *George N. Peek and the Fight for Farm Parity.* Norman: Univ. of Oklahoma Press, 1954.

Fitzgerald, Dennis A. *Corn and Hogs under the Agricultural Adjustment Act.* Washington: Brookings Institution, 1934.

————. *Livestock under the Agricultural Adjustment Act.* Washington: Brookings Institution, 1935.

Freidel, Frank. *Franklin D. Roosevelt: Launching the New Deal.* Boston: Little, Brown, 1973.

Friedrich, Manfred, and Donald Bull. *The Register of United States Breweries, 1876-1976.* Trumbull, Conn.: privately printed, 1976.

Galbraith, John Kenneth. *The Great Crash, 1929.* Boston: Houghton Mifflin, 1954

Gallup, George, *The Gallup Poll: Public Opinion, 1935-1971.* New York: Random House, 1972.

Gipson, Vernon. *Ruby Laffoon, Governor of Kentucky, 1931-1935.* Hartford, Ky.: McDowell, 1978.

Heinemann, Ronald L. *Depression and New Deal in Virginia: The Enduring Dominion.* Charlottesville: Univ. Press of Virginia, 1983.

Hevener, John W. *Which Side Are You On? The Harlan County Coal Miners, 1931-1939.* Urbana: Univ. of Illinois Press, 1978.

Holland, Kenneth, and Frank E. Hill, *Youth in the C.C.C.* Washington: American Council on Education, 1942.

Hood, Fred J., ed. *Kentucky: Its History and Heritage.* St. Louis: Forum Press, 1978.

Hoover, Herbert C. *The Memoirs of Herbert Hoover: The Great Depression, 1929-1941.* London: Hollis and Carter, 1953.

Hoover, Herbert C. *The State Papers and Other Public Writings of*

*Herbert Hoover.* Edited by William S. Myers. Vol. 1. New York: Doubleday, 1934.

Ickes, Harold L. *Back to Work: The Story of P.W.A.* New York: Macmillan, 1935.

Ickes, Harold L. *The Secret Diary of Harold Ickes.* Vol. 2. New York: Simon and Schuster, 1954.

Isakoff, Jack F. *The Public Works Administration.* Urbana: Univ. of Illinois Press, 1938.

Jewell, Malcolm E. *Kentucky Votes.* vol 1. Lexington: Univ. Press of Kentucky, 1963.

Jewell, Malcolm E. and Everette W. Cunningham. *Kentucky Politics.* Lexington: Univ. Press of Kentucky, 1968.

Jillson, Willard R. *The Great Flood of 1937 in Louisville, Kentucky.* Louisville: Standard Printing, 1937.

Johnson, Hugh S. *The Blue Eagle from Egg to Earth.* New York: Doubleday, 1935.

Johnson, John L. *Income in Kentucky.* Lexington: Univ. Press of Kentucky, 1955.

Johnson, Keen. *The Public Papers of Governor Keen Johnson, 1939-1943.* Edited by Frederick D. Ogden. Lexington: Univ. Press of Kentucky, 1982.

Johnson, Palmer O., and O.L. Harvey. *The National Youth Administration* 1938. Reprint. New York: Arno Press, 1974.

Kellner, Esther. *Moonshine: Its History and Folklore.* Indianapolis: Bobbs-Merrill, 1971.

Kennedy, Susan E. *The Banking Crisis of 1933.* Lexington: Univ. Press of Kentucky, 1973.

Kurzman, Paul A. *Harry Hopkins and the New Deal.* Fairlawn, N.J.: R.E. Burdick, 1974.

Leuchtenburg, William E. *Franklin D. Roosevelt and the New Deal.* New York: Harper and Row, 1963.

———. *In the Shadow of FDR: From Harry Truman to Ronald Reagan.* Ithaca: Cornell Univ. Press, 1983.

———. *The New Deal: A Documentary History.* Columbia: Univ. of South Carolina Press, 1968.

Libbey, James K. *Dear Alben; Mr. Barkley of Kentucky.* Lexington: Univ. Press of Kentucky, 1979.

Lindley, Betty, and Ernest K. Lindley. *A New Deal for Youth: The Story of the N.Y.A.* 1938. Reprint. New York: Da Capo Press, 1972.

Lyon, Leverette S., et al. *The National Recovery Administration: An Analysis and Appraisal.* Washington: Brookings Institution, 1935.

Madison, James H. *Indiana Through Tradition and Change: A History of the Hoosier State and Its People, 1920-1945*. Indianapolis: Indiana Historical Society, 1982.

McDonald, William F. *Federal Relief Administration and the Arts*. Columbus: Ohio State Univ. Press, 1969.

McElvaine, Robert S., ed. *Down and Out in the Great Depression: Letters from the "Forgotten Man."* Chapel Hill: Univ. of North Carolina Press, 1983.

McKinley, Charles, and Robert W. Frase. *Launching Social Security: A Capture-and-Record Account, 1935-1937*. Madison: Univ. of Wisconsin Press, 1970.

McKinzie, Richard. *The New Deal for Artists*. Princeton: Princeton Univ. Press, 1973.

Mangione, Jerre. *The Dream and the Deal: The Federal Writers' Project, 1935-1943*. New York: Avon Books, 1972.

Marigold, W.G. and E.S. Bradley. *Union College, 1879-1979*. Barbourville: Union College, 1979.

Marshall, F. Ray. *Labor in the South*. Cambridge: Harvard Univ. Press, 1967.

Merrill, Perry H. *Roosevelt's Forest Army: A History of the Civilian Conservation Corps*. Montpelier, Vt.: privately printed, 1981.

Minton, John D. *The New Deal in Tennessee, 1932-1938*. New York: Garland, 1979.

Nourse, Edwin G., et al. *Three Years of the A.A.A.* Washington: Brookings Institution, 1937.

O'Connor, Francis V., ed. *Art for the Millions*. Boston: New York Graphic Society, 1975.

O'Connor, James F.T. *The Banking Crisis and Recovery under the Roosevelt Administration*. 1938. Reprint. New York: Da Capo, 1971.

Park, Marlene, and Gerald E. Markowitz. *Democratic Vistas: Post Office and Public Art in the New Deal*. Philadelphia: Temple Univ. Press, 1984.

Patterson, James T. *The New Deal and the States: Federalism in Transition*. Princeton: Princeton Univ. Press, 1969.

Peek, George, and Samuel Crowther. *Why Quit Our Own?* New York: D. Van Nostrand, 1936.

Perkins, Frances. *The Roosevelt I Knew*. New York: Viking Press, 1946.

Persons, Warren M. *Beer and Brewing in America: An Economic Study*. New York: United Brewers Industrial Foundation, 1938.

Richards, Henry I. *Cotton and the A.A.A.* Washington: Brookings Institution, 1936.

Robinson, Edgar E., and Vaughn D. Bornet. *Herbert Hoover, President of the United States.* Stanford: Hoover Institution Press, 1975.

Robinson, John L. *Living Hard: Southern Americans in the Great Depression.* Washington: Univ. Press of America, 1981.

Roosevelt, Franklin D. *The Public Papers and Addresses of Franklin D. Roosevelt.* Edited by Samuel I. Roseman. 13 vols. New York: Random House, 1938-50.

Rowe, Harold B. *Tobacco under the A.A.A.* Washington: Brookings Institution, 1935.

Salmond, John. *The Civilian Conservation Corps, 1933-1942: A New Deal Case Study.* Durham: Duke Univ. Press, 1967.

————. *A Southern Rebel: The Life and Times of Aubrey W. Williams.* Chapel Hill: Univ. of North Carolina Press, 1983.

Saloutos, Theodore. *The American Farmer and the New Deal.* Ames: Iowa State Univ. Press, 1982.

Schapsmeier, Edward L., and Frederick H. Schapsmeier. *Henry A. Wallace of Iowa: The Agrarian Years, 1910-1940.* Ames: Iowa State Univ. Press, 1968.

Schlesinger, Arthur M., Jr. *The Coming of the New Deal.* Boston: Houghton Mifflin, 1959.

————. *The Politics of Upheaval.* Boston: Houghton Mifflin, 1960.

Schulman, Robert. *John Sherman Cooper—the Global Kentuckian.* Lexington: Univ. Press of Kentucky, 1976.

Scott, Otto J. *The Exception: The Story of Ashland Oil and Refining Company.* New York: McGraw-Hill, 1968.

Shannon, Jasper B., et al. *A Decade of Change in Kentucky Government and Politics.* Lexington: Bureau of Government Research, 1943.

Sinclair, Andrew. *The Era of Excess: A Social History of the Prohibition Movement.* New York: Harper and Row, 1962.

Slaughter, John A. *Income Received in the Various States, 1929-1935.* New York: National Industrial Conference Board, 1937.

Snyder, Robert, *A History of Georgetown College.* Georgetown, Ky.: Georgetown College, 1979.

Snyder, Robert L., *Pare Lorentz and the Documentary Film.* Norman: Univ. of Oklahoma Press, 1968.

Stokes, Thomas L. *Chip off My Shoulder.* Princeton: Princeton Univ. Press, 1940.

Terrill, Tom, and Jerrold Hirsch, eds. *Such as Us: Southern Voices of the Thirties.* New York: Norton, 1978.

Thomas, Jean. *Ballad Makin' in the Mountains of Kentucky.* New York: Henry Holt and Co. 1939.

Troy, Leo. *Distribution of Union Membership among the States, 1939 and 1953.* New York: National Bureau of Economic Research, 1957.

Wallace, Henry A. *Democracy Reborn.* New York: Reynal and Hitchcock, 1944.

————. *New Frontiers.* New York: Reynal and Hitchcock, 1934.

Wallis, Frederick A., and Hambleton Tapp. *A Sesqui-centennial History of Kentucky.* 4 vols. Louisville: Historical Record Association, 1945.

Warren, Harris G. *Herbert Hoover and the Great Depression.* New York: Norton, 1967.

White, William A. *A Puritan in Babylon: The Story of Calvin Coolidge.* New York: Macmillan, 1938.

Willis, George L. *Kentucky Democracy.* Louisville: Democratic Historical Society, 1935.

Wolters, Raymond. *Negroes and the Great Depression: The Problem of Economic Recovery.* Westport, Conn.: Greenwood, 1970.

Wootton, Clara. *They Have Topped the Mountain.* Frankfort: Blue Grass Press, 1960.

Yater, George. *Two Hundred Years at the Falls of the Ohio.* Louisville: Heritage Corp., 1979.

## Articles

Baxter, W.E. "National Youth Administration." *Kentucky School Journal* 15 (Nov. 1936): 25-26.

————. "NYA Diversified Program Aids Kentucky Cities." *Kentucky City* 8 (July 1937): 9-11.

Beach, Robert. "Book Extension Services in Eastern Kentucky." *Mountain Life and Work* (Summer 1941): 5-7.

Birdwhistell, Terry L. "A.B. 'Happy' Chandler." In *Kentucky: Its History and Heritage,* edited by Fred J. Hood. St. Louis: Forum Press, 1978.

Blakey, George T. "Ham That Never Was: The 1933 Emergency Hog Slaughter." *Historian* (Nov. 1967), 56.

Blayney, Michael S. "Libraries for the Millions: Adult Public Library Services and the New Deal." *Journal of Library History* 12 (Summer 1977): 233-49.

Brashear, L.F. "A Relief Officer Looks at Relief." *Mountain Life and Work* (Oct. 1934), 6-9, 29.

Bubka, Tony. "The Harlan County Coal Strike of 1931." *Labor History* 11 (Winter 1970): 41-57.

Coode, Thomas H. and John F. Bauman. "Dear Mr. Hopkins: A New

Dealer Reports from Eastern Kentucky." *Register of the Kentucky Historical Society* 78 (Winter 1980): 55-63.

Curris, Constantine W. "State Public Welfare Developments in Kentucky." *Register of the Kentucky Historical Society* 64 (Oct. 1966): 299-336.

Davenport, Walter. "Happy Couldn't Wait." *Colliers* 102 (July 16, 1938): 12-13, 49-51.

DeVyver, Frank. "The Present Status of Labor Unions in the South." *Southern Economic Journal* 5 (April 1939): 485-98.

"Doughboys of 1933 Off to the Woods." *Literary Digest* 115 (April 29, 1933): 22-23.

"Federal Aid in Kentucky." *Kentucky City* 4 (March 1934) 5-7.

"Federal Work Relief in Kentucky." *Kentucky City* 9 (April 1938): 5.

Frame, Nat. "Kentucky Mountain Boys in the CCC." *Mountain Life and Work* (Oct. 1935), 21.

Hixon, Walter L. "The 1938 Kentucky Senate Election: Alben Barkley, Happy Chandler, and the New Deal." *Register of the Kentucky Historical Society* 80 (Summer 1982): 309-29.

"The Index of American Design." *Design* 40 (Sept. 1938): n.p.

Kurtz, Russell. "Two Months of The New Deal in Federal Relief." *Survey* 69 (April 1933): 284-90.

Leupold, Robert J. "The Kentucky WPA: Relief and Politics, May-November, 1935." *Filson Club History Quarterly* 49 (April 1975): 152-68.

McCormack, A.T. "The Socal Security Act as It Applies to Kentucky." *Kentucky Medical Journal* (April 1936), 54-58.

MacFarlane, David L., and Max M. Tharp. "Trends in Kentucky Agriculture, 1929-1940." Univ. of Kentucky Agricultural Experiment Station *Bulletin* 429 (June 1942).

Martin, James W. "Kentucky Accounts for Itself: Administration Reports to the People on Four Years of Progress." *State Government* 13 (Feb. 1940): 29, 34.

Miller, Neville. "Relief—the American Way." *Kentucky City* 7 (June 1936): 5-8, 18.

Northrup, Herbert R. "The Tobacco Workers International Union." *Quarterly Journal of Economics* 56 (Aug. 1942): 606-26.

"PWA in Kentucky." *Kentucky City* 6 (March 1935): 24-25.

Pyne, Roland R. "The Civil Works Program in Kentucky." *Kentucky City* 4 (May 1934): 5-8.

Reading, Don C. "New Deal Activity and the States, 1933-39." *Journal of Economic History* 33(Dec. 1973): 792-810.

Robinson, George W. "Conservation in Kentucky: The Fight to Save Cumberland Falls, 1926-1931." *Register of the Kentucky Historical Society* 81 (Winter 1983): 25-58.

Rodes, John B. "Bowling Green Benefits Thru Construction Efforts of RFC Labor." *Kentucky City* 4 (Aug. 1933): 5-6.

"The Roosevelt Handicap." *Time Magazine,* Aug. 1, 1938, 9-12.

Shannon, Jasper B. "Happy Chandler: A Kentucky Epic." In *The American Politician,* edited by J.T. Salter, 175-91. Chapel Hill: Univ. of North Carolina Press, 1938.

Shouse, Francis. "The Mountain Youth in NYA." *Mountain Life and Work* (Summer 1940), 24-27.

Supina, Philip D. "Herndon J. Evans and the Harlan County Coal Strike." *Filson Club History Quarterly* 56 (July 1982): 318-35.

Tugwell, Rexford G. "The Resettlement Idea." *Agricultural History* 33 (Oct. 1959): 159-64.

"TVA Possibilities for Kentucky Cities." *Kentucky City* 7 (Nov. 1936): 21.

Williams, P.E. "The School in the Camps." *Kentucky School Journal* 14 (Jan. 1936): 20-21.

Welch, Austin. "WPA Recreation Programs in Kentucky Cities." *Kentucky City* 9 (Dec. 1938-Jan. 1939): 5-7.

Woodward, Ellen. "WPA Library Project." *Wilson Bulletin for Librarians* 12 (April 1938): 518-20.

Wooten, William H. "National Youth Administration." *Mountain Life and Work* (Winter 1942), 15-19.

# Index

Agee, James, 130
Agricultural Adjustment Administration (AAA), 105-06, 117-22, 135, 170-72, 183, 188, 196, 198, 201; and cotton, 106-07, 116; and tobacco, 106, 113-16, 120; and hogs, 108-12, 116; criticism of, 121
Agricultural Extension Service, 84, 108
Agricultural Marketing Act, 16
Alabama, 28, 91, 133-34, 136-37
Alsop, Joseph, 187
American Bankers Association, 28
American Federation of Labor (AFL), 80, 156-57, 160
American Friends Service Committee, 23
American Guide Series, 68, 200
Amos and Andy, 4-5
*An American Exodus*, 130
Anti-Saloon League, 146
Ashland, Kentucky, 10, 30, 56, 65, 95, 151, 171, 177
Ashland Oil, 152
Aspendale, 36
Atlantic City, New Jersey, 160
Audubon State Park, 85, 89
Aurora, Kentucky, 133
Axton-Fisher Company, 11, 156

*Babbitt*, 6
Bankhead Cotton Control Act, 116
Bank Holiday, 1, 2, 24-26, 172
Banking Act (1935), 29
Barbourville, Kentucky, 17, 20, 94, 170

Bardstown, Kentucky, 57
Barkley, Alben W., 23, 36-38, 60, 75, 89, 92, 112, 115, 146, 149; and politics, 170, 176, 180, 182-88, 194
Baylor, Orval, 187
Beattyville, Kentucky, 56
Beckham, William T., 30
Bell, Urban, 67-70
Bell County, Kentucky, 12, 50, 123, 125, 159
Berea College, 94
Big Sandy River, 134
Bingham, Robert W., 10, 23, 173, 176
Birmingham, Kentucky, 138
blacks, 80-81, 94, 100, 102, 121
Blair, J. H., 158
Blazer, Paul, 152
Bluegrass Park, 36
Bourbon County, Kentucky, 144
Bowling Green, Kentucky, 22, 66, 75-76, 96, 101, 137, 144, 151
Bowman Field, 6
Boyle County, Kentucky, 141
Brains Trust, 27, 180
Brandeis, Alele, 67
Brandenburg, Kentucky, 67
Breathitt County, Kentucky, 64, 68, 131
Brown, James B., 10
Brown and Williamson Company, 11
Brown Hotel, 6, 119, 182
Bryan, Woodrow, 82
Bullock, Harry, 18-19, 21
Butler State Park, 100
Byrd, Harry F., 41, 127, 128, 180